Mirror Images of Evil

THE ROAD TO ISIS

George A. Kinias

Righters Gateway Publishing
http://www.RightersGatewayPublishing.com

Published in the United States of America through:

Righters Gateway Publishing
www.RightersGatewayPublishing.com

info@RightersGatewayPublishing.com

ISBN-13: 978-1475064186
ISBN-10: 1475064187

To Alexandra, who was the inspiration of the Journey, the partner in the quest for the answers, and the cheerleader when the road seemed endless.

And to Asher, our grandson, with the hope that the world he will grow in will be a gentler, safer, cleaner and happier one than the one we are leaving to him. A world where people live together in peace, acceptance and philanthropy.

CONTENTS

Mirror Images of Evil

PROLOGUE

On September 11, 2001, nineteen hijackers crashed two planes into the Twin Towers of New York City, another one into the Pentagon and caused a forth one to crash into a field in Pennsylvania. In a little more than an hour more than three thousand innocent civilians perished in the worst terrorist act on American soil in history. Around the globe, billions of people watched on live television in disbelief and anxiety the horror caused by this demonic act of terrorism. The world financial markets and institutions reeled at the prospects of what this act meant to the already fragile world economies. It was indeed an hour and a day that changed the world forever, as the innocence and sense of security of Americans vaporized the instance that thousands of gallons of jet fuel turned the Twin Towers into an inferno.

In the aftermath of this horrific terrorism, it became clear that America was under attack, the symbols of its economic and military might were the targets, and a message had been sent to the world by a little known group of Islamic militants. Whatever the message was, however, "these nineteen hijackers never represented me, even though I'm an Egyptian, as one of the hijackers" said my wife angrily and concerned. "We don't share the same ideals or goals. They hijacked four American planes to deliver their horrendous message and long before, they hijacked my country and culture." Who were these people, what did they want, and, most importantly, what motivated them to commit this mass murder at the expense of their own lives?

These were questions that began to dominate our thoughts and discussions in the weeks and months ahead and begged answers. We, as the rest of the world, were not prepared to deal with the substance of these questions, much less know the answers. We felt angry, confused and frustrated by the sudden realization that our countries were in danger and our future was uncertain. We were informed adult professionals who had worked and lived in four continents, but were powerless to understand why had all this happened and, most of all, what it meant to our future. Distant conflicts, death and distraction were no longer remote events mentioned casually in the evening news. They had arrived at our neighborhoods and were knocking on our doors.

Anger, confusion and frustration gave way to fear and fear begged action. While the leaders of America and NATO declared a state of war against global terrorism, we were driven to seek answers to what causes and fuels global terrorism. "Every nation in every region now has a decision to make: either you are with us or you are with the terrorists" President George W. Bush told the world leaders, as he unleashed the military might of the world's superpower against the Taliban and Al Qaeda in some of the most treacherous and remote regions of the planet. About the same time, we began our personal virtual journey of mind and soul to the, no less, treacherous and remote areas of human faith and culture. We wanted to learn who these terrorists were, and understand what motivates them and sustains their dedication. Is it hate, injustice, desperation, or blind faith that drove the suicide bombers of Lebanon, WTC, Islamabad, Tanzania, Kenya, USS Cole, and, now, of Twin Towers to these despicable acts of human behavior? Even more, we wanted to fight fear with hope and vindicate the human race. We believed, and still do, that as people are capable of bringing death and destruction to others, they are capable of bringing peace and stability as well.

We were ill prepared for the journey we undertook. We were neither theologians nor political scientists and neither of us had ever ventured into a search that resembled, even remotely, anything of this nature. We were just two ordinary, concerned citizens seeking answers. As we plunged into uncharted waters and began our journey, we quickly realized that our biggest challenge was going to be not the lack of experience, but the acceptance and reconciliation of our findings. As we tried to digest and analyze an enormous amount of research material, we realized that we were opening doors into some very dark rooms of human mind and behavior, and were forced to face our own prejudices resulting from life-long experiences in different cultures and religions. They were many spirited discussions, especially whenever we approached the subject of the ongoing Palestinian-Israeli conflict, or discussed America's global influence or interference, as most non-Americans prefer to call it.

Then, after several months of reading and frequent discussions, we were faced with events that steered our journey to a modified destination. During a visit to the US in the winter of 2002, we were besieged by friends and even casual acquaintances with questions about "our" views concerning not only with what was happening in the Middle East and with the potential war with Iraq, but mainly with "what does the rest of the world really think of America?" It was a stark departure from the lack of interest Americans had shown in affairs outside the US even a couple of years earlier, and one was left wondering, how come in a country where there are more television networks, newspapers, and news magazines than any other place on earth, people wanted to know more from "outside" sources? Perhaps Americans were not, all of a sudden, only interested in what is happening outside their borders, they were suspicious of the objectivity of their news media, and the sincerity of the motives of their government.

Once again overseas, we began to observe the coverage of the news with a more critical eye. With every passing day, we noticed that there were significant differences between the coverage of international news in the US by the major American television networks and the coverage of news abroad by global providers such as CNN International and BBC World News. The differences were not merely in the breadth and depth of news stories, but in the quality of reporting as well. Specifically in the areas of global terrorism and Islamic Fundamentalism, the anchors of the vast majority of domestic news programs exhibited, and sadly still do, at best, a cursory knowledge of the topics they were addressing, and the fast-paced structure of programming allowed only superficial coverage. With a few exceptions, the experts and analysts, who had become permanent fixtures in a growing number of TV shows attempting to address this new threat of global terrorism, were failing to inform the American public of what was really happening. The few, who seemed to understand the real issues and had the courage to speak out, had their voices drowned in a sea of misinformation and demagoguery.

Part of this phenomenon can be explained by the fact that the entire American society was caught totally unprepared to understand the world that emerged after 9/11, and, most important, take action against this new global threat of terrorism. For centuries, the culture of the "West" has been engaged in conventional warfare as it faced a conventional enemy. All of our societal protective systems were designed to understand and deal with such conventional threats. We had been studying our enemies for the greatest part of the last century. We knew who they were, where they were located, what their motives were, their weapons, capabilities, and limitations. Our entire societal mindset was focused on this conventional enemy, but 9/11 changed all that and more. Now we no longer know who our enemies are, where they are located, what their weapons and capabilities, and clearly, as the attack on the Twin Towers demonstrated, what their limitations are. Most important, we do not really understand their motives.

This state of pre-September 11 America began to shed some light into the reactions and actions that the American government has taken since then. It seemed as if America had to identify an external enemy that it could visualize and understand, and, most important, fight effectively. Bin Laden and Al Qaeda proved elusive for the American pride and the political capital of George W. Bush. The administration could not afford not to achieve a clear military victory and began its military campaign against the axis of evil, aiming at Iraq first. Now America had again an enemy it could clearly identify, rally the world against it, and, above all, defeat. (This was written in January 2002 after President Bush's State of the Union Address—sadly it turned out to be correct.)

Assuming that our observations were even partially correct, they made us pause and re-examine our mission. While we had been searching for the roots of an "old" problem, there were even greater problems unfolding right in front of our eyes. During the spring-summer period of 2002, we sensed that there existed not only the danger of a fanatical, and proven extremely lethal, pack of modern assassins that threatened to spread the bloody Middle East conflict to every corner of the globe, but the growing and more grave danger of a spiraling out of control major military US assault against Iraq. The core cause of this probable scenario was, we strongly believed, a serious case of misunderstanding of civilizations—in addition to the usual games of geopolitical control, power, and economic gain—and not the inevitable clash of civilizations, as some, very effectively, have been suggesting for the past several years. The citizens of Islam and those of the Christian West were drifting fast further apart, if that was possible. Osama bin Laden, Saddam Hussein and Yasser Arafat had become both symbols of evil and mujahedeen (holy war warriors). Each side did not understand nor trust, and feared immensely the other. The political and religious leaders of both sides, on the other hand, either exploited the situation and provided abundant inflammatory rhetoric, or, at best, abstained and, thus, strengthened the voices of the cynics. The world was at a standstill as it was drifting towards the abyss.

We were aware that our discoveries thus far had revealed only the tip of an iceberg, but at least we had a clear view of it, and understood that beneath the surface of the water lies a huge, floating and very dangerous iceberg. We decided that we had to continue our journey in search of the truth. To do that, we had to search deep inside us as well, recall our experiences as people who had all of our lives lived, worked, rejoiced, and grieved side by side with ordinary people on both sides of the conflict—Islam and the West—and depend on these experiences to guide us in communicating in a clear, fair and objective way the fears, problems, and misconceptions that plague both sides. We would attempt to de-demonize both Islam and the West, and perhaps, just perhaps, in a very small way our voices might contribute to the chorus of the voices of those who advocate truth, reason, fairness and, above all, peace.

We had been flirting with the notion of writing a book about our findings shortly after we began our research. The drum beatings of war and military mobilizations of the US and Britain against Iraq in the winter of 2002-03 solidified our decision to proceed with the writing of this book, a task that took a very somber nature indeed. By then, we had concluded a fourteen-year cycle of work in the Middle East and we were in the process of repatriating. Our physical presence in the US that allowed more access to information, the probable scenario of a war against Iraq having become a reality, and the start of the 2003-4 primaries and election hype were the major events that led us to discover the existence of a mostly unknown—to most Americans and to us at the time—group of ideologues who had managed to hijack American foreign policy, hurt America's already tarnished image around the world, and posed a major threat to world stability and peace. They were the neo-conservatives (neo-cons), disciples of conservative philosopher Leo Strauss, who cut their political teeth in the sixties working for Senator Henry (Scoop) Jackson, sharpened their skills and gained experience in the arts of fear and deception in the eighties with Ronald Regan, and reached their apogee with George W. Bush.

We had no idea where our research about the neo-cons would lead us when we started this new phase of our journey. As soon as names in the Bush Administration started appearing in the screens of our computers during our search of neo-cons, we realized we were looking at something bigger than we had initially expected. Our surprise turned into concern when we began to trace the history of neo-cons, visit their web sites, and read their articles and books that very clearly stated their political beliefs and strategies for "victory" against the enemies of the state. But we were not merely learning about recent American foreign policy. The most monumental events in American foreign policy and military intervention in, at least, the last forty years were taking place right in front of us. And then our concern grew exponentially when we began to observe the parallels between Strauss' philosophy of deception, power of religion and aggressive nationalism, and the strategy and mindset adopted by Bush and his neo-con cabal, especially after 9/11.

The invasion of Iraq removed any doubts that we might have had about the influence of neo-cons on American foreign policy and militarism in the past fifty years. This time, however, we were not experiencing merely another cold war similar to the one with the Soviets. The Soviets never attacked America and there is a lot of evidence becoming available, as archives on both sides of the cold war begin to be de-classified, that suggests that they never intended to do so. America was at war now with new external enemies-- Islam and terrorism—that were borne mainly out of the failed foreign policy of the United States in the Middle East, especially in Palestine.

Prior to "discovering" the neo-cons and their influence on American foreign policy, we had focused largely on Islamic fundamentalism as the core cause of international terrorism. As we began to learn about the Wilsonian doctrine, the twentieth-century foreign policy, the formation of the modern Middle East in the 1920s, and Leo Strauss and his disciples (neo-cons), we made the startling discovery—for us— that amazing similarities existed between the neo-con controlled think tanks of American foreign policy and Islamic fundamentalists and Wahhabism. Straussian ideology and neo-con policies were harming the West in exactly the same manner that Sayyid Qutb and Wahhabism have harmed and continue to harm Islam. Two evil Mirror Images were emerging. The House of Saud used Wahhabism to bring legitimacy to their shaky control of the kingdom. In return, the Saudi royals allowed, and often supported, Wahhabism to spread throughout the Muslim world the seeds of extreme Islamic fundamentalism and eventually global terrorism. The House of Bush used the neo-cons to bring legitimacy to his questioned presidency and allowed them to formulate and execute his foreign policy—an area that wasn't and still isn't George W. Bush's strong suit. Both the Houses of Saud and Bush have uncapped the evil genies of two very old and powerful forces, that are pushing the world towards a clash of fundamentalists and ideologues. Some call this confrontation a clash of civilizations; others call it a clash of religions; still others call it a war for controlling oil. No matter what the true reasons for the conflict, one thing was becoming abundantly clear. Both sides were driven by conservative ideologies and were reacting to what they perceived were the dangers of liberalism caused by modernity. They believed that the public at large was not capable of grasping these dangers nor making the "correct" decisions to protect itself from them, and used deceptions, religion and nationalism to promote their ideologies and defend their actions.

The US, however, was not attacked by the neo-cons. It was attacked by another brand of fanatic ideologues, the Islamic fundamentalists, who have been taking advantage of the rage of many Arabs—who believe that the foreign policy of the US supports unconditionally the state of Israel at the expense of the Arabs, especially the Palestinians—to recruit many of them who gladly become human bombs or missiles. And here lies the very serious strategic error of American foreign policy. The US does not risk undermining Israel's security, as many here in the US would have us believe, would she choose to being fair and playing the role of "an honest broker" in seeking to resolve the Israeli-Palestinian conflict. On the contrary, continuing on the current course of Israel-Palestine foreign policy, she, most certainly, increases the security risks for Israel, as the Arab world marginalizes the moderates and supports the extremists as a counterbalance to the perceived injustice perpetrated by the US. It should be pointed out at this point, that the threat of terrorism posed by Islamic fundamentalists against the West and particularly against the US is real and should not be underestimated, as critics of the Bush doctrine have attempted to do. Others are suggesting that the terrorism threat will eventually go away if we change regimes and establish democracies in the Arab world. That not only is not going to work, it will fuel anti-American sentiments around the globe, as it is none of our business to mettle in other nations' affairs. Indeed, the people in Muslim and Arab countries should determine how they should be governed and live and not their rulers and definitely not us. The problems in Middle East, however, are very old and very complex and there are no quick and easy solutions. Rushing to establish democracies, though, in regions of the world where religion rules and the majority of the public lacks basic education is a very dangerous proposition. One has to look at Iran, Iraq, Palestine, Egypt, Libya, and Taliban-Afghanistan to appreciate the grave risk of this tactic.

At this point of our research, we realized that it is much easier if one belongs to an ideological, nationalistic or religious camp, when trying to analyze foreign policy, war and territorial expansion. Everything can be rationalized and placed neatly in the appropriate (often misconceived) boxes of our mind. Things tend to be black and white this way. Conversely, when one searches for the truth and tries to analyze and reach conclusions in a fair and rational manner, many things turn gray and it becomes difficult to present findings in an objective way, as there are no absolute right and wrong, good and evil. Everything is relative depending on where you're standing. Challenging as it was, however, we plowed through with our search and writing. The dilemma we were in, though, helped us in a big way to renew and solidify our goals of writing this book. It was important that we tell the story of the threat fundamentalism poses to world stability and peace; and tell it in a clear and convincing manner. Moreover, to tell the tale of two misled empires—America and Islam—and the fanatically driven desire of some of their leaders to control the world under the disguise of freedom, democracy and holy wars.

We decided that the scope of the book should to be narrowed so that it would not overwhelm the common folk. Ideas, philosophies, and concepts presented in the book had to be simplified, partly because of our own limitations, partly to be digestible by the reader. Also, we tried to be as accurate and fair, as humanly possible, in presenting our findings and conclusions; and finally, send a message of warning and hope to the ordinary citizen of the world from two ordinary citizens. What the book did not seek to be is a reference for academics or intellectuals—although we could humbly suggest it might be considered as one of the reading material for those who make and implement foreign policy.

The book as it emerged in its final form consists of three parts: Part One: The Evil Image of Terrorism, is where we started our journey by going back to the birth of Islam in the seventh century and the Islamic empires that followed from Arabia to Andalucía; we covered the emergence of Mongols and Seljuk Turks; the Ottoman conquests and the Golden Age of Islam; then came the fall of the Ottoman Empire and the creation of modern Middle East; we concluded this part with the resurrection of the vision of an Islamic nation, including the birth, evolution and mutation of Islamic fundamentalism movements all the way to present time global terrorist networks. This part, moreover, can be viewed as a historical, religious and cultural journey in the heartlands of Islam, aimed at enriching the knowledge of the reader about Islam and Muslims and dispelling any misconceptions that might exist. In Part Two: The Mirror Images of Evil, we took our journey to the holy wars of Christendom with all the violence and treachery that characterized that era, examined the creation and the rise of neo-conservatives in America in the second half of the twentieth century, and looked at the terrifying mirror images of Islamism and Christianism. Part Three: The End of the Journey, it lists the core causes of Islamic terrorism and concludes that the world is not a safer place after all the blood and treasure that has been sacrificed in the past decade.

This prologue would not be complete without a note of a powerful personal struggle—I guess I could call it my "Jihad"—that I experienced in writing this book. One of the most serious challenges I faced was that many times during the research I came across findings—religious fanaticism and intolerance, and political manipulation—that made me angry and concerned that I was losing my objectivity in presenting my findings. Over and over again I would go back and reread and edit whole sections after I had cooled off, and ask myself, "Am I really being fair and objective about my writings?" I am not sure if I succeeded to depict accurately what I set out to do. I hope I did. I am certain though that even now, whenever I read certain sections of this book, I am deeply saddened and upset about all the misery, death, destruction and injustice that have been caused by power-hungry, greedy, corrupt, and truly evil groups representing religion and government in the course of human history. Perhaps, it is my idealism and belief in the good, that exists in all of us, that causes this sadness and anger whenever I witness manipulation and deceit take over.

George A Kinias
March 2009

POST SCRIPT

When the book was completed, I decided not to publish it. In many ways it had become part of us and it was deemed best that it should remain as a private reference. The journey after all had satisfied many of the initial objectives. Global events, however, tend to get in the way of decisions and force us to re-examined them. The emergence of ISIS, aka ISIL, and the recent terrorist attacks in Paris and San Bernardino, CA were such events. Another election cycle in US politics was in full swing. History was repeating itself once more. The only difference was that this time we were witnessing events instantly in the social media and in HD.

After the Iraq fiasco Americans were hoping for a better foreign policy under the Obama administration. Unfortunately that has not happened. On the plus side, he has kept us out of another war, not a small feat given our recent history in Viet Nam and Iraq. Also, Cuba and Iran were two significant achievements. On the negative side, our performance in the Middle East has been anything but worthy the great expectations we had in 2008.

It is not often that people have the opportunity to witness huge geopolitical blunders more than once in just one decade. But we have. Twelve years ago it was called Al Qaeda, Saddam Hussein and Iraq. In 2015 it is called ISIS (ISIL), Bashar Assad and Syria. And the real bad news is that we still haven't cleaned up the mess we created back in 2003. In fact, these ill-conceived and disastrous events had opened the gates of Hell. And it was time for us to publish the book.

November 2015

PART ONE

THE EVIL IMAGE OF TERRORISM

Islamic Empires

The Early Conquests, 632 - 661

During the first thirty years after the death of Prophet Mohamed, the House (Nation) of Islam was created and its political, social and religious institutions were solidified. The turmoil, infighting, Machiavellian plotting, unprecedented military expansion, and, most importantly, the unwavering Islamic faith that marked this period of patriarchal caliphs, would become the trade mark of the future caliphates over the next 1,300 years.

At the time of Mohamed's death in 632, his followers were confronted with a serious problem—the political and military succession to the creator of Islam. The decision of choosing a successor, however, was not an easy one. They were violent disagreements among Mohamed's followers about the new leader, who should be capable of maintaining unity of the Arab tribes and continuing the quest of territorial expansion and conversion to Islam. While there were strong disagreements as to who this person should be, there was a consensus among the Prophet's followers that this new leader, whoever he might be, had the authority of God behind him. This ruling model was not much different than many other used by ancient civilizations and very similar to the one engineered by the Emperor Constantine, creator of the Byzantine Empire three hundred years earlier, when he established himself as the representative of the Godhead on earth--isapostolos, the Equal of the Apostles. In the end, the man who was chosen to succeed Mohamed was a merchant named Abu Bakr, whose daughter Aisha was Mohamed's favorite wife. Abu Bakr was named the Khalifa (caliph), or "Successor" of Mohamed, and a new religion and a new and untried political form—the caliphate—was created.

The first four caliphs were relatives and followers of Mohamed himself. For that reason they are referred to as "Rightly Guided" caliphs. During this period of their rule, the world of Islam would expand far beyond the borders of the Arabian Peninsula—east into the Persian Empire, north into Byzantine territory, and west across the face of northern Africa [1]. Abu Bakr, who had been with Mohamed throughout all the military campaigns in Arabia and an outstanding military leader, wasted no time after Mohamed's death as he set out for the first Islamic military expedition outside Arabia against the Byzantines. The campaign was led by Osama Bin Zeid and was to revenge an earlier Islamic defeat by the Bani Gassan (the tribe or the people of Gassan). The Bani Gassan were Christians living in the Levant region [2], and under the control of the Byzantines. In the first campaign, Abu Bakr sent to the Levant the Muslim armies which were defeated. Afterwards, Abu Bakr rearranged the army and divided it to four corps. He sent one towards Homs, one headed towards Palestine, another towards Damascus and the fourth towards the Jordan valley.

In a domino effect, several key cities were conquered by the Muslims one after the other. Homs, Aleppo, Antioch, Beirut, Caesarea and Damascus fell to the Muslim armies. In another decisive battle, the stronghold of Ajnadin in Palestine fell and, as a result, the cities of Nablus, Yafa, Askalan, Gaza, Ramallah, and Jerusalem surrendered to the Muslims. By 640, Byzantine Christian Levant had become Arab Muslim.

After the death of Abu Bakr in 634, the Muslims leaders pledged their allegiances to the new Caliph, Omar ibn Al Khatab who had been chosen by the first caliph. Although Abu Bakr died after only two years as the first caliph of the Muslims, his military expeditions had set in motion a global conquest that was destined to create one of the largest empires in history, and have perhaps the greatest and more-lasting impact than any other military event in the history of mankind.

Caliph Omar had not solidified all of the Arab tribes yet and, according to some accounts, Christian Arab tribes were siding with the Byzantines in an effort to regain the lands that had been lost to the soldiers of Islam. A large force came from Egypt from the sea and regained Northern Palestine. The Muslims found themselves surrounded from all sides by Byzantine and Christian Arab armies that were encouraged, although temporarily, by their recent victory in Palestine. Alas, this was not to last for too long. The momentum of the Muslim armies was too much for the Byzantines, as the Muslims mobilized their troops and were able to fight victoriously and regain control. Constantine, the son of Emperor Heraclius, was defeated and the region was again under the control of the Caliph. It was a bitter loss for the Byzantine emperor who, recently after conducting three brilliant military campaigns against the Persians, had handed them a decisive defeat and regained Syria, Palestine, Egypt and the Holy Land. But these campaigns, and the religious and ethnic disunity that was beginning to plague the empire, had rendered it weak and an easy prey to the energized and united Muslim armies.

The raids against the Muslims from the eastern borders of Egypt on the Levant region intensified, however, and the Caliph decided to send an army to invade the land of the Pharaohs. Amr Bin Alas led an army and Egypt was captured in three weeks. Then he followed the retreating army to their stronghold city of Alexandria. After a brief siege, Alexandria fell. With the capture of Alexandria, the Muslims were able to control the whole of Egypt to the southern borders of Ethiopia, and west to the Libyan border. After the occupation of Egypt, Bin Alas was engaged in fighting with some of the tribes along the borders of Egypt. This fighting ended with the conquest of the entire coast till the Libyan city of Tobruk.

Although expanding the military and religious influence of Islam was a principal driving force for Caliph Omar, the Muslim Arabs had a score to settle with the Persians, more so than with the Byzantines. The proximity of Arabia to Persia made the invasions of Persians into Arab territory that easier. The tides of war, however, were running against the Persians this time. Weakened by their constant wars with the Byzantines, the Persians had the same fate as the Byzantine armies in Levant and Egypt. In the crucial battle of Nahawand, the Persian army suffered a crushing defeat in 641 that marked the fall of the once mighty empire. Within a few more years, the strongholds of Basra and Kufa would fall and almost all of Persia would become part of the Islamic empire.

By 642 Persia and Egypt, two of the richest regions in the world, guarded by two of the mightiest armies of the time, had been taken over by Muslims. The founder of Islam had been dead for only ten years and already the world's borders had been considerably redrawn, and although these lands would change hands again and again during the next 1300 years, they would remain Muslim till this date.

The principal contributions Omar made as a ruler were his political and financial innovations, although he continued the conquests that Abu Bakr begun. He realized that the sustainability of the fast-growing empire would require more than faith. An efficient political structure, a strong but controlled military, and a stable and sound financial structure were needed. He did not ignore religion, however. In a series of systematic actions, he established the Islamic calendar and began the process of formalizing and producing the Quran. His caliphate became a milestone in early Islamic history. He would be remembered for his justice, statesmanship, and innovations on social welfare, taxation and financial administration.

Before his death, Omar had the wisdom to appoint a committee of six men to decide on the next caliph. Omar was assassinated in 644, and the committee he had appointed chose the third Caliph Othman ibn Affan. That was a wise decision, since what the growing Islamic empire needed more was the practical and intelligent political and military leader that Othman was. During the time of Othman, the Turks had entered the scene and were raiding the lands of the Muslims from their territories in Turkmenistan. Othman not only defended the Islamic territories and repelled the Turks, he continued to defend the territorial gains against the Byzantines, added Libya to the empire, and conquered most of Armenia. His crowning achievement, and one of much greater importance to Islam, was the compilation of the official version of the Quran, the text of which is accepted to this day throughout the Muslim world.

Othman reigned for twelve years as caliph but his successes were marred by administrative and financial weaknesses. He was accused of favoritism to members of his clan—the Umayyads. Unrest grew throughout the empire, fueled by those who considered themselves as the original followers of the Prophet and, thus, the rightfully heirs of the caliphate, and who were very upset about Othman's selection as the caliph over Ali. In 656, riots broke out in Medina and a mob broke into Othman's house and killed him while he was reading the Quran. The division between the two Muslim groups, vying for nothing less than the right to the caliphate, widened greatly with the selection of Ali ibn Abu Talib, cousin and son-in-law of the Prophet, as the fourth caliph. At issue was the legitimacy of Ali's caliphate. Othman's relatives—in particular Muawiyah, the powerful governor of Syria—challenged the legitimacy of Ali's election because he was supported by those responsible for Othman's unavenged death. This conflict eventually led to a major division of Muslims in 657 and the formation of the two major sects in Islam—the Sunnis and the Shiites. Although there are minor theological differences between the Sunnis and Shiites, the major debate had been political rather than religious, centered on the selection of caliph or successor of Prophet Mohamed.

Abu Bakr's military genius and loyalty to Mohamed, the political genius of Omar, the intelligence of Othman, and practical-unreligious approach to ruling the faithful were the precise ingredients that the new caliphate needed at this formative time of its existence. But the seeds of discontent and rivalry, that were sown with the by-passing of Ali, son-in-law and companion of the Prophet that many felt should have been the first caliph, had finally sprouted and led to a civil war between Ali's followers and the Syrian-based Umayyads. A few years after the indecisive battle of Siffin near the Euphrates between the two warring factions, Ali was murdered in 661 by one of his formal supporters who had grown dissatisfied with him. Ali's son Hassan was proclaimed the new caliph but after a short reign he wisely abdicated in favor of Muawiyah bin Abi-Sufyan who had been proclaimed caliph in Jerusalem by the Umayyads in the previous year. The election of Muawiyah as the fifth caliph recognized by all Muslims ended, at least temporarily, the dispute over the successor of Mohamed, and ushered in the Umayyad dynasty which ruled for the next ninety years. Muawiyah established Damascus, where he had ruled for seventeen years under three caliphs as the emir (prince) of Syria, as the capital of his caliphate.

The European and African Expansion

Muawiyah was not merely the founder of the Umayyad dynasty and the fifth caliph of Islam. He was a very intelligent and shrewd ruler as well. A master manipulator and a geopolitical visionary, he chose bribes and negotiations over military conflicts, and was the first Muslim strategist to realize the importance of a navy as an essential tool in the ambitious global expansion of the young empire. One cannot be sure whether Muawiyah realized the military and political significance of attacking Europe, since the Arabs did not really have a concept of geographical borders in the sense that the West did and does. But nonetheless, he was the first caliph to expand Islam into Europe and bring his warriors right to the front door of Byzantium, by laying siege to its capital Constantinople. It is ironic that the West knows so little about Muawiyah, if anything at all, considering that the military achievements of all of his well-known European counterparts pale in comparison to his.

Since he became the emir of Syria, Muawiyah realized the benefits of conquering new territories in the Mediterranean and was against the lack of a naval force and the reluctance, perhaps even fear, of the caliphs to venture into territories that were not land bound. It was not until Othman's reign that Muawiyah was able to persuade the caliph to allow a naval expedition to attack Cyprus on the promise of considerable loot. So, in 649 Cyprus became the first European island to be invaded by the Muslims.

"The Cyprus expedition was not only the first major Arab naval enterprise. It was also the first of these raids by what Americans, more than a thousand years later, were to call 'the Barbary Coast pirates'; those who haunted and terrorized Mediterranean Europe until the French took Algiers in 1830 and ended the flourishing enterprise of slave raiding in the Mediterranean."[4] It appears that from their inception, the Islamic conquests had very little, if anything at all, to do with spreading Mohamed's religion, and a lot to do with land–grabbing, power and plunder—just as so many other conquerors had done from the beginning of time.

The islands of Crete and Rhodes followed next, as they promised lucrative payoffs. It is interesting to note that the Arabs were not particularly keen in settling in these islands and solidifying their presence there. They would raid the territories, kill as many of the defenders as they could and go away with the spoils of the victors—gold, females, and slaves. In 668 Sicily and Sardinia were the next targets of the Umayyads and this time Muawiyah was no longer the emir of Syria but the caliph of all Muslims and free to strengthen the empire's naval capacity.

The Umayyads did not limit their military exploits to those against the Mediterranean islands. Muawiyah launched a campaign in 663 to complete the conquest of North Africa. Libya was soon under the control of the Arabs and by 670 Tunisia was taken as well. Shortly after, the city of Qairawan was built and would become the Arab base in North Africa and the third holiest city in Islam after Mecca and Medina during the medieval period. One last prize remained in North Africa—the ancient city of Carthage. After several raids the Arabs conquered Carthage in 695 and with this victory the Byzantines were defeated in virtually all North Africa.

Although the Arabs had achieved remarkable military victories and territorial gains against the Persians and Byzantines, they had not launched a direct assault against the crown jewel of the Byzantine Empire—Constantinople. Muawiyah was about to change that. Sometime between 668 and 672 (the historians do not seem to agree on the exact year), Muawiyah's warriors headed towards Constantinople aboard a sizable naval armada and laid siege to the capital. After a few years of siege, the invaders were to discover what others before them and many after them would: Constantinople was a city almost impregnable. The location of the city—surrounded by water on three sides—its masterful fortification, and the use of a secret weapon known as "Greek fire" made it impossible for the Muslims to succeed.

After seven years, their greatly diminished army started a perilous journey by sea and land back to Damascus. Although their first assault on the Byzantine capital failed, the armies of Mohamed would continue their stubborn attacks against Constantinople for the next eight centuries until the exhausted and morally weak empire succumbed in 1453.

The Invasion of Spain

Muawiyah died in 680 shortly after the failed invasion of Constantinople and was succeeded by his son Yazid who became the second caliph of the Umayyads and reigned for only five years. Yazid's reign was as brief as was turbulent. A second civil war broke out between the Umayyads and Ali's followers in Arabia. Ali's son Hussein was assassinated and Yazid died in Mecca while trying to put down the revolt. Abd El Malik ibn Marwan became the next caliph of the Umayyads, and after seven years he was finally able to defeat the rebels and place Arabia once more under the control of the Umayyad clan. The victory came at a heavy price as during the civil war, in addition to the human losses, the holy places of Mecca and Ka'aba were destroyed.

With the end of the second civil war in 692, Islam began a period of relative stability and the Muslim armies, free from internal strife, once again aimed their swords at the infidels in Europe as they poised to begin the latest conquests that would take the empire to its farthest limits. Spain became an irresistible prize to ignore. The conditions in Spain couldn't be better for the Muslims. King Roderick was immensely unpopular among the peasants and Jews of Iberia. Moreover, the governor of a Byzantine colony near Morocco, Count Julian, had a score to settle with the king of the Visigoths. According to the legend, the king had forcefully seduced the daughter of the governor who now sought revenge. [5] He approached the emir of Qairawan, Mousa bin Nossair, and persuaded him that attacking the Visigoths by crossing from Africa to Iberia in the narrow straits of Gibraltar would bring an easy victory and much loot. He argued that the peasants who provided the bulk of the Visigoth army would not fight for their despised king. Moreover, the governor had properties and supporters near Gibraltar and he knew the territory well.

Whether the legend is correct or not does not matter. The Muslims have been thinking and preparing for this opportunity for some time. After recapturing Qairawan from the Berbers who had rebelled against them, the Muslims turned their attention to converting the Berbers to Islam and recruiting them into the Arab army. This strategy would prove vital for the Muslims in their invasion of Spain in 711. Mousa succeeded to secure the approval of Caliph El Walid ibn Abd El Malik, who ruled from Damascus, to invade Spain using mostly Berber warriors and promising the caliph huge loot. Paul Fregosi in his book *Jihad* writes: "There was nothing holy about this Jihad. It was a magnificent illustration of implacable Mediterranean revenge (on the part of Count Julian), and of planned mass abduction and mass robbery on the part of the Muslims). The Jihad, throughout these ages, inspired from its pre-Islamic tradition of Arabian tribal raids, was already a mighty instrument of what in the twentieth century we could bluntly call white slave traffic." [6]

Mousa chose as the commander of the Muslim invading forces Tarek, a former Berber slave who had proved himself as a soldier and leader. Tarek landed in the Iberia shore in the spring of 711 with an estimated army of twelve thousand soldiers, consisting mostly of Berbers and with Count Julian at his side. The landing site was near a rocky mountain that is known since then as the famous Gibraltar—Jabal Tarek or Mountain of Tarek–-in honor of commander Tarek. King Roderick met the invading army northwest of Gibraltar with as many as one hundred thousand men. "The knights on their horses wore armor; the infantry, dragged from their fields and dressed in rags, carried spears, scythes, and hoes." [7] What the king didn't know was that the catholic Bishop Oppas of Toledo, primate of all Spain and brother of Witiza, the former king of Spain, had secretly defected to the Muslim side. When the battle started, the Muslims suffered heavy losses but eventually Tarek's Berbers, joined at a critical time of the battle by Bishop Oppas and Witiza's sons, prevailed. At the battle of Sedonia, King Roderick was killed and his head was sent as a trophy to the caliph in Damascus. So, in 711 the Muslims successfully invaded Spain and would remain there for the next eight hundred years. [8]

Spain was now at the mercy of the Muslims and Tarek. At the encouragement of Count Julian, the Muslims marched towards Toledo, capital of Spain. On the way to Toledo, the Muslim armies captured Cordoba, Malaga, and Grenada. When the armies arrived to Toledo, they captured it without a fight. By 712, Mousa Bin Nossair, the emir of the West, received the news of the fall of Spain. Envious of Tarek and worried that he was being upstaged by the young and successful commander, Mousa advanced quickly to Spain with more troops to complete the conquest that Tarek had started. He marched towards the east. His troops captured Seville, where a large Jewish population welcomed him as a liberator, and Merida, once the capital of Spain. He met with the armies of Tarek in Toledo where they joined forces and advanced towards Aragon. On the way, more cities in the north surrendered as Barcelona and Tarragona. In less than two years all of the Iberian Peninsula was in the hands of the Muslims until the Pyrenees Mountains. They established Cordoba as their Spanish capital in 717 and named the newly acquired territory Al Andalus. A region of southern Spain retains the name Andalusia to this day. In few more years, they were able to capture Portugal and considered it a separate state known as Al Garb (the West).

Mousa continued his march and advanced with his army towards France. He captured the regions that were under the Spanish control in the Languedoc region. Historians say that as he ascended the mountains of Pyrenees and gazed at the continent, he thought that all of Europe was within his reach and someday could come under the banner of the Prophet. France would be nothing more than the gateway to Rome, Greece and Constantinople and this would have meant the ultimate triumph of Muslims and the Islamization of Europe. Mousa, however, would never realize his dream. Upon returning to Damascus loaded with treasure and slaves he was arrested by the new caliph, Suleiman, and narrowly escaped decapitation. Instead he was allowed to return to his native village in Yemen where he lived the rest of his life as a beggar. "Thus ended Mousa, conqueror of Spain and dreamer of an Islamic trans-European empire stretching from Gibraltar, north to France, east to Baghdad and beyond, and south to the Red Sea — an empire that was never to be." [9] As an emirate of the Umayyad caliphate, Spain was a long distance from Damascus and while this gave a great deal of independence to the emir of Spain, it hindered the ability of the caliph to govern effectively this vast empire, and it contributed to its downfall in 750.

The Battle of Poitiers-Tours

In the year 719, the new Emir of Andalusia, Al Sameh Bin Malik, advanced with his armies towards Toulouse, the capital of Aquitaine, besieged it but was not able to advance any further as the duke of Aquitaine came from Bordeaux to the rescue with a large reinforcement. The Muslims were defeated, their Emir was killed in combat and they withdrew back to Spain after losing a lot of their leaders in this battle that took place in 721.

The Muslims, however, were not deterred. In 732, Abdel Rahman El Gafki, the new emir of Andalusia, advanced with his troops to the north towards the French border. He reached Bordeaux and captured it. Abdel Rahman was able to capture Burgundy, as well, and raise the banner of Islam on the castles of Leon. From there, he advanced towards the capital. Beyond laid Poitiers and Tours with their churches rich in gold and silver. There, the two armies met and one of the most decisive battles in history was fought for eight days resulting to extreme losses to the Muslims. On the ninth day Abdel Rahman was killed in combat. This caused a major upheaval among the soldiers who fled. Historians say that the Muslims may have lost as many as 360,000 soldiers in this crucial battle, that may very well have saved Christendom and Europe from the armies of Islam.

Although the Umayyads suffered a crushing defeat in France at the Battle of Poitiers, by the year 743 the Arabic empire was at its glory. In Europe, it was controlling the south of France, and the Iberian Peninsula except of some hills that were the strongholds of some of the rebels. In the Mediterranean Sea, the Arabs were controlling the Islands of Majorca, Minorca, Efeikia, Corsica, Sardinia, Crete, Rhodes, Cyprus, a part of Sicily and several islands in the Aegean Sea. In Africa, they were controlling the lands from Gibraltar to the Gulf of Suez and in Asia, from Mount Sinai to the hills of Mongolia. By the year 755, however, the Franks were able to expel the Arabs out of France finally after besieging and fighting them for several years.

The Second Siege of Constantinople, 717-718

In the West, the Franks had succeeded to halt the breathtaking expansion of Arabs and Moors into the rest of Europe. In the East, there was another major historical event, of which very little is known, some fifteen years earlier that also changed the course of history. In the year 717, Caliph Suleiman sent an army of 120,000 by land and under the command of his brother to capture Constantinople, the capital of the mighty Byzantine Empire. Another 120,000 Muslim warriors sailed from Syria and Egypt aboard 1,800 galleys. [10] The Muslim armies besieged the city, since they knew from their first siege nearly forty five years ago that Constantinople was impregnable. The only thing they could hope to accomplish was to starve the besieged Byzantines. That strategy would prove futile, however, as the city had food and water supplies to last them as long as three years.

The Byzantines, moreover, were aided by the winter weather that befell on the besiegers and by the Greek fire that destroyed most of the ships of the invading Muslim force. Leo the Isaurian, Byzantine emperor, was a borne soldier and organizer. He had risen through the military ranks and shortly before the Muslim invasion was proclaimed emperor by his troops by being risen on their shields, in the traditional and honored Roman manner, and proclaimed Caesar and Emperor. Leo lured the Muslim navy into the Bosporus, where the Byzantine smaller and more maneuverable ships were able to wreak havoc on the enemy by destroying a large number of their ships with all their soldiers and supplies. [11]

On land, the Muslim armies did not fare any better. Their invading strategy was to starve the besieged Byzantines. During the harsh winter of 717, however, they found themselves freezing and starving. More supplies and reinforcements that arrived in the spring of 718 did not alter the fortune of the invaders. The Muslims, defeated and humiliated, lifted the siege of Constantinople and tried to return to Damascus. Unfortunately for them they faced in the Aegean Sea almost the same fate as those of the first invasion. It is said that only five galleys returned to Syria undamaged. The crushing defeats of Muslims in Poitiers and Constantinople took the wind out of the sails of the soldiers of Mohamed, at least for the time being. The world took a deep breath as it was shown, in the battlefields of France and in the straits of Bosporus, that the Muslim armies were not invincible. It would be hundreds of years before Islam would pose again a serious threat to Europe and the Byzantine capital.

Moreover, the caliph was facing more serious problems in the heartland of Islam. The Umayyad dynasty had begun fracturing internally. Many of the non-Arab Muslims became increasingly unhappy with the discrimination shown towards them by the Umayyads. The opposition, unified under the leadership of the descendants of Mohamed's uncle, Abbas, and after several military conflicts between the two groups, succeeded in overthrowing the Umayyads and bringing to an end an empire that in ninety years had dramatically changed the world map. After the fall of the Umayyad Dynasty, the capital of the Islamic empire moved from Damascus to Baghdad and the Abbasids began their five hundred-year reign.

The Abbasids, 750 – 1258

The early years of the Abbasid dynasty were marked with unfulfilled expectations on the part of the non-Arab subjects of the empire, that were instrumental in securing the overthrow of the Umayyads, and the systematic, almost barbaric, extermination of the Umayyad clan throughout the empire. In today's jargon the latter objective of the Abbasids would be known as ethnic cleansing and genocide. There would be no more military conquests and territorial expansions of Islam of any significance, with the exception of Sicily's invasion, during the Abbasid dynasty, as Islam began a period of looking inwards and focusing on stabilizing its own internal affairs. While this section's focus remains the colonial nature of Islam and its military conquests and territorial expansion, it would be unfair and inaccurate, however, to downplay or, worse, ignore the artistic, scientific and cultural achievements of the Abbasid dynasty, especially those in the ninth and tenth centuries when the empire reached its apex.

Ibn Rushd: In the midst of brutality that only wars and military conquests bring out at its worst, it would be a serious historical omission not to mention Abu'l Walid ibn Rushd, undoubtedly the greatest philosopher, physician, scientist and overall thinker that Islam ever produced. Ibn Rushd stands out as a towering figure in the Arab-Islamic thought. Born in Cordoba in 1128 he is believed to have influenced Western thought from the 12th to the 16th centuries. His books, the ones that survived the wrath of the caliph of Spain and Morocco, were included in the syllabi of many European universities, including Paris. A common theme throughout Ibn Rushd's writings was that there is no incompatibility between religion and philosophy when they both are properly understood. This might sound very logical to most people, but runs contrary to the interpretation of the Quranic teachings according to Islamic Fundamentalists.

Although the mass assassinations of the Umayyad leadership eliminated any possibility of return of the Umayyad caliphate in Persia, the new center of the Abbasid dynasty, they did not end the rule of the Umayyads altogether. One of their leaders, Abdel Rahman, was fortunate to survive a well-orchestrated assassination and able to escape to Andalusia where the Umayyads still had power and support. There in Cordoba, he succeeded to reestablish the Umayyad rule and declare himself, initially, an emir. After defeating the army that the Abbasids sent to overthrow him, Abdel Rahman I, as he is known in history, became the de facto ruler of the Moors, and established a rival Caliphate to that of Abbasids. The Muslims remained in power in Spain till 1248, just ten years short of the end of the rule of Abbasids in 1258.

Golden Age of Islam: After the Abbasids quenched their thirst for Umayyad blood, they turned their attention to administrative and financial matters, a trade mark of ancient Persians. In the pursuit of that goal, they established the position of vizier, or vice-caliph, in the government and placed the administrative affairs of the empire in the hands of the Persian

Barmakid family. Moreover, during the early centuries of their reign, the Abbasid caliphs promoted intellectual life. The great period of Islamic philosophy and art that started in Baghdad and continued, for much longer in Cordoba, reached its zenith during the reign of Harun Al-Rashid (786-809), who is better known in the West for his role in the famous collection of Persian and Arab fables, The Thousand and One Nights. The principal reason for this sort of renaissance could be attributed to the fact that the new empire sat between two intellectual giants, Byzantium and India, and it adopted and expanded ideas and systems from both.

After Harun Al-Rashid's death, civil war broke out between his two sons and the slow but steady decline of the Abbasid dynasty begun. Rebellions in Persia were increasing and by granting independence to Maghreb—today's Morocco—the caliph allowed a revival caliphate to flourish, that would eventually unite with the Moors of Spain and form the Almoravid dynasty. The Abbasids never ruled west of Egypt again. In the east, the empire was on the defensive against the Byzantines in Syria and Anatolia and against the Khazars in Armenia. Even in Iraq, the disintegration of the Abbasid dynasty continued. As more people converted to Islam, as a way to reduce their taxes, there were fewer revenues collected to support the lavish style of the Abbasid caliph and his court, a great departure from the simple and austere style of the earlier caliphs. About the same time, the caliphs started to import Turkish slaves as soldiers, the Mamluks, who eventually rose to prominence and controlled the military, thus, rendering the caliph to nothing more than a figurehead and spiritual leader of Islam who wielded no direct authority over the Muslim lands.

The Conquest of Sicily, 827-902

Sicily, Cyprus, Crete and Malta, have always been the targets of conquerors throughout history because of their strategic locations in the Mediterranean. This was the case once more with the invading armies of Islam. Sicily was first invaded by the Muslims in 668. A Byzantine territory at the time, the island fell quickly into Arab hands during the early Muslim expansion that had spread with breathtaking speed. The invading armies at that time, however, were more interested in looting and pillaging than land holding. They continued to invade and loot Sicily, almost at will with little resistance and support from the Byzantines, for another one hundred and sixty years.

By the beginning of the ninth century, the territory of Maghreb in North Africa gained its independence from the Abbasids in Baghdad and founded the Aghlabid dynasty. While the Umayyads in Andalusia were facing the slow but steady threat of the Christian Reconquista of the Iberian Peninsula, the Aghlabids would seek to expand their territory by invading Sicily. In the first invasion, Sicily had surrendered without any resistance, and Spain was in Arab hands in a few years. This time, Sicily would prove a very tough and stubborn opponent. It took the Muslims seventy five years to bring the entire island under their control and it would remain so for two centuries.

Although the territorial gain of Sicily is miniscule when compared with the vast land expansion of the early Arab conquests, its capture by the Muslims is noteworthy for its strategic significance. Moreover, it would become the last real land addition to the Arab-Muslim caliphates, the disintegration of which had already begun. Meanwhile, in Cairo, the Fatimids (909-1171) established themselves as the rivals of the Abbasids, maintaining political control over all the lands from Tunisia to Palestine. The Fatimids were Shiites who claimed decent from Ali's wife and Mohammed's daughter, Fatima. The next two centuries would bring to the Arab Muslims civil wars, loss of control over their vast territories, the creation of rival caliphates, and the eventual collapse of the Arab reign with the destruction of Baghdad by the Mongols in 1258. The first six centuries of Islam had been marked with rapid but bloody conquests, civil wars and massive genocides against the Christians and the Jews, even their own people. There was nothing *holy* about these Islamic conquests.

The Seljuk Conquest of Anatolia

The Seljuk Turks were descendants of the Turkic Oguz tribe who had migrated from the Punjab region in Central Asia, accepted Islam in the tenth century and established themselves in the Transoxamia region under their khan, Seljuk. While in the service of the Abbasid caliphs, as paid soldiers, defending the frontiers of the crumpling empire, the Seljuks defeated the Ghaznavids in 1040 and took Khorasan. From there, they advanced to crash the Persian Buyid chiefs who had been controlling the Abbasids in Baghdad for more than a century. The caliph, in reality nothing more than a spiritual leader by now, was unable to protect the caliphate from the Seljuks and in 1055 their khan, Tugrol Bay, advanced to Baghdad, occupied the capital and became the de facto ruler of the Abbasid Empire. The caliph had no choice but to recognize Tugrol as sultan (temporal ruler) of Persia and Mesopotamia, and later of Syria. The Arabs were removed from the administration of the Tugrol and the Great Seljuk Sultanate was established. Although the caliph of Baghdad had ceased being the effective temporal ruler of Islam for some time now, the recognition of the Turkish sultan ended officially the reign of the caliphs, who till the fall of the Ottoman Empire in 1924 remained as the spiritual leaders of Islam.

Soon the Seljuks became the controlling power over Asia. When the Sultan died, his nephew Alp Arslan—the "Lion Hero"—came to power and the caliph recognized him as the Sultan. Arslan was able to capture Armenia but his main objective was the rival caliphate of the Fatimids in Egypt. The Seljuks had become staunch supporters of the Sunnis and the Fatimids, be ing Shiites, were both a military target and a religious adversary. Alp Arslan began preparing for a major military campaign against the Fatimids, and in the spring of 1071 started his march towards Cairo for the eventual confrontation between these two major Islamic forces in the East. Fate, however, took him to a different battlefield in what was destined to become one of the most significant battles in history and one that changed the course and destiny of the Byzantine Empire, and consequently the history of all Balkan nations.

The Battle of Manzikert, 1071

About the same time that the Great Seljuk Sultanate was founded, Byzantium was facing one of its worst internal conflicts. As a result of decades of weak leadership in Constantinople, the institutions of state and church were controlled by the families of Michael Psellus and John Ducas, two of the most treacherous persons—and there were plenty during the eleven hundred years of the empire—that were to roam the halls of the Byzantine palaces. In 1068 Romanus IV Diogenes became the emperor and was confronted with two imminent dangers: Psellus and Ducas in the inside, and the Seljuk Turks outside. Being concerned about the real threat of a coup d'état by his archenemies at home, Romanus was reluctant to venture outside of Constantinople in pursuit of the Seljuks. Instead, he concentrated on strengthening and improving the military, while staying within the walls of the capital. A recent truce made between the Byzantines and Alp Arslan which allowed Romanus to direct his energies to the military and other internal affairs, was not destined to last long. The ghazi (warriors of the faith) were Turkish tribesmen who often broke the truce as they invaded and looted Byzantine territories according to their tribal traditions and with little respect for Alp Arslan's truce.

The ghazi's raids forced Romanus to act. He knew that sooner or later he had to confront the growing threat of the Seljuks, but he chose a terrible time to do it. About the same time that Alp Arslan had started his campaign against the Fatimids, Romanus marched towards the Seljuks with an army of about one hundred thousand men. This move by Romanus caused a reluctant Alp Arslan to divert his army towards the Byzantine forces but made clear to Romanus that he wished no war with him (at least for the time being). Romanus, being an arrogant man and needing a victory to boost his fragile reign, refused Alp Arslan's offer for peace and thus failed to take advantage of the growing feud between Arslan and the Fatimids.

The two armies met near the garrison town of Manzikert sometime in late August 1071. Romanus and the Byzantine army, although no longer the formidable fighting force of past centuries, still had a chance to deliver a major blow at the Muslim warriors, or even defeat them, should the circumstances of the engagement had been different. One of the Byzantine generals with the larger part of the army headed for Lake Van near Manzikert. It is not clear what happened to the general and the army but they never joined Romanus at the main battlefield of Manzikert. Some believe that he was attacked by the Muslims and his army dispersed. More credible sources suggest that he was an agent of John Ducas and he betrayed the emperor.

Romanus was left with the remaining of the army and was supported by two more generals, one of whom, unfortunately for Romanus, was Andronicus Ducas, nephew of John Ducas, tasked to cover the flank of the emperor. During the engagement of the two armies, an order of orderly withdrawal by Romanus was miss-communicated to the soldiers by Andronicus as a general retreat caused by the emperor's death. This created panic and confusion to the troops who fled the battlefield leaving Romanus without rear protection and alone to face Alp Arslan's army with only his personal guards. The emperor was captured alive and the once invincible Byzantine elites melted away in the Anatolian wilderness.

Alp Arslan, in a rather uncharacteristic manner for an Arab ruler of that period, treated Romanus with all the respect and courtesy appropriate for the emperor of the Byzantines. Romanus was allowed to remain as a guest of Alp Arslan at his camp and the terms of surrender were very merciful for the Byzantines. Alp Arslan was anxious to resume his march towards Cairo and made truce with Romanus at the cost of a small territorial loss and tribute to be paid by the Byzantines. Romanus would be allowed to return to Constantinople and resume his duties as emperor.

Michael Psellus and John Ducas had different plans, however, for Romanus. In a palace coup, they decided that Michael VII Ducas and his mother would share the crown of Byzantium. The treaty with Alp Arslan was denounced; Romanus was blinded, before he even returned to the capital, and died shortly after. With him died the hope that the Muslim armies could be contained in Asia and that the Balkans would be spared several hundred years of occupation by the new emerging power of Islam – the Turks.

...the Empire had suffered at the hands of the Seljuk Turks, just outside the little garrison town of Manzikert a few miles to the north of lake Van, the most disastrous defeat in all its history: a defeat which had resulted in the capture of the Emperor Romanus IV Diogenes, the ignominious flight of the once-invincible Byzantine army and the gradual spread of the conquerors across Anatolia until some 30,000 square miles of the imperial heartland had been overrun by Turkoman tribesmen. At a stroke, Byzantium had lost the source of much of its food supply and most of its manpower. Its very survival was now in doubt. [14]

The Sultanate of Rum

The disaster of Manzikert was not the only problem facing the internally corrupt and self-destructive rulers of the Eastern Roman Empire. In the West, Robert Guiscard, the Roman conqueror, had taken Sicily from the Saracens and Bari, the last Byzantine outpost in Italy, had fallen to Norman hands in 1071. Guiscard's ambitions, however, were much greater. Constantinople, the crown jewel of Europe and Asia Minor, was a challenge and a prize of such proportions that Guiscard found too difficult to resist. In 1081, he set out to accomplish his dream. He crossed into Greek territory from Italy and dealt a humiliating defeat to the Byzantines lead by their emperor, Alexius Comnenus, in Durazzo. Guiscard would have marched all the way to Bosporus and may have taken Constantinople were it not for a number of distractions back in Italy and a typhoid epidemic that struck his army and caused his death in 1085. [15]

While Comnenus was fighting the Normans in Greece and Italy, the Seljuks, within ten years of the defeat of the Byzantines in the Battle of Manzikert, had overrun and controlled Anatolia, a predominantly Greek and Armenian Christian territory with a sizeable Jewish minority, thus, adding a large and rich area to their sultanate. The migration of ghazi tribesmen into Anatolia and Persia continued and, aided by the huge land gains in Anatolia, contributed to the creation of a number of independent states under the suzerainty of Baghdad. The strongest and most significant of these states was the sultanate of Rum—from Roman Empire, as the term Byzantine was not used at the time—

which was located in Asia Minor and comprised mostly of the territory won from the Byzantines. Benefiting from its diverse and cultured populace, the sultanate of Rum reached a level of cultural and artistic excellence unparalleled in the other Seljuk states. After conquering Iconium from the Byzantines in 1072, they made it the capital of their sultanate and renamed it Konya.

Although the sultanate of Rum was the longest lived of all Seljuk states, it too was destined to decline, as so many other great states in history had done before it. Its decline may be attributed to the practice of dividing the state between the sons of sultan in a tribal tradition. While this made local rule strong, it made the sultanate weak to attacks from external enemies. Alexius Comnenus fearing the expansion and strength of Seljuks, asked for help from the West Roman Empire and Roman church to prevent the onslaught of Christians by the armies of Islam. Instead, he got a lot more than what he bargained for. Pope Urban was successful in rallying European Christendom and he unleashed the crusades against the Muslims which were to cause, by far, more damage to Christendom than Islam. The Seljuks were defeated in the first Crusade and Konya fell in crusader hands in 1097. The Turks triumphed, however, over the crusaders in the second Crusade in 1147 and with this victory the sultanate of Rum entered a century, its last, of significant cultural and territorial growth.

The Mongol Invasions

The Mongols can be traced back to the fifth century when Turkic speaking tribes migrated from Siberia to the steppes from where the Huns emerged. Although the Mongols became the greatest conquerors of all time, surpassing even Alexander the Great in terms of territorial gains, they did not become the subject of our research because of their conquests, since they had not converted to Islam during these invasions. As will be shown below, their eventual clash with the Muslims and the resulting demise of Baghdad and of the Abbasid dynasty in the thirteen century gave birth to the justification for Jihad, that has been used by the modern Islamic revivalists and terrorists from Sayyid Qutb to Ayman El Zawahiri. It is for this reason that we detoured briefly into the vast, complex and intriguing culture and warfare of the Mongols.

The Invasion of Islam and the Sacking of Baghdad

The great conquests of the Mongols culminated during the reign of Temujin who is known in the West as Genghis Khan or Universal Ruler, as he took the Mongols to China and Crimea. By 1225 he controlled everything between the Caspian Sea and Korea. The Mongols believed that Genghis Khan was immortal and they were destined to rule the world—not unlike the Islamic belief of creating the Dar al-Islam (nation of Islam). It would not be long before these two mighty tribal powers would clash for world dominance.

As it has happened very often in history, the successors of great rulers or great conquerors find it very difficult to measure up to the achievements of their predecessors. It was no different with Genghis Khan's successors. Although there was further expansion of the Mongols into Europe and Persia, after the great khan's death the empire was divided into several khanates and the central power and control of the Mongols weakened. We witnessed the same pattern in the sultanate of Rum almost two centuries earlier with similar results. Of particular importance are two khanates that were ruled by two of Genghis Khan's grandsons: The Golden Horde which controlled the Russian territories and ruled by Berke Khan, and the Ilkhanate that controlled Persia. Hulagu Khan was the infamous, to the Muslims and especially the Iraqis, ruler of the Ilkhanate. Berke Khan became the first Muslim ruler but was unable to establish Islam as the official religion of the Mongols and his faith caused a serious rift between him and his cousin Hulagu who was shamanistic with Buddhist sympathies.

As mentioned earlier, it was inevitable that the Mongols would eventually challenge the Muslims in their own turf. In 1251, Hulagu led a successful Mongol invasion of Persia and established the Ilkhanate. He was able to wipe out the Assassins (Ismaili Shiite Muslim sect who used assassinations as a political weapon and who are considered to be the first terrorists in history) in Persia in 1256 by capturing their fortress in Alamut and bring an end to their systematic series of murders that had terrorized Muslims and Christians alike for almost two centuries. Hulagu's principal targets, however, were Baghdad and Damascus—the seats of Muslim power outside of Andalusia at that time. He marched west towards Baghdad and demanded from the last Abbasid caliph the complete surrender of the city. The caliph refused to surrender and what followed was not merely the collapse of a once proud city and of a glorious dynasty, but an event of much greater historical significance to Baghdad and Muslims, the effects of which are felt to this day.

Hulagu laid siege to the capital which unable to defend itself against a much stronger Mongol force fell in 1258. The caliph and all male members of his family were executed thus officially bringing to an end the Abbasid Caliphate. Baghdad was utterly destroyed and tens of thousands, perhaps one hundred thousand, were massacred in one of history's worst pillages that lasted almost a month. It is this battle that Saddam Hussein referred to a few days before the collapse of Baghdad on 9 April 2003 during the US – Iraq War. He referred to President Bush as the modern Hulagu in a desperate last minute effort to rally the Iraqi army and Muslims around the world in a Jihad against the invading modern Mongols. There can be no sympathy for a brutal dictator who terrorized his own people for the great part of a quarter of a century, but one needs to recognize that such characterization of the American president and the invading army greatly resonates among all Muslims, especially Arab Muslims, and inflames their rage against America and the West.

After Baghdad fell, other cities followed. Damascus surrendered and was spared destruction. Aleppo resisted and had the same fate as Baghdad. Hulagu was not done yet as Egypt was next to his list. Events, however, were to alter his plans and the Mongol – Muslim relations. Berke, khan of the Golden Horde and Hulagu's cousin, was appalled with the destruction of Baghdad, a famous Islamic city, and the execution of the caliph himself. Although Hulagu was his cousin and a fellow Mongol, the Abbasids were Muslims after all. The resulting animosity between the two leaders led to war, the first to pit Mongol armies against each other. Although there were other rivalries between the two cousins over control of the Caucasus Mountains, the main cause of the feud was their religious differences.

Hulagu concerned about Berke's anger over the treatment of the Abbasid caliph and the sacking of Baghdad, decided to head north toward Russia with part of his army and send one of his generals to deal with the Egyptians. In 1260, the Mamluks, who were the de facto rulers of Egypt, aided purportedly by the Mongols of the Golden Horde were able to deal Hulagu's Mongols a decisive defeat, the first ever suffered by the Mongols.

The sacking of Baghdad and the defeat of the Mongols by the Mamluks changed the dynamics in the Middle East dramatically. Eventually the Mongols of the Golden Horde and of the Ilkhanate were assimilated into the Islamic Turkish culture of the south, rather than the Christian Russian culture of the north. The young Mamluk sultanate was now the leading power in the region, and it was this power that would lead the final offensive against Europe. After the collapse of the Abbasid Caliphate, the house of the Caliph moved from Baghdad to Cairo which became the capital of the Caliph. The Mamluks retained control of Egypt until the Ottoman conquest in 1517 when the house of the Caliph moved from Cairo to the new Ottoman capital of Istanbul (Constantinople).

To the Muslim empire, the Mongol conquests were politically and economically disastrous. Some regions never recovered fully and the empire, already weaken by internal strife, never again regained its previous power. The Mongol invasions, in fact, were a major cause of the subsequent decline that set in throughout the heartland of the Arab East. In their sweep through the Islamic world, the Mongols killed or deported numerous scholars and scientists and destroyed libraries with their irreplaceable works. The result was to wipe out much of the priceless cultural, scientific, and technological legacy that Muslim scholars had been preserving and enlarging for some five hundred years.

Ibn Taymiyya (1263-1328): The Roots of Islamic Jihad

Five years after the sacking of Baghdad a child was born in Persia to an Islamic scholar who had escaped to Syria for fear of the

Mongols that occupied his land. The child proved to be a brilliant student, followed in the footsteps of his father, was able to complete his studies at age 19, and became a professor of Islamic studies himself. Well versed in Quranic studies and theology, the young man started issuing fatwas (religious decrees) without following the rules of any of the traditional legal or religious schools. Eventually, his radical views made him a target of the traditional Orthodox Islamic schools that consequently were able to imprison him. The young rebel, however, would make his imprint in Islamic history not because of his rather heretical interpretations of the Quran, but rather because of his unprecedented declaration of Jihad against another Muslim.

This energetic Islamic activist was Ibn Taymiyya and would become the most prolific Islamic writer of all time, with the exception of Ibn Rushd. Ibn Taymiyya declared that a ruler who fails to strictly enforce the Shariah, including the performance of Jihad, forfeits his right to rule. He became a strong advocate and participant of Jihad against the Crusaders and Mongols who occupied parts of what he considered Dar al-Islam. Ibn Taymiyya developed his arguments by building upon the tradition of previous Islamic dissidents, including the Kharijis of the seventh century and the Assassins of the eleventh century. Ibn Taymiyya and his predecessors directed Jihad against rulers they considered as apostates because they did not follow the true faith.

He became the conservative voice of Islamic thought in the Middle Ages, and his thinking inspired the late eighteenth century Wahhabi school of thought, as well as many twentieth century Islamic revivalist movements, including The Islamic Jihad that was responsible for the assassination of the late Egyptian President Anwar Sadat in 1981. Ibn Taymiyya would die in prison in 1328 and become the role model for Sayyid Qutb, Mohamed Farag and Ayman Zawahiri.

The Ottoman Empire

The Ottomans, as the Seljuks, were members of the Oguz confederation of Turkic tribes that had settled in Asia Minor. Although a significant number of these tribes had migrated into the more fertile lands of Anatolia, the Ottomans might have been refugees escaping the Mongol invasions and seeking relative security in the Seljuk controlled territories. As the other Turkic tribes, the Ottomans were originally shamanistic nomads that had been converting to Islam en masse.

The Ottomans or Osmanlis derive their name from their Ghazi tribal leader Osman (Othman in Arabic) who came to power in 1299. A minor tribe initially, the Ottomans had been assigned by their Seljuk overlords to the border area of the Byzantine Empire. It was their role as guards of a constantly contested frontier that allowed them to develop their highly disciplined organization and strengthen their military skills. As the Seljuk sultanate began to crumble, the Ottomans emerged as the dominant power in Anatolia and would become a dynasty that ruled much of Europe and Asia in one of the most remarkable chapters of history. Within two centuries after Osman came to power, they had established an empire that included not only the former Byzantine territories of southeast Europe and Anatolia, but also Hungary and the Arab world. Not since the Muslim invasion of Spain in the eighth century, had Islam been poised to establish a European presence as it did in the sixteenth and seventeenth centuries.

Early Expansion

During the early period of the twenty five year rule of Osman, the Ottomans began to systematically chisel away Byzantine villages and garrisons and thus eroding the already precarious Byzantine control of the border areas of the empire. Using the captured forts as a base and aided by an inflow of Ghazi warriors, the Ottomans laid siege to Bursa and Nicaea, the largest Byzantine cities in Anatolia. Bursa, which laid just fifty miles south of Constantinople, was the first to collapse in 1326 after a seven-year siege and subsequently became the first capital of the Ottomans during the reign of Osman's son, Orhan.

Orhan continued his father's military strategy and the siege of Nicaea, which crumbled under the stubborn Muslim offensive in 1331. Nicomedia followed six years later. This gave Orhan complete control of the Asian shore of Marmara and enabled him to build a naval force which he used to attack the European shore. Meanwhile, the once mighty and proud Byzantine Empire had started hemorrhaging. External enemies—the Serbs, Bulgarians, Turks, the Venetians, the Knights of St John (Crusaders), and especially the Genoese—civil wars, and serious financial and morale problems were plaguing her. To thwart the Genoese, Emperor Andronicus and his Grand Domestic, John Cantacuzenus, entered to an alliance with Umar Pasha, one of Orhan's emirs. Umar hated the Genoese who the Byzantines considered as a more serious threat than the Turks. This alliance which eventually grew into a lasting friendship between the emir and John Cantacuzenus proved more pivotal than the Grand Domestic might have anticipated or wished. Both Umar and Orhan came to the aid of Cantacuzenus in 1342 and later in 1346, when a revolt had spread through the empire and the newly crowned and reluctant emperor found himself desperately fighting against many adversaries in the palace and the patriarchate. The friendship and alliance between Cantacuzenus and Orhan were farther strengthened with the marriage of Theodora, daughter of the emperor, to Orhan. [16]

This alliance with the Ottomans would come to haunt the empire in the not too distant future. In seeking the military support of Orhan against his enemies, Cantacuzenus had allowed the Turks free passage into Thrace—west of Constantinople—and for the first time Muslims crossed the Bosporus. They would remain there till present time. The emperor's miscalculation wasn't as bad as the consequences of a natural disaster that struck Thrace in the spring of 1354. A violent earthquake destroyed a large part of the region and in the once-great city of Gallipoli not a house was left standing. [17] Most of the inhabitants of the city escaped by sea and the rest died of hunger and exposure to cold. Gallipoli became a ghost town overnight, but not for long. For Suleiman Pasha who was stationed on the Asiatic side of the Bosporus this was an opportunity that he couldn't afford to miss. He marched to Thrace with as many Turkish families as he could find and had them settle in the devastated areas. Most of them moved into Gallipoli and within a few months they were able to rebuild the city and its walls. [18] Gallipoli, a Greek city and an important crossing point for the empire between Thrace and Asia Minor, was now an exclusive Turkish city right in the back yard of the Byzantine capital. The Muslims had gained a stronghold on European soil that they would use as their base in future attacks against Constantinople and other European cities.

Murad I

The loss of Gallipoli to the Turks alarmed Western Europe, but conflicts between Venice and Genoa delayed any possible intervention. Then in 1362, Orhan's son and successor, Murad I (whose mother was Princess Theodora) marched into Thrace through Gallipoli and captured Adrianople and Philippopolis, and forced the Byzantines to pay tribute. In 1366 the count Amadeus VI of Savoy (cousin to John V Palaeologus, Byzantine emperor) initiated a minor crusade to aid the Byzantines. The count drove away the Turks from all Europe except Gallipoli. The next year, however, Murad marched against the Byzantines and regained most of Thrace, including Adrianople.

In 1371 Murad, who had proclaimed himself Ottoman Sultan, realizing that he was not yet ready to Attack Constantinople, marched his forces deeper into Europe. On the river Maritsa, that lies about twenty miles west of Adrianople, Murad met a sizable force of Serbs led by their king. In the first major battle fought on European soil, the Ottomans annihilated the Serbs and dealt a severe blow not only to the Serbs but the Byzantines and European Christians as well. There was nothing any longer left that could stop the advance of the Ottomans to Serbia, Bulgaria and Greece.

After a brief pause, Murad's armies were on the march again. One of the armies advanced into Bulgaria and took the cities of Sardica and Nish. To the east and south, the monasteries of Mount Athos had submitted to the Sultan. Thessalonica, the second most important city of the empire, after Constantinople, and a strategic port was all of what was left of the crippled empire. In October 1383, the Sultan's Grand Vizier laid siege of Thessalonica and gave the city an ultimatum: surrender or be massacred. The city held up for three and a half years and would have not fallen into the hands of the Ottomans, had the European Christendom sent by sea the badly needed provisions and reinforcements, that the emperor had urgently requested. Murad lacked the naval force required to enforce an effective blockade. At the end, the exhausted Thessalonicans opened their gates and surrendered to the armies of the Sultan. The circle was closing on Constantinople. [19]

The Battle of Kosovo: After the Serbs had suffered a crushing defeat in Maritsa, one would think that they had lost all appetite for war. Not so. The Ottoman conquest was halted when in 1387 the Serbs, in the absence of Murad, won several skirmishes against the Turks and the battle of Plocnik, and regained some of their lost territory. But Murad was back two years later and in one of the greatest medieval epics, the Serbian army was utterly destroyed in the battle of Kosovo. Sultan Murad I, however, was killed either during the battle or by a Serb assassin shortly after the battle. The battle of Kosovo, disastrous for both the Serbs and the Byzantines, proved beyond any doubt that the Ottoman armies were virtually unstoppable in the fourteenth and fifteenth centuries.[20]

Beyazid I

With Murad's death, his oldest son Beyazid proclaimed himself Sultan and immediately ordered the execution of his popular and brave brother to eliminate any possible future claims to the throne. This action would establish the tradition of imperial fratricide that would become law under Mehmed II. Beyazid, known also as the Thunderbolt, had an insatiable ambition even for a Muslim Sultan that could be rivaled only by his mercurial temper and quick actions. He bestowed on himself the title of Sultan of Rum to enhance his image and to signal a more aggressive military policy than those of his predecessors.

During Beyazid's reign the Byzantine Empire had sunk to depths unimaginable. Even during periods of military defeat, civil wars, bankruptcy, or religious upheaval the state had retained its dignity and pride. Under Emperor John V, she was humiliated beyond description and became the laughing stock of Western Europe. The emperor's policies of appeasement had made him an impotent vassal of the Sultan. Indeed the empire was at her worst militarily and financially, and the emperor was challenged by his own nephew; but he people of Byzantium and the crown deserved more as John's successors would prove in the next six decades. [21]

When John V died in 1391, his son Michael II and successor to the throne was a hostage of the Sultan in Adrianople. Michael was able to escape, however, and return to the capital where he received the imperial diadem by the Patriarch. Beyazid, who openly supported John's VII (nephew of Michael) bid for the crown, was furious that Michael did not ask for his permission to be crowned emperor. Soon became clear to the Sultan that Michael was determined to end the policy of appeasement that so disgracefully his father had instituted. After refusing to comply with one of the frequent summons of the Sultan, Michael knew that he had also terminated the vassalage; to Beyazid this would only mean declaration of war. [22]

Michael's only hope against the endless army of Beyazid was the impregnable walls of Constantinople, that had withstood countless invaders for more than one thousand years. The siege began in 1394 and would last for eight years. Were it not for the determination of its emperor and the occasional aid from the princes of Christendom in the West—who were mainly motivated from the prospect of having to face the Ottoman tide themselves in the near future—the city might have surrendered to the Turks. But the city could not hold out forever. By the summer of 1402, when it was becoming increasingly clear to the Byzantine leadership that no substantial help might be forthcoming from the West, it is said that they decided to surrender the keys of the city to the Sultan. Then, as in a miracle, help arrived not from the West but the East. The Mongols under Tamburlaine (Timur–lenk) had destroyed the Ottoman army at Ankara. Beyazid himself had been taken prisoner and would die in captivity in 1403. Constantinople had been spared again; but not for long. [23]

Murad II

After the defeat at Ankara the Ottoman Empire fell into total chaos. Although Tamburlaine died in 1405, the Mongols roamed free in Anatolia and the political power of the sultan was broken. Beyazid's sons fought each other for ten years for control of the sultanate. In 1413 Mehmed I stood as the victor and his task was to restore the Ottoman Empire to her former glory. Many of the Christian kingdoms of the Balkans had broken free of Ottoman control, and Anatolia had suffered greatly from the civil war. Mehmed moved the capital from Bursa to Adrianople, reinstated control over Bulgaria and Serbia, drove the Mongols from Anatolia, and assaulted Albania and the Byzantine controlled areas in southern Greece.

When Mehmed died in 1421, one of his sons, Murad II, became sultan and continued his father's task of united the Ottoman's and bringing rebellions, most notably the revolts of the Serbs, under control. In 1423 Murad laid siege of Constantinople but after only a couple of months he lifted the siege and directed his efforts to Thessalonica and the Venetians who had taken control of the city at the request of the inhabitants. When the Turks stormed the city, the Venetians fled to their ships but as the invading army entered the city and started pillaging it, the Venetians started bombarding them from the sea and forced the Turks to flee. The first siege of Thessalonica by the Ottomans had failed.

The outcome of the battle of Thessalonica was a setback for Murad but worst troubles were waiting for him. The Serbs and Hungarians allied with the Venetians against the Ottomans, and in Anatolia the emirate of Karaman attacked the Empire from the back. Murad was forced to split his army. His main force headed to the Balkans and his reserves marched to Anatolia. Murad crushed the Serbs and the Hungarians in separate battles and sent his main army to Anatolia, where he defeated the emir of Karaman in 1428. The Ottomans had proved once again that they were formidable.

Murad also had unfinished business in Thessalonica. In 1430, he launched a massive attack against the second city of the Byzantines by sea and land. The city was helpless against such a force and its defenses crumbled. The Ottomans entered the city and what followed was one of the saddest chapters of the mortally wounded empire. While the Venetian leaders, entrusted with the protection of the city, were fortunate to escape by sea to Venice, the city was reduced to a smoldering pile of bodies and ruins. For the traditional three days, Murad's soldiers pillaged the city where some seven thousand are believed to have been massacred.

The capture of Thessalonica was an important victory for Murad but his troubles with his many enemies were far from over. There would be no new conquests or territorial gains for the Ottomans for the remaining of Murad's rule. He would spend the next twenty years fighting battles in the Balkans and Anatolia against the Christians and Mongols, just trying to hold on to past gains. By the time of his death in 1451, Murad had succeeded to stabilize the Ottoman Empire, had gained some lands in Greece and lost others in Serbia and Bulgaria. The empire was poised now for its final quest for the ultimate prize in the western world: Constantinople.

The Fall of Constantinople, 1453

Mehmed II became the new Ottoman Sultan after Murad's death and many doubted the young Sultan would be able to continue the restoration of the Empire. They were to be proven wrong. By conquering and annexing the emirate of Karaman and by renewing the peace treaties with Venice and Hungary, he proved his skills both on the military and the political front and was soon accepted by the noble class of the Ottoman court. When he in 1452 proposed to attack Constantinople, though, most of the divan, especially the Grand Vizier, was against it and criticized the sultan for being too rash and overconfident in his abilities. Mehmed would prove them wrong very soon.

On April 1452, Mehmed ordered the construction of a castle on the Bosporus side. The Rumeli Hisar, as the castle will be known, was completed in a breathtaking period of nineteen weeks and its ominous presence so close to the Golden Horn must have sent a terrifying message to the protectors of Constantinople and the princes of the West. Despite his relatively young age and inexperience, Mehmed proceeded with the siege of the Byzantine capital as a master strategist and technician. Being humbled by the impregnable walls of the city, all past invaders had resorted to tactics of attrition by laying siege to the capital and hoping the defenders would surrender. But without a superior naval force a siege could not succeed without an effective sea blockade. Mehmed was determined and prepared to overcome both of these weaknesses.

First a vast armada sailed past Gallipoli and dropped anchor into the Sea of Marmara. Meanwhile, in Thrace the army was gathering. A huge force of one hundred thousand soldiers (by the most conservative estimates) equipped with armor, weapons and siege engines set up a camp surrounding the city. As awesome as his army and navy might have been, there was nothing in comparison to Mehmed's cannon. A German engineer was commissioned to build a super-cannon for the Sultan, that measured some twenty seven feet long and had a barrel two and a half feet in diameter. An ultimate weapon for the period, the cannon would play a pivotal role in the assault of Constantinople. On April 5, 1453 Mehmed presented emperor Constantine XI Palaeologus with an ultimatum but the emperor refused to surrender the city. The last siege of the capital was on. [24]

The Sultan began a bombardment of the city unprecedented in the history of siege warfare, thus far, that continued uninterrupted for the next fifty five days. The outer walls slowly started to collapse despite the heroic efforts of the defenders to try to repair them after nightfall each day. It was a gallant but futile effort. [25] On Tuesday, 29 May 1453 the Ottomans broke through the crumbled walls. The remaining exhausted but brave defenders fought to the end – their emperor among them. The last great epic in the history of the Middle Ages had ended. Norwich provides the most eloquent epitaph for a once mighty and proud empire:

> The Roman Empire of the East was founded by Constantine the Great on Monday, 11 May 330; it came to an end on Tuesday, 29 May 1453. During those one thousand, one hundred and twenty-three years and eighteen days, eighty-eight men and women occupied the imperial throne – excluding the seven who usurped it during the Latin occupation. Of those eighty eight, a few possessed true greatness; a few were contemptible; the vast majority were brave, upright, God-fearing, unimaginative men who did their best, with greater or lesser degrees of success. Byzantium may not have lived up to its highest ideals – who does? – but it certainly did not deserve the reputation which, thanks largely to Edward Gibbon, it acquired in eighteenth- and nineteenth-century England: that of an Empire constituting, 'without a single exception, the most thoroughly base and despicable form that civilization has yet assumed'. So grotesque a view ignores the fact that the Byzantines were a deeply religious society in which illiteracy – at least among the middle and upper classes – was virtually unknown, and in which one Emperor after another was renowned for its scholarship; a society which had with difficulty concealed its scorn for the leaders of the Crusades, who called themselves noblemen but could hardly write their own names. It ignores, too, the immeasurable cultural debt that the Western world owes to a civilization which alone preserved much of the heritage of Greek and Latin antiquity, during these dark centuries when the lights of learning in the West were almost extinguished.

Mehmed renamed Constantinople Istanbul and made it the capital of his empire. Aghia Sophia, the holiest shrine of the Byzantine Christians was converted into a mosque. After Constantinople was captured and the Byzantine Empire extinguished, Mehmed turned south to Morea (Peloponnese) where a last Greek kingdom still remained in Christian hands, and west to the Balkans. In 1456 Mehmed laid siege to Belgrade but he never succeeded in taking it. He entered Athens in 1460 where until then emperor Constantine's two brothers ruled. The following year, Mehmed launched a campaign into Anatolia defeating Armenia and strengthening the Ottoman control of the region.

The Ottoman Golden Age

In addition to conquering the Byzantine Empire, Mehmed began a vigorous reconstruction program of the new capital of the Ottomans that had been devastated by the bombardment and the looting. Large number of Muslims moved into the city and soon it became again the center of commerce and culture. The Sultan worked hard in consolidating the central control of the empire and establishing an effective administrative and tax system. He was assisted greatly in this task by the vast and very efficient Byzantine bureaucratic structure that fell into his hands.

After Mehmed's death, Beyazid II became the Sultan of the Ottomans and expanded the Empire into the Balkans and outposts along the Black Sea, and brought under control the revolts in Anatolia. Although Beyazid II was responsible for modest territorial gains, he is known more for encouraging European Jews to settle to Istanbul and rebuilding the city after it was damaged by an earthquake. It is ironic that about the time Columbus was headed for the New World and European Christians were persecuting the Jews who were expelled from Spain, Sultan Beyazid welcomed them to Istanbul and Thessalonica. He encouraged them to move there and helped them reach a high level of prosperity and achievement. The Sultan also turned the Ottoman fleet into a major naval power that displaced Venice and Genoa in the eastern and central Mediterranean as the dominant seafaring states.

His son and successor, Selim I, was more militant and extended Ottoman rule southward conquering Syria and Palestine. In 1517 he drove out the last of the Mamluk sultans in Cairo and made Egypt a satellite of the Ottoman Empire. Selim I was also recognized as guardian of the holy cities of Mecca and Medina and it was from this time that the Ottoman sultans adopted the title of caliph. Ottomans held now the keys to the gateway of the East–West trade routes and Selim was successful in increasing significantly the revenue to the Empire. This however, forced the Europeans to seek new routes around Africa and it might have contributed to strengthening the naval superiority of the Europeans and expanding the colonization of Africa.

Selim's son, Suleiman I (1494-1566) was called the Kanuni (lawmaker) by his Muslim subjects and the Magnificent by the Europeans. He came to the throne in an opportune time. New revenues from the expanded empire and new trade routes brought to the empire wealth and power unparalleled in Ottoman history. During his long reign of forty six years (1520-1566), the Ottoman Empire experienced its golden age and ranked foremost among world powers in cultural, social and military achievements. Although almost constantly at war, the Ottoman Empire brought its diverse peoples the benefits of peace. The population grew, roads and caravan networks expanded, and an unprecedented, for the Ottomans, explosion of building projects, including bridges, mosques and palaces, that rivaled the greatest projects of the world of this period, took place during Suleiman's rule. The Ottoman lands became a bridge between the East and West where the different cultures and communities living within the borders of the empire in large parts of Europe, Asia and Africa merged and coexisted.

Moreover, Suleiman greatly cultivated the arts and he is considered one of the great poets of Islam and an accomplished goldsmith. He earned his nickname the Lawmaker from his complete reconstruction of the Ottoman law system. Races and religions coexisted under his rule; Muslim, Christian and Jewish families lived together in the Ottoman capital and Christians and Jews freely practiced their religion, customs, and laws. The sultan used to consult theologians on crucial decisions. He attached importance to justice and fairness.

The most important contribution, however, that Suleiman might have made to the world, especially when viewed from a post 9/11 perspective, is that he demonstrated that modernity, science, culture, arts and Islam are not mutually exclusive and that Muslims and other religions can coexist and benefit from each other. In this respect, and this respect alone, he towers above all other Muslim rulers, before him and since him, that have walked on this historically rich but turbulent region of the world. He is indeed a role model worth being emulated by all aspiring reformist contemporary Islamic leaders.

The Battle of Mohacs and Siege of Vienna

Suleiman's military campaigns may be viewed both as a continuation of the Islamic conquests, deeply engrained in the psyche of all Muslim rulers and warriors, and a response to an aggressively expanding Europe. Like most other non-Europeans, Suleiman fully understood the consequences of European expansion and saw Europe as the principal threat to Islam. After succeeding his father, Suleiman began a series of military conquests, starting with the capture of Belgrade in 1521 and of Rhodes in 1522. He correctly grasped the strategic importance of Hungary and the country became the battleground of several clashes between the Ottomans and Europeans. At Mohacs, in 1526, Suleiman dealt the Hungarians a crushing defeat; the Hungarian king, Louis II, was killed in the battle. This, as decisive a victory as it might have been for the Ottomans, set in motion a series of events, however, that would spell more troubles for Suleiman in the not too distant future. The vacant throne of Hungary was now claimed by both Ferdinand I, the Habsburg archduke of Austria, and Janos Zapolya, lord of Transylvania. Suleiman sided with Janos (John) and recognized him as the vassal king of Hungary. Moreover, in an effort to resolve this dual claim to the Hungarian throne, Suleiman laid siege to Vienna in 1529. The resistance of the Christians, who saw this battle as a crucial event in stopping the Ottoman tide, bad weather and lack of supplies forced Suleiman to lift the siege.

The siege of Vienna proved successful in another respect though; it might have discouraged the Habsburg archduke from further interfering in the affairs of Hungarians. Janos was able to rule Hungary uncontested until his death in 1540 and Suleiman, preoccupied with other events in the East, granted a truce to the Habsburgs. The death of Janos created an opportunity that the Austrians could not resist, as they advanced once more into Hungarian territory; an event that may have caused Suleiman to regret that he had not dealt decisively with the Habsburgs earlier. The wars in Hungary and over Hungary continued till the end of Suleiman's reign. At the end, old and broken by the death of his eldest son Mustafa, the heir apparent of the Ottoman throne, by no other than Suleiman himself, and the deadly rivalry between his surviving sons that ended in the defeat and execution of prince Beyazid, Suleiman died while besieging a Hungarian fortress. While he died like a true Muslim ghazi, fighting in the front lines for Islam, Suleiman deserved a better end and, definitely, a better successor.

The Battle of Lepanto

The naval strength of the Ottomans became formidable during the reign of Sultan Suleiman with the help and under the leadership of Barbarossa, the most famous of the Barbary pirates, whom Suleiman appointed Grant Admiral of the Ottoman fleet. Until his death in 1544, Barbarossa ravaged the coasts of Mediterranean. In 1538 in a naval battle off the coast of Preveza, Greece, he defeated the combined fleets of Spain, Venice and the Pope and confirmed the naval superiority of the Ottomans in the Mediterranean, that would go unchallenged for another three decades.

The combined forces of these three major naval forces of Christian Europe, however, would have another opportunity to limit the control of the seas by the Ottomans. In 1571 and not far from the site of their earlier defeat they met a very formidable armada of more than three hundred Ottoman ships commanded by admiral Ali Pasha in the Gulf of Lepanto (currently the Corinthian Gulf that separates the mainland Greece from the Peloponnesian peninsula). The battle that followed was a crushing defeat for the Ottomans who lost all but about forty ships, and is considered one of the most decisive naval battles fought in the Mediterranean. During the course of the battle, Ali Pasha's flagship was captured, the admiral beheaded and his head was displayed from the mast of the Spanish flagship.

The Battle was the first major victory of any European army or navy against the Ottoman Empire and as such it had great psychological importance. Despite the massive Ottoman defeat, European disunity prevented the allied forces from capitalizing on this victory or achieving a lasting naval or land superiority over the Ottomans. The Sultan began an immediate massive rebuilding of the fleet and within six months the Ottomans were back again ruling in the seas. What the defeat accomplished, though, was that the Ottomans lost their control of the western part of the Mediterranean and the widely held perception that the Ottomans were invincible was broken.

The European March of the Ottomans Comes to an End

The man who succeeded Suleiman the Magnificent to the Ottoman throne in 1566 was one, whose character and performance as Sultan rightfully raises the question, that certainly must have been asked countless times in history in similar situations: how can a person like Selim II have been an offspring of Suleiman? Selim was the first Ottoman Sultan entirely devoid of military virtues, who was willing to abandon all power to his ministers, provided he were left free to pursue his orgies and alcoholic stupors. While the Ottomans were fortunate to conclude an honorable treaty with the Holy Roman Emperor Maximilian II in 1568, they were less fortunate against Russia. In 1569 they suffered a sea and land defeat against the Russians and were forced to sign a treaty with Ivan the Terrible in 1570. Also, it was during Selim's reign that the Ottomans suffered the humiliating defeat of Lepanto. The Ottoman Empire was fortunate that he reigned only for eight years. Is a relatively short period the throne of Othman had been occupied by Suleiman "the Magnificent" and Selim "the Drunkard."

The general decline of the Ottomans that started with the defeat in Lepanto was halted periodically by able state administrators, notably Grand Vizier Mohamed Kuprili, who would fight corruption, sustain vital services of the sultanate, and encourage military superiority and conquests. The tide, though, had turned against the Ottomans and it culminated in the defeat they suffered in the Battle of Vienna in 1683.

The Ottomans had waged wars against the Austro-Hungarians on and off for more than one hundred and fifty years. In 1683, Kara Mustafa, a greedy and villainous Ottoman leader, led a considerable Ottoman army, estimated at some 140,000 men, to a final assault of Vienna – an unfinished business since the unsuccessful siege by Suleiman in 1529. The defending European forces were led by Polish King Jan Sobieski, who came to the aid of the Austrians and Germans honoring

Poland's commitment according to the Treaty of Warsaw between King John III and the Holy Roman Emperor Leopold.

On September 12, 1683, the Austrians and their Polish allies took advantage of Mustafa's poor disposition of his troops and won the Battle of Vienna with a devastating flank attack led by Sobieski's terrifying Polish cavalry. The Turks retreated into Hungary never again to threaten central Europe. In 1699, the Ottomans signed the Peace of Karlowitz by which they handed over to Austria the provinces of Hungary and Transylvania, leaving only the Balkans under Ottoman control. The age of Ottoman conquests had come to an end and the mighty empire was clearly in decline.

The End of the Ottoman Empire

The Decline

There has been much speculation about the factors that contributed to the decline and subsequent fall of the Ottoman Empire, most of them probably correct, and as tempting as it is to add our views to those of others, we have concluded that this exercise would be outside the scope of this book. We will be content with the findings of historians and analysts. Regardless of the reasons for its decline, though, there is one undisputed fact; the once mighty Ottoman Empire had entered a new era of steady decline precipitated largely by the defeats in Lepanto and Vienna. Turkey had become known as the "Sick Man of Europe". The outside world was still largely unaware of the extend of this decline until the 1820s when it became clear that the Ottoman armies were unable to bring under control the revolt that was spreading in Greece. Backed by the great powers of Europe, Greece became the first nation to gain its independence from the Ottoman Empire. A few years later in 1839, the Sultan lost Egypt after his Viceroy, Mohamed Ali Pasha, rebelled against him and established Egypt as an independent state.

The Crimean War, 1854-1856

Then came the Crimean war that was fought between Russia and the joined forces of Britain, France and Ottoman Empire. The war grew out of a dispute over the guardianship of holy places in Palestine and the protection of Orthodox Christians. Russia used this dispute as a pretext to invade Moldavia and Walachia which were semi-autonomous vassals of the Ottoman Empire. When the Russians sank the Ottoman fleet at Sinope in 1853, however, the defeat of the Ottomans raised fears among Britain and France about a Russian expansion and naval domination of the Mediterranean. The Ottomans were joined by Britain and France and when Austria threatened to enter the war on the Ottoman side, the Russians withdrew from the occupied territories.

Though the immediate cause of war had ended, the allied forces landed in the Crimea and laid siege to the city of Sevastopol, home of the tsar's Black Sea fleet. Sevastopol fell into the hands of the allied army in 1855. In the same year, the Russians occupied the former Armenian city of Kars, now in the hands of the Ottomans. Peace negotiations followed and the Crimean War ended with the Treaty of Paris in 1856.

The Crimean War illustrated the lack of modern technology and superior weaponry in the Ottoman army. While fighting alongside the Europeans, the Ottomans realized how far they had fallen behind. While Europeans were reaping the benefits of the industrial revolution, the Ottomans were still largely relying on medieval technologies. The vast empire had no railroads and few telegraph lines. It took days before the Port (the Administration of the Sultan in Istanbul) learned of the major naval defeat at Sinope. The Crimean War, thus, brought some needed positive changes to the Ottomans. The western powers who had invested a great deal of resources in the war did not wish to have to come to the rescue of a crumbling empire again. That forced the Ottoman Empire to begin a period of reconstruction and revitalization as a flood of businessmen, engineers and administrators from Britain, France and Austria arrived in the Turkish capital. The banking and tax systems were completely revised and strengthened; the legal system was altered to be based on the Napoleonic Code; and the Orient Express was constructed, as well as other railroads, along the cost of Anatolia and into the Balkans. The Empire was undergoing a revolution as a new Ottoman nationalism was emerging. It appeared for a while as though the Empire might be able to survive.

The Ottoman Empire's euphoria was not destined to last long. The Vienna stock market collapsed in 1873 and with it the hopes for an Ottoman revival. The money and loans that have been flowing into Istanbul came to a screeching halt, and The Port unable to repay the foreign loans was forced to default on them. A bad economy, an ambitious Russia, and frustrated Christian Orthodox Serbians and Slavs under the Ottoman domination became an explosive mixture that ignited into a series of revolts against the Turks. Although the Ottoman armies were reequipped and fought better than had in a very long time, they were not an equal match to the rebel states which were aided by the superior Russian forces. The British navy intervened again and Russia not wishing to engage Britain agreed to a treaty which resulted to major territorial losses for the Ottomans in the Balkans. The Sultan unhappy with the results of the treaty asked the Germans to help him broker better terms in another treaty. This started a special relationship between Turkey and Germany which would continue through World War I and until the end of the empire.

The Young Turks

The beginning of the twentieth century found an Ottoman Empire struggling to stand on its own crumbling feet. Internally, she was undergoing a period of relative stability under the three-decade reign of the ruthless and autocratic, even by Ottoman standards, Sultan Abdul Hamid. But under the surface, there was considerable political turmoil. The Sultan had suspended the constitution and disbanded Parliament, and his secret police was feared everywhere, especially in the capital. This drove all political life and dissent underground and a large number of secret societies of progressive students and military cadets proliferated. While Abdul Hamid's secret police succeeded in crashing these societies in Constantinople, elsewhere in Thessalonica one such group was about to make history. Founded by Mehmed Talaat, who lived and worked in Thessalonica, one such group developed close ties with the Turkish Third Army which was headquartered there. [27]

Talaat's secret cell merged with a group called the Committee of Union and Progress (C.U.P.) and became its principal faction. The group was also known as the Young Turkey Party and its members became known as the Young Turks. Two more members who would play a key role in Turkey's future were recruited by Talaat and joined the Young Turks. They were Ahmed Djemal, a staff officer, and a junior officer named Enver. In a bloodless coup, led by the army officers in Thessalonica in 1908, the C.U.P. took control and officially deposed and exiled the Sultan in 1909, and placed a puppet Sultan, Mehmed IV. The Young Turks would rule the Ottoman Empire from 1908 until the end of World War I in 1918. [28]

The C.U.P.–led government was ruled by a dictatorial triumvirate: Mehmed Talaat who became the Minister of Interior; Enver Pasha who was the Minister of War; and Ahmed Djemal Bey who became the Minister of Navy. Although committed and energetic, the Young Turks were unable to slow down the territorial disintegration of the Empire. Under different circumstances, they might have succeeded. The events unfolding rapidly before them were too powerful indeed. Albania had revolted against the Ottomans, and during the two Balkan Wars of 1912 and 1913, all the European territories previously held by the Ottomans for five hundred years were gone. Greece, the successor to the once mighty Byzantine Empire, was one of the greatest beneficiaries of the Balkan Wars, as it regained northern Greece, including Thessalonica, Epirus, and the Aegean islands. The invading armies reached the edge of the Ottoman capital. Elsewhere, Russia was looking for territorial expansion and Britain, ruling one quarter of the world in the dawn of the twentieth century, was determined to prevent other nations become too powerful. In this backdrop of geopolitics, the Young Turks sought to ally themselves with Berlin during World War I against public opinion, which was largely anti-German at the time. Soon, this decision would seal the fate of the critically ill empire. [29]

The Great Arab Revolt and World War I

What the West knows about the Great Arab Revolt, most likely comes from the 1962 Box Office hit movie Lawrence of Arabia in which British officer E. T. Lawrence—Lawrence of Arabia—comes to the aid of Arabs rebelling against their Ottoman occupiers during World War I. Under the reign of the very unpopular Sultan Abdul Hamid, the Ottomans were becoming nationalistic, at the expense of other nationalities under their occupation, especially the Arabs. Following the Young Turk rebellion, the Ottomans abandoned their pluralistic and pan-Islamic policies, pursuing instead a policy of secular Turkish nationalism. This policy was a great departure from the past practices of tolerance and began, in turn, to create in the Arabs, under the Ottoman rule, a sentiment of pan-Arab nationalism which continues to this day. The champions of this Arab nationalist movement were the Hashemites of Arabia under the leadership of Sharif Hussein bin Ali, the last Hashemite Emir of Mecca and King of the Hejaz, who claimed direct lineage to Prophet Mohamed.

Hussein's dream--the catalyst of the Great Arab Revolt—was to establish a single independent and unified Arab state stretching from Aleppo (Syria) to Aden (Yemen), based on the ancient traditions and culture of the Arabs and the upholding of Islamic ideals. [30] Hussein was a strong-minded and influential leader and shared with his fellow Arabs a strong dislike for his Ottoman overlords. In June 1916, as head of the Arab nationalists and in alliance with Britain and France, Sharif Hussein initiated the Great Arab Revolt against the Ottomans which was led by his two sons, Abdullah and Faisal.

Captain E.T. Lawrence traveled to Jeddah to meet Hussein and together they agreed on the terms under which the British and Arabs together would fight the Turks. Moreover, Britain promised her support for a united kingdom for the Arab lands. Hussein told his son Faisal, "a British promise is like gold. No matter how hard you rub it, it still shines". A special friendship was born between Lawrence and Hussein. Together these two warriors commanded an army that carried out a guerilla campaign against the Turks, that culminated with the capture of the strategic port of Aqaba. Elsewhere, Faisal's forces liberated Damascus in 1918. At the end of the war, Arab forces controlled all of modern Jordan, much of southern Syria, and most of the Arabian peninsula.[31]

Unfortunately, Britain's promises were not genuine. While they spend millions to support the Revolt, they were unable to deliver a united Arab nation at the Paris Peace Conference in 1919. Prior to the Paris Peace Conference, significant events had been unfolding for several years before and during WW I, that would affect the Middle East in a much more profound way than WW I and WW II ever did, and the consequences of which are felt throughout the Arab world and the Middle East to this day.

The Creation of Modern Middle East

Those who ignore the lessons of history are destined to repeat them

When looking at the constant turmoil and frequent bloodshed that has plagued the Middle East region for almost sixty years, one does not have to be an expert in political science or foreign affairs to realize that something must have been wrong with the "blueprints" that were used to create it. So, naturally from the very beginning of our journey we were drawn to research the events and the main characters that were responsible for the creation of modern Middle East. What we learned, indeed explains the mess that exists in this troubled region of the world, and why peace remains an elusive task for the several warring factions vying for "their rights". While we poured through dozens of books and articles in our research, our first and, by far, best source was David Fromkin's book *A Peace to End All Peace*, a must read book for all of those who want to learn more about the events that took place during the last years of the Ottoman Empire, and the creation of modern Middle East and Turkish Republic.

The European Great Game

"Turkestan, Afghanistan, Transcaspia, Persia – to many these names breath only a sense of utter remoteness…To me, I confess, they are the pieces on a chessboard upon which is played out a game for the dominion of the world."
George Curzon, British Viceroy of India

It must be embarrassing to some nations how revealing history can be when decades or centuries later they stand unrobed in front of the eyes of the world, especially when the audience includes those whose lives (borders, religion, culture, rights, and freedom) have been dramatically altered or, worse, lost. As the above quotation reveals, a Great Game indeed was what the great powers of Europe were playing at the close of the nineteenth century! The Ottoman Empire was in decline, but still a power to be reckoned with. As Russia continued to threaten Britain for control of Asia and Asia Minor, the Brits allied with the French and the Japanese against the Russians. French eventually would ally with the Russians. The Germans had entered the scene as well, and their meteoric rise in industrial production and international investments posed a threat to Britain and France, who allied against the Germans. Britain wanted to limit Russian territorial gains over the Ottomans, but did not want the Ottoman Empire to regain its old strength either. This threw the Ottomans right into the lap of Germans who eagerly wanted to become a player in the Great Game. [32]

While the British politicians regarded their traditional rivals, France and Russia, as friends and allies in the post-Victorian era, British officers and civil servants, serving in the African and Asian outposts of the British Empire, continued to view Russia and France as their enemies. Politicians and field officers, however, shared the common view "that what remained of the independent Middle East would eventually fall under the European influence and guidance." [33] This assumption would prove to be the driving force that created the "blue prints" of modern Middle East.

The Middle East that existed in the early years of the twentieth century was very different than the one that even the oldest of us remember. Iraq, Syria, Jordan, Saudi Arabia, and Israel did not exist then. For more than four centuries this region, which constituted the majority of the domains of the Ottoman Empire, was in relative tranquility under the sluggish style of governance of the sultans. The fire of Islam, that drove the faithful into the remote corners of the globe under the banner of the Prophet in the early centuries of Islamic conquests, was only a glow in the beginning of the twentieth century. Although the Ottoman Sultans bore very few of the positive traits of the early caliphs as champions of the Islamic faith, Muslims under their rule appeared to be content with the territorial holdings of the empire and the fact that the Ottomans, who were Muslims like them, were a dominant military and economic world power. This sense of superiority was sufficient tranquilizer to the rulers and subjects of Islam. All this was about to change largely by external plans and events.

The Players

Trying to cover the events that led to the dismemberment of the Ottoman Empire and the creation of modern Middle East is a formidable task for novices, as we are, and a very lengthy one to boot. Moreover, whole books have been written about these short years that led to the 1922 Middle Eastern Settlement. We will suffice to present in this section only a brief summary of the major events, and most importantly, the misunderstandings and miscalculations that ironically and tragically greatly influenced the initial and final maps and agreements of the Middle East. And to begin this very tall order, we will rely on David Fromkin's introduction in his book *A Peace to End All Peace*. Describing the 1914-22 period, Fromkin writes:

> It was an era in which Middle Eastern countries and frontiers were fabricated in Europe. Iraq and what we now call Jordan, for example were British inventions, lines drawn on an empty map by British politicians after World War; while the boundaries of Saudi Arabia, Kuwait, and Iraq were established by a British civil servant in 1922, and the frontiers between Moslems and Christians were drawn by France in Syria-Lebanon and by Russia on the borders of Armenia and Soviet Azerbaijan.
>
> The European powers at that time believed they could change Moslem Asia in the very fundamentals of its political existence, and in their attempt to do so, introduced an artificial state system into the Middle East that has made it into a region of countries that have not become nations even today. The basis of political life in the Middle East – religion – was called into question by the Russians, who proposed communism, and by the British, who proposed nationalism or dynastic loyalty, in its place. Khomeini's Iran in the Shiite world and the Moslem Brotherhood in Egypt, Syria, and elsewhere in the Sunni world kept that issue alive.

The creation of the map of Middle East, as we know it today, was the product of many individuals and it reflected the geopolitical plans of Britain, France, the United States, and Russia. During the eight-year (1914-1922) gestation period, there were two towering, powerful, ambitious and very dissimilar personalities which more than any event or other person contributed, most probably unwillingly, to the contents of the disastrous Middle Eastern settlement of 1922: they were a young politician, Winston Churchill, and an old soldier, Field Marshal Kitchener.

While Churchill is known in the West as the World War II British Prime Minister that rallied the free world and defied the Germans, very little is known about him during the first world war and we will not venture off course, as tempting as it may be, to provide an early portrait of his complex and turbulent political career. Instead, we will suffice to say that during this period of British imperial supremacy, Churchill was obsessed with the notion of invading the Ottoman Empire and bringing it under the British dominion. An obsession which, we may add, he was unable to bring into fruition with the failed naval campaign at the Dardanelles in 1915 and the disastrous defeat of the British army in Gallipoli in the following year. One cannot help but wonder what might have happened with the Middle East and the creation of modern Turkey if the outcome of war at the Dardanelles and Gallipoli had been different for Britain. One thing is certain though. Destiny drove Churchill and the Middle East to interfere repeatedly in one another's political lives as David Fromkin writes: "This left its marks; there are frontier lines now running across the face of the Middle East that are scar-lines from those encounters with him."

Field Marshal and Earl of Khartoum Kitchener, on the other hand, unlike Churchill became an unwilling player in the Middle Eastern Game. In August 1914 and while visiting England from his post in Egypt, as the British Agent and Consul-General, for the ceremonies elevating him to the rank and title of Earl Kitchener of Khartoum, Kitchener was appointed War Minister by Prime Minister Asquith. Germany had just declared war against France and Churchill, First Lord of Admiralty at the time, had recommended to the Prime Minister to appoint the legendary war hero to the post of War Minister. Kitchener, who was eager to return to his post in Egypt and had asked King George to appoint him Viceroy of India when the post became available in 1915, had reluctantly accepted the position. [34] This desire to return to the East, and especially India, would influence many of Kitchener's decisions that would prove crucial in how the Middle East was formed.

During the successful Sudan campaign, Kitchener had greatly expanded the Arab territories controlled by Britain. Egypt was such a recent addition and the officers that served there with Kitchener were limited in their knowledge of Arab affairs. "Neither Kitchener nor his aides demonstrated any real awareness of the great differences between the many communities in the Middle East" writes David Fromkin. "Arabians and Egyptians, for example, though both Arabic-speaking, were otherwise different--in population mix, history, culture, outlook, and circumstances. Even had they been the experts on Egypt which they believed themselves to be, that would not necessarily have made Kitchener's aides the experts on Arabia they claimed to be." He adds, that British Cairo was "an enclave that possessed (wrote one of Kitchener's aides) all the narrowness and provincialism of an English garrison town." From this provincial background, Kitchener and his aides emerged. [35] Sadly, the Cabinet ministers who deferred to Kitchener on Middle Eastern matters were not aware how little the War Minister and his aides in Cairo and Khartoum understood Middle East.

While the major players were Churchill and Kitchener, and to a lesser extent Woodrow Wilson and Lloyd George, there were others who, although of much less stature and position, left their imprints on the final settlement of the Middle East. Among them were Mark Sykes of Britain and George Picot of France, authors of the Sykes-Picot Agreement signed in 1916 by Britain, France and Russia which divided the Middle East into zones of permanent colonial influence; and British Foreign Secretary Arthur Balfour who issued the controversial Balfour Declaration in 1917 promising Britain's commitment and support for a Jewish home in Palestine.

To the Victor Go the Spoils

It was not too long before World War I when victors of wars proudly displayed their spoils. These perhaps were simpler and more honest times. It was easier to tell who the aggressors and villains were. And most important, the motives for going to war were unpretentious and primitive—territorial gains and control, wealth and dominance. World War I ushered an era in which the word imperial had lost most of its luster. It was beginning not to be politically correct or wise to flaunt militaristic expansionism and colonialism. It is on this changing stage of geopolitics that the Middle Eastern Settlement would be played.

During WW I, the Middle East affair was a sideshow for Britain, at least initially. For more than a century British policy had been to side with the Turks as a counterweight to the growing Russian threat. Although oil was not discovered yet in large quantities in the region and, thus, not a major factor in the formulation of the Middle East, France seems to have had her eyes on the coastal areas of Syria and Lebanon and the Kurdish region of Iraq for a long time. And the Americans, who were reluctant latecomers to WW I, had joined the war because, according to President Woodrow Wilson, the world had to be made "safe for democracy".

There is no doubt that the West and Islam have never understood each other well and that this is one of the reasons that led to the ill-conceived creation of the Middle East and continues to plague the relations of these two very different worlds to this day. But the quarrel with the Middle Eastern settlement, Fromkin writes, is not that Britain failed to satisfy the needs and desires of the peoples of the Middle East.

> It is that they were trying to do something altogether different. For Lord Kitchener and his delegated agent Mark Sykes the Middle Eastern Question was what it had been for more than a century: where would the French frontier in the Middle East be drawn and, more important, where would the Russian frontier in the Middle East be drawn?

And things got worse. Between 1914 and 1922, Britain and the officials and politicians involved in the remaking of the Middle East changed. By the time the settlement was signed, they no longer believed in it. Fromkin continues:

> It may well be that the crisis of political civilization that the Middle East endures today stems not merely from Britain's destruction of the old order in the region in 1918,

> and her decisions in 1922 about how it should be replaced, but also from the lack *of conviction* [emphasis added] she brought in subsequent years to the program of imposing the settlement of 1922 to which she was pledged.

The Republic of Turkey and the Lost Sultanate

The final blow to the aged and crippled Ottoman Empire came with the end of World War I and from this disastrous defeat the Turkish Republic was born. In November 1918 Turkey signed the armistice with the Allies. Italy, who had agreed to come into the war on the Allied side in return for a share in the partition of the Ottoman Empire, began to move troops into Anatolia in the spring of 1919 supposedly to restore order. Britain and the US fearing that Italy's presence in Anatolia would become permanent, asked Greece to sail to Smyrna and pre-empt the Italians. The Greek landing, however, assumed a different—and more permanent—character from the start. The British and the Americans believed that the Smyrna enclave ought to be detached from Turkey and incorporated into Greece—a vision of Greece's historic mission promoted brilliantly by the charismatic Greek Prime Minister Eleutherios Venizelos. Moreover, Lloyd George favored a plan whereby the United States, Greece, Italy and France would partition Turkey. Events in Turkey, however, would derail this plan.

At the end of 1919, elections were held throughout the Ottoman Empire and Turkish nationalists headed by the Young Turks won an overwhelming victory. Ottoman war hero Mustafa Kamal Ataturk moved to Ankara deep in the interior of the country and declared the National Pact—stimulated by the Greek occupation of Smyrna—which called for the creation of an independent Turkish Muslim nation-state. With this declaration of independence, Mustafa Kamal and the Chamber of Deputies signaled the beginning of the end of Europe's rule over its neighboring continents. General Mustafa Kamal organized the remnants of the Ottoman army into an effective fighting force and rallied the people to the cause of nationalism. By 1923 Ataturk and his nationalist government had driven out the invading armies, abolished the Sultanate and the Caliphate, and by constitutional amendment introduced the principle of secularism as an anchor of the new democratic and republican constitution. As a result of this new direction, all laws, rules and regulations, and theocratic institutions that had greatly influenced the dealings of state and social order were abolished and various political and social reforms introduced along Western lines.

Drastic reforms aimed at bringing medieval Ottoman society into the 20th century were carried out. Polygamy was abolished, women were granted equal rights with men, state and religion were separated, the Arabic alphabet was replaced with the Latin alphabet, and the fez and the veil were outlawed. But the task of bringing Turkey in line with the free and democratic nations of Europe was not easy. It was difficult to teach democracy to a people who had been ruled by an absolute monarch for 600 years and by nomadic rulers before that for all its existence. Until Ataturk's death in 1938, Turkey remained a one-party state and the armed forces have been to this day the guardian of the Turkish constitution.

What Ataturk accomplished by creating a secular state in a predominant Muslim country and at the hills of perhaps the greatest Islamic empire ever cannot be overestimated. It was a courageous, visionary, and even revolutionary act that has served Turkey well for eighty years and one worth emulating elsewhere in the Muslim world. Not everyone was or is happy about it, however. The collapse of the Sultanate and Caliphate enraged and humiliated the Arab spirit and is haunting the Arab psyche to this day. Moreover, the partition of the Middle East and the European colonialism that followed with the 1923 settlement spawned the resurrection of Islamic fundamentalism in Egypt a few years later. Osama bin Laden has referred to these events as the "great catastrophe" and the period from then until now as "eighty years of humiliation and disgrace".

It's very difficult for non-Arabs to fully understand how deep Arab nationalism runs. Arabs throughout their long history have been notorious about undermining and even attacking each other. When there are no external enemies, they turn against each other. But when their religion and pan-Arab pride are threatened or humiliated, they become amalgamated. The degree of the unity they achieve and the extent of sacrifices they are willing to undergo are beyond the comprehension of the West.

We were in the Middle East when the news of the collapse of Baghdad reached the Arab media on 9 April 2003. While many rejoiced, at least momentarily, with the Iraqis for having ridden a brutal dictator and, perhaps for a brief precious moment, dreamed of a similar event in their own troubled country, many more had tears in their eyes because one more time fellow Arabs were humiliated by the West. They simply could not understand why the West was striking back at them once again. They longed for the glorious days of the Islamic Golden Age of and of the victorious expeditions of the caliphs of past. And they grieved for their lost Sultanate and despaired for what they saw as their future.

1. Richard Hooker, *The Caliphate, World Civilizations*
2. Levant: The region now known as Lebanon, Syria and Jordan.
3. "The Islamic World to 1600", The University of Calgary, The Applied Research Group
4. Paul Fregosi, *Jihad*, p 80.
5. Paul Fregosi, *Jihad*, pp 90-92
6. Ibid.
7. Paul Fregosi, *Jihad*, pp 93-100
8. Ibid.
9. Ibid.
10. Paul Fregosi, *Jihad*, pp 103-106
11. Ibid.
12. Paul Fregosi, *Jihad*, pp 123-126
13. Ibid.
14. John J. Norwich, *Byzantium: The Decline and Fall*, pg 1
15. Ibid, pp 13-28
16. Ibid, pp 300-302
17. Ibid, pp 320-322
18. Ibid.
19. Ibid, pp 341-343
20. Ibid.
21. Ibid, pp 345-348
22. Ibid, pp 349-364
23. Ibid.
24. Ibid, pp 417-420
25. Ibid, pp 423-424
26. Ibid, pp 448-450
27. David Fromkin, *A Peace to End All Peace*, pp 39-44
28. Ibid.
29. Ibid., pp 45-50
30. Official website of Kingdom of Jordan; http://www.kinghussein.gov.jo
31. Ibid.
32. David Fromkin, *A Peace to End All Peace*, pp 26-32
33. Ibid.
34. Ibid. pp 79-87
35. Ibid.
36. Ibid. pp 96-106

We continue our Journey with the birth of Muslim Brotherhood, the largest and most influential Islamic revivalist movements of the twentieth century and the first one to be founded in the Arab world. Most of the writings on Islamic Fundamentalism (pre- and post-September 11) focus on the activities of Muslim Brotherhood in the 1950s and beyond. We chose, instead, to go back to the creation of the movement and follow it through its evolution to the current Jihadist movements. Moreover, the 1920s mark the fall of the last Islamic Caliphate (Ottoman Empire) and the beginning of "…80 years of humiliation and disgrace..." according to Osama bin Laden. (*) The restoration of the Fallen Caliphate has been the goal and obsession of all Islamic movements. It is ironic, however, that while the movements strive to restore the Caliphate, none of the past Caliphs would qualify as a true Caliph under the current interpretation of Islamic state

(*) Osama bin Laden's videotaped address, aired shortly after US strikes against the Taliban in Afghanistan in October 2001, aimed to incite Muslims in a holy war against the West.

The Resurrection of the Vision of an Islamic Nation

Stage One: Revival of Islamic Fundamentalism

Islam is faith and worship, a country and a citizenship, a religion and a state. It is spirituality and hard work. It is a Quran and a sword.

Islamic fundamentalism is not a late twentieth century radical Islamic movement, as many would like us believe. Its origins go back to the seventh century and the ancient, early Islamic movement of the khawarig (separatists) who vehemently opposed Ali, the fourth of the "Righteous Caliphs" and the cousin of Prophet Mohamed. It is ironic that the foundation of Islamic fundamentalism as it exists today was laid by Ibn Taymiyya (1263-1328), a medieval religious scholar, whose loathing of the khawarig was only second to that of Mongols, who sacked Baghdad and brought the Abbasid Caliphate to an end in 1258. Driven by his dedication to rally the Muslims against the Mongol invaders, Ibn Taymiyya went to Cairo and incited the Mamluks to wage Jihad (holy war) against the Mongols.[1] But he faced a problem. How could he convince Muslims to take arms against Muslims, since the Mongol King Mahmud Ghazan had converted to Islam in 1295? With great skill and ingenuity, Ibn Taymiyya constructed a theological theory by which the Mamluks could still fight the Mongols who, although they were Muslims, were considered apostates because they did not apply Muslim Shariah law. In Islam, there is no greater sin than being an apostate, and King Ghazan by allowing his soldiers to follow customary Mongol law (Yasa code of laws) rather than Islamic law, had committed the ultimate crime of apostasy and should be treated as the arch enemy of Islam. [2]

A convenient theory at the time, devised by Ibn Taymiyya to unite the Mamluks in a holy war against the Mongols, it would be rediscovered in the 1920s, greatly influence all modern Islamic fundamentalists and dominate the debate on politics and religion within modern Islam. Ibn Taymiyya thus became the most influential medieval scholar-activist on radical Islamic ideology. Though he was providing a remedy to his society's problems in the thirteenth century, later generations—from the Wahhabi movement in Saudi Arabia to Sayyid Qutb, Abdel Salam Farag and Islamic Jihad in Egypt, and Osama bin Laden and Ayman Zawahiri—would use the rationale of Ibn Taymiyya's fatwa (religious ruling) on the Mongols to declare Jihad against, what they considered, the apostate Muslim rulers and the infidels of the West.[3]

For more than four centuries the Islamic fundamentalists hibernated, or so it seemed. This was the glorious age of the dominance of the Ottoman Empire. The Mongols were defeated and eventually absorbed by the Turks. The mighty Byzantine Empire had finally crumbled as its crown jewel and capital, Constantinople, fell to the Turks in 1453. The Muslims were content with their conquests, although they failed to conquer Western Europe, and once again there was an Islamic Caliphate (Ottoman Empire). Their hunger for territorial conquests and holy wars was greatly diminished.

The speed by which Islam had spread and the dominance of Islamic Caliphates from Arabia to Andalusia, for more than a thousand years, was sufficient proof and an historic validation to Muslims of the truth of the Quran and Islam's claim as the true and universal religion. From the eighteenth to the first half of the twentieth century, Western colonialism and a wave of uprisings by many Eastern European nations aimed at regaining national independence, though, seriously challenged Islamic geopolitical dominance, and the notion that Muslims were destined to be the true inheritors of the earth. To many Muslims, this Western dominance and the growing Muslim weakness were the result of unfaithfulness, and a sign that Muslims were drifting away from the true path of Islam. [4]

This conclusion became a convincing and powerful argument that encouraged Muslims to struggle (Jihad) to bring the Ummah (nation) back to the path of "true" Islam. This new call to arms in the eighteenth century marks, for the first time, a global emergence of Islamic revivalist movement that remains till today the foundation and driving force of all Islamic fundamentalism activists. The most noteworthy eighteenth century revivalist movement is the Wahhabi movement in Arabia. Mohammed ibn Abd al-Wahhab (1703-1791) was an Islamic scholar who lived in Arabia and whose hero was Ibn Taymiyya. Abd al-Wahhab's theology and movement called for a fresh, strict and fanatic interpretation of Islam and became known as Wahhabism or Wahhabi movement. Among the most early and infamous acts of Wahhabism is the destruction of the sacred tombs of Mohammed and His Companions in the holy cities of Mecca and Medina, as the movement considered any manmade artistic and religious symbols idolatrous.[5]

As Wahhabism was spreading through Arabia, an alliance of mutual benefits, that merged religious zeal with military might, was forged between Mohamed ibn Saud, a local tribal chief and ancestor of the current Saudi Royal Family, and Abd al-Wahhab. The former sought unification and control of the Arabian tribes and needed Wahhabism to legitimize his Jihad; the latter desired the spread of Wahhabism through the Muslim world and he needed money and power. This merger of politics and religion formed the foundation of the dynasty of the House of Saud, and, with the enormous wealth that came with late twentieth century oil revenue, Saudi Arabia began to export the puritanical and often militant brand of Wahhabism to all corners of Muslim world and the West. This legacy has infuriated moderate Muslim leaders, and caused a great deal of embarrassment to the Saudi Royal Family, because of the growing accusations by the West that Saudis not only tolerate terrorism, but they incubate it and fund it as well. It is ironic that the Saudi Royal Family has become one of the major and well-identified targets of Al Qaeda and Islamic fundamentalists that have spawned from Wahhabism. [6]

The first part of the twentieth century brought not only the First World War, it also marked the collapse of the Ottoman Empire and the creation of a secular Turkish state in its place, the remaking of the Middle East, and the start of the creation of an Israeli state at the expense of Palestinians. These were profound and highly traumatic events that wounded Islamic pride and humiliated Muslims all over the world. This notion of Wahhabism that the decline of Islamic supremacy was caused by the drift from the path of true Islam was re-ignited after the collapse of the Ottoman Empire and led to the birth of the Muslim Brotherhood in Egypt shortly thereafter.

Hassan El Banna

The Muslim Brotherhood is the largest and most influential Islamic revivalist movement in the twentieth century. It was founded in Egypt in 1928 by Hassan El Banna, a 22-year-old school teacher, and its initial purpose was to oppose the growing influence of secular and western ideas and practices in the Middle East. Conservative Muslims feared that Egypt would follow Turkey's example and form a secular government. Unlike the liberal nationalists who sought to reconcile Islam with modernity, El Banna was determined to reject modernity and restore the rule of Islamic virtues. [7]

El Banna was born in 1906 in a small village in Egypt to a simple and conservative Muslim family. His father, who repaired watches for a living, was an El Azhar scholar with a sizable Islamic library and a wide knowledge of Islamic literature. He served as Imam (prayer leader), was a teacher in his village mosque and the author of few books on Islamic subjects. After work, Hassan's father spent his time studying the Sunnah (Prophet Mohamed's Traditions), and discussing his studies with friends and scholars at home or in the mosque in the presence of his children, including young Hassan. [8]

At the age of eight, El Banna joined the kutab (village school) where the emphasis was on memorizing and studying the Quran. He was very bright, grew up with strong religious values and at the age of twelve he became a member of a moral organization for students. This organization encouraged the students to behave properly, avoid the use of bad words or fighting each other. It wasn't long before he became the president of this organization. [9] At the age of fourteen, he joined an elementary school for teachers, where he and his fellow members from other moral organizations were active in founding more organizations and targeting cultural and social reforms. They sent letters to people urging them to pray, stop drinking and gambling, and asked women to get veiled. They also targeted Christian missionaries and fought their influence on Muslims. His involvement in these organizations had a profound influence on young El Banna who came to believe that the Islamization of society starts with the moral reform of the individual.[10]

In 1923 and at the age of only sixteen, El Banna moved to Cairo to join the Dar-El-Ulum (High Institute for Teachers). He studied and lived in Cairo until his graduation in 1927. Moving from the small village to the big capital, he looked at the mega city of Cairo with the eyes of a simple religious villager. He noticed how the influence of secularism had penetrated the society. He saw that people, especially the young ones, were drifting away from the old ways of Islam and this greatly disturbed him. He observed that people's behaviors and mannerisms were becoming more Western. The social liberal activists within the Egyptian society encouraged this new phenomenon of secularism and modernity. Some liberals advocated that the universities should become secular by rebelling against the laws and traditions of the Islam. El Banna believed that magazines, books and newspapers were instrumental in promoting these ideas that aimed at weakening the influence of religion in public life.[11]

The four years he spent in Cairo also exposed him to the political turmoil in Egypt under the British occupation. At that time, the Muslim world was broken up into pieces after the collapse of the Ottoman Empire and re-mapped into its present shape.[12] El Banna was very concerned about this decline of the Islamic civilization in relation to the West. He was greatly influenced by Wahhabism and believed that Egypt had lost its political and economic independence, and, because of the influence of western secular ideas, people had drifted away from the path of the true faith that had been laid down by God.[13] He often stated how he was in misery seeing all the social diseases that had affected the lives of the people, and while he and his followers were trying to find solutions and remedies for the nation, the people were roaming the streets of Cairo between cafes and nightclubs.[14]

It should be noted that, notwithstanding the direction El Banna's future activism took, as a young man he cared immensely about his country and Islam and was tormented by the collapse of the Islamic supremacy, the British occupation of Egypt, and, most importantly, the decay of, what he believed, the moral values of Islam. As he describes in his own words, as he met with his friends and colleagues he used to cry in despair about the state the country and the Muslim world had reached. In these meetings, they would ask themselves what can they do to stand against these secular ideas of the West, and what change can they bring in the lives of their own people. These questions kept lingering in young Hassan's mind and he kept discussing them with his close friends.[15]

At the age of 21 and after his graduation from Dar-El-Ulum in 1927, he accepted a teaching position in Ismailia after rejecting a scholarship to continue his studies in Europe. Ismailia was the headquarters of the Suez Canal Company and there were a lot of British living there with their families, as employees of the Company and as soldiers in the military camps. The presence and influence of the British in Ismailia strengthened the beliefs that El Banana had harbored since his days in Cairo about the political conditions, military occupation and economic exploitation, as the city's utilities and the Suez Canal were in the hands of the British. The burning issue for El Banna, however, was the secular western influence that the British had on the people of the city.[16]

He observed the community of Ismailia for a while before he started getting involved in it. He realized that the influential persons in the community were the religious scholars, so he acquainted himself with them. Eventually he started preaching in coffee houses, mosques and youth clubs to the astonishment of his friends and bystanders, who were not used to this type of public display of religious fervor.[17] El Banna, even conducted night classes for his student's parents. Also, he founded a religious library with his own books and circulated them among the people.

This type of preaching served a purpose for a little while, but it was only affecting people's emotions rather than solving any problems. El Banna was astute to realize that preaching and lecturing people will not rid the country and the Islamic nations from the secular western influence, and will not bring back the country or the people to the true path of God.[18] He started having direct encounters with several important religious scholars who he had been observing for some time. He even took his concerns further to El Azhar and met with its scholars, but their answers were inadequate and unsatisfactory to him. Some religious scholars, unhappy with the status quo and mainly because of El Banna's efforts, started a magazine named El Fatah (The

Conquest) where El Banna served as one of its reporters. The magazine's objective was to stand against western and secular ideas published in other magazines, and to promote the formation of Muslim NGOs aimed at reforming the youth and bringing them back to the right Islamic way. One of the NGOs formed was the Young Men Muslim Association (YMMA) modeled after the YMCA clubs that were present throughout the country. El Banna became a member of the YMMA and remained as such until his death in 1949.[19]

The Birth of Muslim Brotherhood

The passionate preaching and tireless efforts of El Banna eventually began to bear fruits in a more significant way. In March 1928, he was visited by some colleagues who were influenced by his preaching, and complained to him about the deterioration of the Muslims under the British occupation, the loss of their dignity and pride and being exposed to their secular ideas and western behavior and lifestyle. El Banna knew that the time had finally arrived and with emotion declared, "Let us promise God to become soldiers of Islam, country and Islamic nation." Following El Banna's declaration, they all took an oath to live and die for Islam. El Banna's companions then asked him, what should they refer to themselves, a club, an organization, or a syndicate? He responded, "Since we are all brothers serving Islam, then we are the Muslim Brotherhood." And there and then, the foundation of Muslim Brotherhood (MB) was established and its first cell was formed. The MB attracted more members and by the end of 1928, the membership grew to more than seventy.[20]

After the historical meeting of March 1928, El Banna rented a small room where they could meet and operate and called this operation "The MB Reform School." The school's aim was to educate people of the true belief of Islam and its history, and, most importantly, of their duty to fight the influence of West and its missionaries. Since initially the MB Reform School's objective was strictly to reform and educate, it did so by producing Islamic publications and by preaching. The MB was registered as a religious and charitable NGO as any other small association that existed at that time.[21] The movement was led by Supreme Guide Hassan El Banna, who was assisted by a general guidance board, an executive body responsible for formulating policies and running the group's activities. There was also an Assembly of Members, called the Shurah Council.[22]

As the MB grew and more members attended its functions, the small rented room became inadequate. From funds the Brother's contributed, the first physical structure was built that served as the headquarters of the brotherhood and they referred to it as the Dar (Home) of the MB. The Dar opened to the public in February 1930 and included a mosque. This was an important milestone in the activities of MB and the Islamic revivalist movement, as it did not only provide a badly needed space for its activities, it provided a concrete evidence of its presence and sent a message to the Islamic world that it was there to stay.[23]

The immediate objective of the MB in the first three years was to increase the number of its membership. In his own words, El Banna said he preferred gathering men than gathering information in books.[24] For recruiting new members, the MB established social projects such as schools, youth centers, technical institutes for school dropouts, and built mosques, factories, and clinics. The economic, social and psychological support such projects provided to the Muslim community played an incredible role in the MB ability to generate loyalty between its members and attract new recruits.[25] This aspect of MB services to Muslims is to this day one of the most important pillars of the organization, and a major factor in its unparalleled appeal to the masses. Moreover, it is a testimony of El Banna's caring personality and, most of all, his marketing genius.

To spread the MB ideology and attract new members, El Banna also visited small villages and towns on his weekends and met with the public in the mosques. By the year 1932, the MB had established fifteen branches in different cities and towns in Egypt.[26] Each branch included a center or an office, a mosque, a school, a clinic and a youth center where young males could play sports. He supplemented the traditional Islamic education for the male students with physical training.[27]

In 1932, and after spending five years in Ismailia, El Banna was transferred to a school in Cairo at his own request. He realized that operating out of a big capital city like Cairo would be more beneficial to the MB than being in a small city like Ismailia. In the short span of five years, El Banna had seen his dream and passion become reality, and the success and growth of the MB in Ismailia encouraged him to enlarge the operational theater and relocate the MB headquarters to Cairo.[28]

After his move to Cairo, he continued to concentrate on the MB expansion. The single and most important factor that made this dramatic expansion possible, was the organizational and ideological leadership provided by El Banna, who was a charismatic leader, and played an important role in the formation of the organizational structure of the group.[29] He was the center of authority and the sole decision maker for the group. The members pledged obedience and loyalty to him. This was reflected on the unanimity of the members on all decisions. His control over the group members was unlimited and he had absolute power in his hands. He emphasized building the organization and establishing its internal rules in a way that it would operate effectively in his absence. In other words, single handedly he developed and institutionalized the structure, policies, and practices of Muslim Brotherhood. The importance of this accomplishment is fully appreciated when one realizes that the same structure, policies, and practices that El Banna created are, in most part, still in effect to this day, and have been the paradigm to all other sister fundamentalist movements, including *Al Qaeda*, that have spawned through the Muslim world in the past eighty years.[30]

The first stage of the Islamic revivalism movement, thus, was completed with the formation and institutionalization of Muslim Brotherhood. This period can best be summarized in the words of Gilles Kepel, a scholar of Islam and Middle East, in his book *Jihad: The Trail of Political Islam.*

> In the 1920s, when the Society of Brothers was founded, the Muslim world was in disarray. Ataturk abolished the Ottoman caliphate in Istanbul in 1924, which for so long had symbolized the unity of the faithful, and replaced it with the secular Turkish nationalist republic. The land of Islam was divided up by the Christian powers at the same time that it was being eaten away from the inside. The

Muslim Brothers formed their society in Egypt in order to reclaim Islam's political dimension, which had formerly resided in the person of the now-fallen caliph. Confronted by the Egyptian nationalists of the time—who demanded independence, the departure of the British, and a democratic constitution—the Brothers responded with a slogan that is still current in the Islamic movement: 'The Quran is our constitution.' ...Everything was made clear in the Quran, whose moral principles, the Brothers claimed, were universal. This doctrine was shared by the entire Islamic movement, whatever their other views. All agreed that the solution to the political problems facing Muslims lay in the setting up of an Islamic state that would implement the law of the sacred texts of Islam—the Shariah—as the caliph had done in the past.[31]

1. Johannes J. G. Jansen, *The Dual Nature of Islamic Fundamentalism*; pp 26-39
2. Ibid.
3. John L. Esposito, *Unholy War: Terror in the Name of Islam*; pp 45-46
4. Ibid; pp 47-49
5. Ibid.
6. Ibid.
7. Arabic Trends, The International Magazine on Arab Affairs, Special Report, Hassan Al Banna, Founder of the Muslim Brotherhood, by Guilain Denoeux.
8. Ibid.
9. Zyad Ahmed Salama, *The Biography of Sheikh Hassan Al Banna*, , pp 11-19
10. Ibid.
11. MAS Chicago
12. Ibid.
13. Arabic Trends
14. MAS Chicago
15. Ibid.
16. Zyad Ahmed Salama, *The Biography of Sheikh Hassan Al Banna*, pp 85-86
17. Ibid.
18. Ibid, pp 25-28

19. Ibid.
20. Ibid, pp 92-93
21. Ibid, pp 24-25
22. "Politics in God's Name", *Ahram Weekly* #247,
23. Zyad Ahmed Salama, *The Biography of Sheikh Hassan Al Banna*, p 96
24. Muslim Brotherhood Movement homepage, www.ummah.org.uk
25. Arabic Trends
26. Zyad Ahmed Salama, *The Biography of Sheikh Hassan Al Banna*, p 97
27. "Politics in God's Name", *Ahram Weekly* #247,
28. Zyad Ahmed Salama, *The Biography of Sheikh Hassan Al Banna*, p 91
29. Arabic Trends
30. Muslim Brotherhood Movement homepage, www.ummah.org.uk
31. Gilles Kepel, *Jihad: The Trail of Political Islam*; pp 27-30

This section traces the phenomenal growth of Muslim Brotherhood, and focuses on the second stage of evolution of this Islamic revivalism movement, as the ideology and tactics of Islamic fundamentalism have not remained static since its most recent revival in 1928. This stage posed a great intellectual challenge to us. The plethora of information was rivaled only by its complexity and even contradiction. Socialism, communism, Marxism, capitalism, Fascism, and Islam were often mingled, in attempting to classify the Islamic movement according to models familiar to social scientists, and contributed to a mystification of the ideology of the movement. It is worth presenting here a quotation from Diaa Rashwan in which he articulates the character of the Islamic movement: "The influence of religious ideology extends to all aspects of the Islamic movement, from symbols and terms of reference to tactics and strategies, a factor which alone distinguishes this movement in general from all other social and political movements, however similar they may appear on the surface."

At the risk of presenting an oversimplified version of the phenomenon of Islamic movement, we attempted to present to the lay reader, in the second stage of the movement, the "big picture" without leaving out important details that influenced its next stage.

Stage Two: Islam and Political Activism

God is our purpose, the Prophet our leader, the Quran our constitution, the Jihad our way, and dying for God's cause our ultimate objective.
Muslim Brotherhood

The Ideology of Muslim Brotherhood

Since the foundation of the MB in 1928 and until the mid-90s, the fundamental principles of the MB remained unchanged. They might have deviated from their original approach, but the objective remained the same. These principles are based on a fundamentalist approach of Islam. El Banna outlined these principles in his address to the MB in their fifth convention in 1938. The MB, he said, seeks a return to the pure sources of Islam, the Holy Quran and the Sunnah of the Prophet Mohamed. El Banna believed that Islam was not only a religion, but a system covering all aspects of life. Muslims should understand Islam as the companions of the Prophet Mohamed and the generation of the first followers understood it. Islam was a universal religion.

Islam should not be limited within the walls of the mosque, El Banna believed. People who restrict Islam to a system of worship and they think this is its core, they are wrong. As a result, the MB rejected the secularist approach of restricting Islam to only a relationship of faith between man and his creator, and wished to establish a political body in the form of an Islamic state and demanded governmental reform. This structure of the nation must be driven from the pure sources of Islam and become an Islamic lawful system. Moreover, the MB believed that the rules and teachings of Islam are so comprehensive that they address all of the affairs of people in this and in the life after. Those who think that these teachings address the worship aspects, or the spiritual aspects alone were wrong in their thinking. Islam was faith and worship, a country and citizenship, a religion and a state. It was spirituality and hard work; the Quran and a sword.

The following brief summary, in the words of El Banna [1], provides a glimpse to the ideological worldview of the MB and its mission:

> You can say that the MB is a call for people to take the Islam back to its pure sources and reject any action or principle which contradicts with the Koran and the Sunnah which should be implemented in every aspect of life. The MB has dedicated itself to increase Islamic faith by concentrating on the purity of the hearts and souls. It's a political organization that demands the reform of the government for the purpose of Islamizing the governments in the Muslim nations. It is an athletic group because a strong believer is better than a weak believer, as the Islamic duties as praying, fasting and pilgrimage cannot be performed with a weak body. It's a scientific, educational and cultural association because a good Muslim has to seek knowledge to train the body, the soul and the mind. It is a business corporation because Islam cares for fund raising and earning money in a proper way. And it's a social idea as maintaining brotherhood links among the members of the Islamic society, enables it to find proper remedies and cure to its diseases.

It would be difficult for anyone to argue against this ideology espoused by El Banna. But not everybody, of course, accepted that this was the true ideology of the Brotherhood. The following excerpts from the book *Religion in Egypt* by the Al-Ahram Center for Strategic Studies provide a somewhat different evaluation of the ideology of Islamic fundamentalism in general, and Muslim Brotherhood in specific. Moreover, they present another example of the debate that continues to this date about the merits of the Brother's Islamic ideology, and illustrate the socially ambiguous nature of the early stage of modern Islamic revivalism movement.

> El Banna established political Islam. For him Islam was a political ideology, as it governs all aspects of human existence. The Muslim Brotherhood movement seeks a whole social change just like any other fanatical social and political group. Although is started as religious movement, it evolved to a political movement that used Islam as the

> framework for certain interpretations of the religion that was implemented by El Banna. As he used Islam as his guideline for building the movement's ideological structure, it made it appear as a religious movement. This movement is still imprisoned in the same ideological structure set by El Banna. The Muslim Brotherhood group has a certain view of Islam that otherwise no other view is correct.
>
> The Muslim brotherhood group since it was founded and until the present time, didn't get rid of their mysterious ideology or its political maneuvering, so it is believed by analysts that both are part of their motives for the continuation of the group and the attraction of more followers. When El Banna wanted to start getting involved in politics, he wrote an article in an Islamic magazine saying, "we are now moving forward from preaching by using words only, to preaching by using words accompanied with action and Jihad. But we are not deviating from our original plan by getting involved in politics, as ignorant people may say. We are moving a step forward in the direction of our Islamic way. It is not our fault that politics is part of the religion and Islam consists of both leaders and followers."
>
> It is clear that the group is deliberately putting a big frame around its general ideology that enables it to deal with both the governing and political powers with a big freedom of movement, so it wouldn't fall under certain laws and systems like the rest of the political parties. At the same time, it helps in attracting more followers who are attracted by its different religious slogans with unidentified meanings. This means that it was a deliberate act of disguising their true identity, to give the group a chance of dual talking. When it is under pressure, it talks about its peaceful religious reforms and when it feels its power and political ascendancy, it starts talking about the enforcement of Islamic laws and demands government reforms forgetting the moral and social reform, they talked about earlier.

Whether one agrees with the views of the Al-Ahram Center for Strategic Studies, one fact remains clear. Within a few years the Brotherhood had evolved into a populist movement that succeeded in enlisting the masses—particular the urban lower-middle classes—and managed to politicize their religious vision of the world, as no other group and movement had done thus far in Egypt and within Islam since Ibn Taymiyya .

Although anti-Western, El Banna was not against technological and scientific modernization, and he raised the standard of *Islamic modernity* as an alternative to the modernity of Europe. His Islamic version of modernity consisted of a "complete and total" blend of society, state, culture, and religion, a blend with which everything began and ended. [2] As El Banna pointed out, the Quran renders the acquisition of knowledge, in both the spiritual and moral domains, a religious duty.

> Hassan El Banna established political Islam as an all-encompassing endeavor—the logical consequence of the idea that Islam governs all aspects of existence. Faith guides man's being in the universe. The Shariah (Islamic law) establishes his duties and rights with respect to society, and defines the principles of conduct and modes of interaction with others, whether Muslim or non-Muslim. Islam, in Hassan El Banna's political ideology, is a philosophy, a code of law, and a moral ideology that demands the believer's full mental and emotional commitment. [3]

Moreover, while El Banna was quick to denounce imperialism and the danger of westernization, he knew that the Muslim predicament was first and foremost a Muslim problem.[4] He believed that the only route to Islamic revival begins with reforming the Muslim individual by acquiring strong faith, good manners and correct worship, it then passes to building the proper Muslim family, and by reforming both, the community will be reformed, then the government and the Muslim state will be reformed. By doing so, the Muslims can restore their lost Caliphate and with it they can master the world with Islam. He was, in this respect the forerunner of Islamic reform.

El Banna saw the Muslim Brotherhood (MB) as the vehicle to this Islamic reform and laid down three stages for its expansion. The first stage was the **Introduction Stage**, in which the MB's message was communicated to people. The second stage was the **Formation Stage**, which aimed at attracting new supporters and recruiting more members. The third stage was the **Implementation Stage**, where the MB executed its plans. The

MB took several steps to promote the nature and understanding of their movement as it began to act on the three stages by holding several conventions over the next few years.

The main objective of the first convention held in 1933 was fighting missionary schools. El Banna and fifteen other members representing the different MB branches signed a letter and sent it to King Fouad of Egypt. In this letter they requested the King to cancel the license of any school or hospital that was used for missionary purposes. Subsequently, sending letters became one of his means of communicating with the government officials. El Banna over the years sent letters to officials, members of the royal family and religious scholars, requesting them to work for Islam and reform the social and moral corruption in the country. One of these letters was sent to the prime minister criticizing him of mentioning in a public speech his admiration of Kamal Ataturk, who changed Turkey from an Islamic state to a secular one.

Overall, these letters summarized his views of reforming the conditions of the Islamic world, which were presented in fifty requests. These requests included dissolving the political parties, modifying existing laws to Islamic laws, allowing prayers in universities, strengthening the military, bonding Islamic nations, especially Arabic nations, as a first step to the revival of the lost Caliphate, spreading the Islamic spirit in governmental offices, observing the manners and behaviors of employees, and outlawing prostitution, gambling, alcohol drinking, horse racing, dancing and mixing between men and women. Another mean of communicating his message was a weekly meeting he held every Tuesday, where El Banna spoke to his followers. Over the years the popularity of these meetings grew, and by the year 1936 the government and the British became aware of the growing influence of this movement on the people.

In 1934 and during the second convention, the MB formed a company to establish a printing house where they published and printed their weekly magazine. The magazine helped in expanding their message to a wider range of audiences. By the end of 1934, the MB had established 50 branches nationwide—all styled along the model that El Banna had used earlier in Ismailia. Each branch included an office, a mosque, a school, a technical institute and a youth center.

After its successful spreading through Egypt, the MB was ready to go global. In the year 1935 and during their third convention, the MB discussed that they have to start working and spreading their ideology outside of Egypt. They also discussed and encouraged the formation of an Islamic league for Islamic revival. In 1935, the Djibouti branch was established and in 1937 the Syria branch followed. At present time, more than seventy branches are established worldwide in countries as Jordan, Libya, Algeria, Sudan, Iran, Pakistan, Indonesia, Malaysia and others. By the late 1930s, MB had established branches in every Egyptian governorate.

The MB dedicated their fourth convention in 1937 in support of young and hugely inexperienced King Farouk who had suddenly and prematurely inherited the Egyptian throne. A big crowd of some twenty thousand Muslim Brothers marched to Abdein Palace in Cairo cheering in support of the king and its regime, "God is great, The Quran is the universal constitution, Islam is the savior of humanity, the MB is supporting his Royal Highness, and we only want the Islamic law to be implemented." [5]

Their main objective continued to be strictly religious, anti-Western and fighting moral and social corruption. Their means of reforming was limited to preaching, spreading their ideology through conferences, meetings and the articles published in their magazine. Until the year 1938, the MB had never sought reform through political power, but the political events in the country at that time took them in a different direction, as the Brotherhood deviated from its original objective and it began changing from a movement for spiritual and moral reform into an organization directly active in Egyptian politics. El Banna declared that there is no difference between religion and state and demanded this time an Islamic reform for the government.

1. Hassan El Banna, *Memoirs of Hassan el Banna*
2. Gilles Kepel, *Jihad: The Trail of Political Islam*, p 28
3. *Al-Ahram Weekly*, 9-15 December 1999, Issue No. 459
4. John L. Esposito, *Unholy War: Terror in the Name of Islam*; pp 51-56
5. Hassan El Banna, *Memoirs of Hassan el Banna*

Stage two covered the formative years of the modern Islamic revivalist movement, i.e. Muslim Brotherhood. This was mainly a period of political activism that sought the return to the purest form of Islam, the Quran and the Sunnah, through government reform. Stage three follows the transformation of the movement from political activism to political violence. This form of violence, however, was still very different than the kind of violence that became the trademark of the Islamic movements ever since the mid-sixties. The El Banna brand of political violence aimed at achieving specific political objectives, while subsequent violence was part of the Jihad (holy wars) against the apostate rulers and leaders.

Stage Three: Political Reform Turns Violent

God's rule on earth can be established only through the Islamic system, as it is the only system ordained by God for all human beings, whether they are rulers or ruled.

Sayyid Qutb

In 1941, in what is considered to be the MB's first serious conflict with the government, El Banna was arrested and detained for one month because of a reported incident that he had attacked the British in one of his speeches. By that time, El Banna had started getting involved in politics and becoming influential in the political stage. He tried to run for parliamentary elections twice. In 1942 and after El Banna registered his name for the elections in the city of Ismailia, he met Prime Minister El Nahas Pasha who advised El Banna to withdraw from the elections because the government was pressured by the British. El Banna withdrew from these elections and in return El Nahas allowed the MB more freedom of action, and agreed to act on some of El Banna's demands for reform. These demands included: the celebration of Islamic religious days and making them national holidays; outlawing prostitution throughout the country; using the Arabic as the language of communication in all companies and organizations in the country; and moving towards the formation of the Arab League, which eventually was formed in 1944. These concessions by the government were seen as a big gain for the MB, as they were indeed.

The truce between El Banna and the government, however, was short lived, as he and five of his followers made a second attempt to run for election again in 1944 against the wishes of the government represented this time by Prime Minister Ahmed Maher. El Banna lost in the election and afterwards declared that the elections were marred with fraud. Whether these failed attempts to gain political power were the reason for the violence that would mire the activities of the Brotherhood for the next several years remains a subject of controversy to this day. What is certain, though, is that the Islamic movement was mutating from one of political reform to one of political violence.

On February 24, 1945 Prime Minister Ahmed Maher was shot dead in the parliament, as he was reading the declaration that Egypt was joining World War II. The MB had previously objected to this decision and had asked the prime minister to reject this option. El Banna and two of his assistants were arrested by the orders of the new Prime Minister El Nokrashy Pasha, but eventually released for insufficient evidence. This incident shows not only that the MB started interfering with the decision making of the government, but also showed their dissatisfaction with these decisions had led them to violence.

In 1946, four attacks, in which guns and explosives were used, were directed at British occupation forces, injuring more than 100 people. Several MB members were arrested and convicted by Judge Ahmed El Khazendar. Few months later, two members of MB assassinated the judge in front of his house as he was on his way to work. One of the assassins was the personal secretary of El Banna. Also, in the same year several members of the MB were arrested in the city of Ismailia where they were experimenting with the manufacturing and use of bombs and explosives.

It was becoming apparent by then that the, long suspected but still secretive, paramilitary wing of the MB had gone into action. According to *Al-Ahram* Center for Strategic Studies, some claim that the paramilitary wing was established from the very beginning with the foundation of the MB, while others say it was not established until just before WWII. Also they were allegations that the paramilitary members were selected from the MB boy scouts division and were under the direct supervision of El Banna. Regardless of when the militant seeds were sown, the paramilitary wing had been kept secret from most members, who started knowing about it only after the assassination of Judge El Khazendar, and the eventual arrest and conviction of some MB members.

Jihad for Palestine

By 1947, major international and regional events were unfolding which would prove extremely important not only in the ideology and tactics of the Islamic movement, but to the peace and stability in the Middle East, and which unquestionably have dominated global geopolitics for more than fifty years, as no other events have. Palestine was fractured as a nation and the Israeli state was born in its midst.

The Muslim Brothers could not ignore this decision by the international community. On October 1947, El Banna ordered all branches of MB to prepare for *Jihad* in Palestine. The first wave of mujahedeen (holy warriors) traveled to Palestine after the UN declaration of the division of Palestine in November 29, 1947. Then a big demonstration led by the MB took place in the streets of Cairo on December 15, 1947 in support of the Palestinians. In a speech he gave that day, El Banna urged the leaders and rulers of the Arab world to intervene to save Palestine. He announced that he had 10,000 men under his command ready to go fight and die for Palestine, and to that end he asked the government to allow them to go and fight. The Egyptian government agreed, supplied them with weapons and money and the Brotherhood started military training. This was a fateful decision by the Egyptian government that would come to haunt them in the not too distant future. By March 1948, MB entered Palestine and joined the fighters from Syria, Libya, Tunis, Iraq, and Jordan in their *Jihad* against the Israelis.

Back in Egypt in a statement issued by El Banna, as the group celebrated its 20th anniversary in 1948, he boasted that MB had two thousand branches in Egypt, five hundred in Sudan and others in Palestine, Jordan, Syria, Pakistan, Iran and Turkey. The group's two immediate objectives, he continued, were reviving and applying the Islamic social system and contributing to social service. So, while El Banna's mujahedeen were fighting in Palestine, he didn't want his followers back in Egypt lose sight of the initial goal of the Brotherhood.

The Movement Gains Weapons and Training

The 1948 war in Palestine gave the paramilitary wing the golden opportunity to collect weapons and to be trained in military camps by army officers. It also introduced its members to *Jihad* as a way of fighting for the cause they believed in. By the end of the war, the paramilitary wing had expanded, its members were well trained, organized, well equipped, and with combat experience. They were ready to die for whatever cause their leader deemed vital. More than three decades later, history would repeat itself in another war theater—Afghanistan—with another charismatic leader—Osama Bin Laden.

In the domestic front, violence continued to escalate. In 1947, in Ismailia, a bomb exploded in King George Hotel injuring several people including the bomber. While members of MB with other Arab fighters were waging Jihad in Palestine, national security files in Egypt had recorded several crimes of violence conducted by MB members during 1948. Fifteen members of the group were arrested in a military training camp that the paramilitary wing had established in the area of Mokatam Mountain near Cairo. They were arrested while they were engaged in one of their weapon training sessions. Several bombs exploded throughout Cairo during that year, targeting Jewish owned shops, businesses and residential areas. It should be noted that until this time Muslims and Jews lived and worked side by side in relative peace, as they had done throughout the Muslim world for more than thirteen hundred years. These attacks against Jewish interests mark a turning point in the attitude of Arabs towards Jews.

In October 1948, in searching the ranch of Mohamed Faragallah, the MB president of the Ismailia branch, the police found boxes containing bombs, explosives, rifles, guns, ammunition and cannons. The police also found documents indicating that the group was planning to launch big attacks against the government and the security forces of the country. And in December 1948, bloody attacks led by MB students took place in one of Cairo's universities. The students set fires on the campus and attacked the police throwing rocks, firing guns, and hurling hand grenades at them. During the clashes, Selim Zaki, the chief of

Cairo police was killed. The MB was blamed for the incidents but because of insufficient evidence nobody was identified as responsible for the attacks and nobody was charged with the murders.

Violence Escalates

After the university riots and on December 8, 1948, the prime minister met with the national security officials to address the growing level of unrest in the country. The meeting lasted until late in the night, and the country was placed at the highest state of emergency at the conclusion of the meeting. The deputy minister of interior, Abdul Rahman Ammar, issued a statement about the MB, where he said "The group is seeking power by using violence. They are using crime to reach their objective. They have trained a group of its members, calling them the Boy Scouts. They have established youth centers for them, where they provided military training for them. They have collected weapons, bombs, guns, ammunition and explosives. They are using the Palestine war to reach their objectives, as the war is making their mission of collecting weapons and get military training easier. They became very dangerous for the national security and a big threat to the regime [King Farouk]… Since this group was founded, they called themselves MB, and announced that their objectives and motives are religious and social reforms with no political objectives. But as soon as they attracted more members and its popularity grew, they revealed their true objectives that are all political. They seek power to change the regime of the country by overthrowing the government"

By midnight the same evening, a large police force advanced to the MB headquarters, surrounded it and went in where they confiscated all the documents they found. Following the raid to the MB headquarters, Mahmoud Fahmy El Nokrashy, the military governor, issued an order whereby he dissolved the MB as an organization and banned all its activities throughout the country, on the grounds that it had secretly plotted to overthrow the regime. The police confiscated all of their documents, closed down all their offices and newspapers, and banned all meetings of its members. El Banna mentions in his memoirs that, by this military order, more than one thousand people were arrested, their money confiscated from their houses and their bank accounts frozen; employees were fired, students expelled from their schools and universities, their cars and radios were confiscated and their phones were disconnected.

This was the first drastic action taken by the Egyptian government to reign in the growing and worrisome disobedience and violence caused by the Brotherhood. El Banna tried to persuade the government to revoke the banning order and release those detained in the jails, but the government refused. Twenty days after the ban decree was issued and on December, 28, 1948 as Prime Minister El Nokrashy Pasha was entering the ministry of interior building, he was shot dead by Abdel Meguid Ahmed Hassan, a twenty-one years old member of the MB who had joined the organization in 1944.

The El Banna Era Comes to an End

It was becoming clear by now that El Banna had lost control over his paramilitary wing. In less than three years, two prime ministers, one judge, and the Cairo chief of police had been assassinated. As El Banna tried to control the situation, he contacted the new prime minister, Ibrahim Abdel Hadi, and offered to help him bring order to the country and, in return, secure the release of the detainees and return of their confiscated assets. Abdel Hadi not only refused, he ordered the arrest of an additional four thousand members of the MB.

El Banna, though, was not arrested and he proceeded to issue a statement condemning the assassination of the prime minister. But the *jinni* was out of the bottle and, in a rapid deterioration of events, the MB tried to blow up the Court House on January 13, 1949, where all the trials' papers and documents were kept. They wanted to destroy all evidence against them. One of the employees, though, suspected a bag left behind by someone, and took it out of the Court House where it exploded. And an attempted assassination of Ibrahim Abdel Hadi, the new prime minister who had dealt very harshly with the MB by placing large numbers of them behind bars, also failed.

The MB had gone too far. The government had to react and react quickly and decisively. On February 10, 1949, as El Banna was walking in the streets of Cairo, he was shot dead. There were no arrests made for the assassination, but Prime Minister Ibrahim Abdel Hadi and the Egyptian government were widely believed to be responsible for it. El Banna was dead at the age of 43 and the Brotherhood never recovered completely from the death of its charismatic leader, although the organization remained a significant political force in several Arab countries. El Banna's writings were translated into several languages, and have inspired religious activists and Islamic revivalists throughout the Muslim and Arab world to follow his ideology.

The Struggle for New Leader

After El Banna's assassination in 1949, there were disagreements among the MB members about who should be selected as his successor. There were four main candidates including El Banna's brother. The group's Supreme Guidance council wanted to appoint someone who could dispel the MB group's reputation as a terrorist movement, following the string of assassinations carried out by its paramilitary wing in the late 1940s. After considerable and heated debate, Hassan El Hodeiby was named as the Supreme Guide of the MB group in 1950. He was an outsider to the movement, and although he stood outside of political activism, he strongly believed in an Islamic state. However, he was very different from El Banna. He was a judge, less charismatic than the late leader, and had very close ties to the king. He was not accepted as the Supreme Guide by some from within, who considered themselves more worthy of the post than he was. The paramilitary wing led by Abdel Fatah El Sanadi did not accept his authority as leader either. [1]

Although the MB was not satisfied with their new leader, they could not change him, as the Supreme Guide's position was a lifelong one. As a result, there were only few people within the movement that Hodeiby really trusted. He had little confidence in Abdel Fatah El Sanadi and he never gained full control over the paramilitary wing, which he proceeded to dissolve on the grounds that it was not proper for a religious group to have a militant component. At the same time, though, he started forming another paramilitary group consisting of members who were loyal to him. While doing so, the new members tried to get rid of the old ones by expelling them from the movement. There is even a documented incident of an assassination of a member of the former paramilitary wing. A bomb, sent to him inside a parcel, exploded in his face and killed him as he tried to open it. This created a further sense of confusion, division and conflict among the MB members.

On October 18, 1951, the Egyptians declared military resistance against the British in the Suez Canal zone. To the surprise and dismay of everybody, El Hodeiby didn't approve the MB joining the resistance. He advised the MB to go and pray rather than fighting. He said violence would not rid the country of the British and this statement alarmed not only the members of Muslim Brotherhood but Egyptians in general, as well.

Analysts have suggested that the close ties of El Hodeiby to the king of Egypt may have been the reason for his strong opposition to the 1952 revolution that forced the king into exile. After he was selected as the new Guide, he had met with the king on several occasions and pledged his allegiance. Upon the king's request he consolidated the MB fifty branches in Cairo to only four. The king in return promised him a ministerial position which never materialized as the king was removed by the revolution. Ayman Zawahiri comments on this relationship.

> The Islamic movement in Egypt, even though it made an effort against what it considered the enemies of Islam in the past, its general line was not against the ruling regime but against the external enemy [The Brits and the West]. The movement's ideology and media continued to try to get close to the head of the ruling regime (the king) and to recognize him as the legitimate authority in the country. This arbitrary separation between the external enemies and their internal agents led to many disasters and setbacks because the movement's members faced their enemy with their chests but left their backs exposed to this ally. Thus, they were stabbed in the back on the orders of those whom they faced with their chests. [2]

The "Nasserite Regime"

The relationship between the MB and the revolution was a controversial and complicated one, although on the surface it seemed like a strong one. It started in the 1940s when the revolution was still an idea in the minds of a handful of young army officers. These young officers eventually formed the Free Officers' movement. Several of them were members of the MB.

On the morning of July 23, 1952, Egyptians woke up with the news of the revolution. The revolutionaries called the MB Supreme Guide asking for his support. Although the Brotherhood did not fully support the revolution until the king was deported, the first days of the revolution marked a brief period of collaboration between the MB and the revolution leadership which released the assassins of Judge A. El Khazendar and El Nokrashy Pasha. Later the revolution pardoned all political prisoners—mainly Brotherhood members—arrested in past political crimes.

After the revolution, the Nasser regime dissolved all political parties, but kept the MB on the reasoning that it was a religious movement and not a political one. It even invited the members of the Brotherhood to join the new government cabinet. When the revolution decided to dissolve the political parties in Egypt, they advised the MB, which at that time wanted to change their movement to a political one, to stay as a religious organization, so that the law that was issued to dissolve the political parties would not apply to them.

Cracks began to appear on the façade of the alliance between the Brotherhood and the Nasser regime, however, as MB started placing demands on the revolution. President Nasser met with MB spokesmen who demanded no law should be issued in the country without the approval of the MB, and that no decision was to be taken without their approval. In other words, they wanted to rule from behind the scenes. Nasser, naturally, refused that.

Nasser also met with the Supreme Guide El Hodeiby who requested that Nasser should pass a law for all women to get veiled, close down all theaters and movie theaters and implement Islamic laws. Nasser refused these requests as well. Following these meetings, El Hodeiby started openly showing his disapproval of and disappointment in the revolution. The Brotherhood went farther and accused Nasser of deceiving them and everyone else with whom he collaborated prior to the revolution, and started working against him.

On January 12, 1954, a big march in Cairo University took place. This day was dedicated to the memory of the martyrs of the Canal Battle. The march turned violent and clashes started as MB students attacked other students, especially the ones that were members of a youth organization that supported the revolution. Bombs and other weapons were used in these clashes. One day later, the revolutionary board decided to dissolve the MB. El Hodeiby was arrested together with other 450 members. When King Saud of Saudi Arabia visited Egypt and met with President Nasser, he asked Nasser, in what can be considered as one of the many mistakes the Saudis made regarding Islamic militants, to release them. The revolution decided to release them and give the MB their last chance, on the condition that they do not get involved in politics again.

Once they were out of jail, however, the Brothers continued working against Nasser and his regime. On October 26, 1954 as Nasser was giving a speech in Alexandria, an attempt was made on his life when a gunman fired bullets at him. The attempt failed as the gunman missed and was arrested. This incident is considered to be the turning point in the relationship between Nasser and the MB. Thousands of MB members were arrested in what was considered to be the biggest arrest movement in the history of Egypt after the 1952 revolution. The government dissolved the MB for one more time, sentenced seven of its members to death including El Hodeiby, but later his verdict was commuted to life sentence and another nine members of the Brotherhood received life sentences, as well.

By October 24, 1955, the number of Brotherhood members arrested had reached almost three thousand and 700 of them were scheduled to go on trials. A year later, less than six hundred were still in prison and among them Sayyid Qutb, a top lieutenant of the MB, who was sentenced to a fifteen years prison term. Qutb would become the most important theorist of modern Islam, and his writings would dramatically influence the ideology and actions of all future Jihadist movements.

1. From an interview with Mamoun El Hodeiby, son of Hassan El Hodeiby to *Al-Ahram* weekly newspaper, issue # 592
2. Excerpt from Part Three of the book titled *Knights Under the Prophet's Banner* by Ayman Zawahiri. This book is considered to be his "Last Will", and it was made available by the London *Al-Sharq al-Awsat* publishing house on 2 December 2001, shortly after the invasion of Afghanistan by US forces in retaliation of the attack on the Twin Towers and the Pentagon by *Al Qaeda* on 9 September 2001.

In this section, we followed the path of Islamic movements in the sixties and seventies. This period marks the transition from political violence to one of religiously legitimized violence, aimed at assassinating the rulers and leaders (internal enemies of Islam) of Muslim countries and restoring the true Islam. Although this ideologically driven violent movement spread from Egypt to Algeria and Pakistan, where local groups and leaders played a vital role in the local struggle against the "apostate" rulers, we focused mainly on the Egyptians Sayyid Qutb and Mohammed Abdel Salam Farag. Their lives and works revolutionized the Islamic movement and became the inspiration, justification, and model of all subsequent Jihadist movements around the globe, and remain so until today.

This section, moreover, contains several excerpts from Ayman Zawahiri's book 'Knights Under the Prophet's Banner" which present a rare insight into the inner working of these movements, and a glimpse at Zawahiri, the revolutionary and strategist.

Stage Four: Egyptian Jihad against the Internal Enemies of Islam

The Muslim Brothers had welcomed the revolution led by Abdel Nasser in July 1952. Now power was in the hands of the "sons of the Egyptian people" who were socially very similar to the majority of the Brotherhood's members. They were also pleased with Nasser's dissolution of all political parties, except the MB, that were disrupting Muslim unity and diluting their message. Moreover, they hoped that Nasser's revolution would lead to a society without social and economic divisions, and governed by the laws of Islam that they have been advocating for a quarter of a century. The honeymoon did not last long, however. Nasser's socialism soon collided with the Brotherhood's Islamism, as they competed for the same grassroots support—the lower middle class Egyptians. [1]

This conflict led to violence and an attempted assassination of Abdel Nasser in 1954. The Brotherhood was dissolved, thousands of its members imprisoned or exiled, and several of its leaders executed, or sentenced to life. It appeared as the movement had been dealt a fatal blow, an assumption that proved to be erroneous time after time for the next fifty years, as the movement would spread to other Islamic countries and, during the next decade, renew itself and surface in the Egyptian scene more potent than ever.[2]

Sayyid Qutb and Milestones

With the approval of a new Supreme Guide, the immediate tasks of the underground activities of the resurrected movement were recruiting new members, contacting old members, and developing educational programs that would become the cornerstone of future activities. By 1962, the Brotherhood, with the permission of the Supreme Guide and through the help of his sisters, contacted Sayyid Qutb in jail and solicited his advice about their educational programs, and sought his guidance in general. Responding to this request, Sayyid Qutb sent them a section of a book, called *Milestones* that he was writing in jail and preparing to publish it. He suggested that this book could be used as a core subject in educating the young members of the Brotherhood in Islamic ideology. With the blessings of the Supreme Guide, who not only approved of the book but also described Sayyid Qutb as a bright hope in the call for an Islamic nation, *Milestones* and Sayyid Qutb were on their way to immortality. (Zeinab El GhazAli, *Days from my Life*; p 43)

With the instructions of Sayyid Qutb, who had been delegated power of leadership from the Supreme Guide, the group decided on the following strategy: a period of education, formation, preparation, and implanting the creed of *La ilaha illa Allah*—Islamic monotheism—in the minds and souls of their followers should last for a period of thirteen years, the same duration that Prophet Mohamed used to secretly proselytize his followers in Mecca before he went public with Islam. The MB would be the driving force for the foundation of the Islamic nation that was committed to the Quran and its laws. After thirteen years of preaching, they would survey the country. If they found that more than 75% of people were supporting them and believed that Islam should take over, they would demand an Islamic state to be formed. If the number of supporters were less than 75%, they would keep preaching for thirteen more years and so on, until the nation was mature enough to accept the new system.

After the Supreme Guide gave his permission for the book to be published, the government authorities strongly objected to its publication. President Nasser, however, read the book and allowed its publication. In less than a month, it was printed for the second time and in less than six months it was printed three more times. When the information reached the president that the book was on its way to be printed again, he read it for a second time, perhaps a little more carefully, and sent the book to the general bureau of investigation with a note suggesting that a new organization of MB was in operation and ordered its investigation. But the *jinni* was already out of the bottle one more time and though *Milestones* was banned from future publication and circulation, its importance in the struggle to create the Islamic nation was strengthened significantly.

The *Milestones* of Sayyid Qutb, according to Islamic movement analysts, stands on top of all of the ideological references that have influenced and shaped the Islamic radical groups until this day. In the book, Qutb describes how the society we are living in is in a state of ignorance, as it is neither following the path of God nor His laws. Humans have to free themselves from the servitude of other humans in the form of their leaders and rulers, because following the rules made by man is a worship to man. This is sinful, as worship is for God alone. No man should have any authority over another because by doing so man becomes a servant to other men, while man should be a servant to God only. Or else this would be a jahili society. It is, thus, the duty of all Muslims to end the rule of man, by any means, and restore the "true" Islam.

Jahiliyyah and Jihad in the Cause of God

Sayyid Qutb's *Milestones* consists of twelve chapters in which he presents his ideology and his concept of using "milestones" to track the struggle of the faithful for the realization of their ultimate goal, which he calls "a waiting reality about to be materialized." Of all the chapters, the one that attracted our attention mostly was number four—*Jihad* in the cause of God—where Qutb in chilling clarity and detail presents his theological justification of *Jihad* against the apostates and infidels. Following are excerpts from this chapter. We advise our readers that the following does not represent Islamic doctrine, and we have attempted to provide a counter view, by including comments from the prestigious *Azhar* (Islamic University) that are presented in a following section.

> The method of this religion is very practical. This movement treats people as they actually are and uses resources which are in accordance with practical conditions. Since this movement comes into conflict with the *Jahiliyyah* (un-Islamic societal behavior) which prevails over ideas and beliefs, and which has a practical system of life and a political and material authority behind it, the Islamic movement had to produce parallel resources to confront this *Jahiliyyah*. This movement uses the methods of preaching and persuasion for reforming ideas and beliefs; and it uses physical power and *Jihad* for abolishing the organizations and authorities of the *Jahili* system which prevents

people from reforming their ideas and beliefs but forces them to obey their erroneous ways and make them serve human lords instead of the Almighty Lord.[7]

After establishing the conflict between the *Jahili* system and Islam, Qutb continues, in a fashion typical of Islamic scholars, his justification of *Jihad* against the earthly rulers that he legitimizes with numerous references to Quranic verses, and concludes:

> It is clear that obedience to laws and judgments is a sort of worship, and anyone who does this is considered out of this religion (apostate). It is taking some men as lords over others, while this religion has come to annihilate such practices, and it declares that all the people of the earth should become free of servitude to anyone other than God.
>
> If the actual life of human beings is found to be different from this declaration of freedom, then it becomes incumbent upon Islam to enter the field with preaching as well as the movement, and to strike hard at all those political powers which force people to bow before them, and which rule over them, unmindful of the commandments of God, and which prevent people from listening to the preaching and accepting the belief if they wish to do so. After annihilating the tyrannical force…, Islam establishes a new…system.
>
> It is not the intention of Islam to force its beliefs on people, for Islam is not merely 'belief.' As we have pointed out, Islam is a declaration of the freedom of man from servitude to other men. Thus, it strives from the beginning to abolish all those systems and governments that are based on the rule of man over men and the servitude of one human being to another.[8]

According to Qutb, the reasons for Jihad are: to establish God's authority on earth; to arrange human affairs according to the true guidance provided by God; to abolish all the satanic forces and satanic systems of life (*Jahiliyyah*); and to end the lordship of man over another. All men are the creatures of God and no one has the authority to make them his servants or to make arbitrary laws for them. These are his reasons for proclaiming *Jihad,* and he continues, in his distorted way of thinking, by saying that one should always keep in mind that there is no compulsion in religion; that is, once the people are free from the lordship of men, the law governing civil affairs will be purely that of God, while no one will be forced to change his beliefs and accept Islam.[9]

To understand the dynamism of Islam with clarity and depth, says Qutb, it is necessary to remember that Islam is a way of life for man prescribed by God. It is not a man-made system, nor an ideology of a group of people. God's rule on earth can be established only through the Islamic system, as it is the only system ordained by God for all human beings whether they are rulers or ruled.

Zawahiri on Sayyid Qutb and Milestones

Ayman Zawahiri in his book, *Knights under the Prophet's Banner,* that he wrote while hiding in the Afghanistan caves at the end of 2001 during the American coalition's military operation against the Taliban and Al Qaeda, describes the importance of Sayyid Qutb's *Milestones* this way. "He [Sayyid Qutb] affirmed that the issue of unification in Islam is important and that the battle between Islam and its enemies is primarily an ideological one over the issue of unification. It is also a battle over to whom authority and power should belong—to God's course and Shariah, or man-made laws and material principles and those who claim to be intermediaries between the Creator and mankind. This affirmation greatly helped the Islamic movement to know and define its enemies. It also helped it to realize that the internal enemy was not less dangerous than the external enemy was, and that the internal enemy was a tool used by the external enemy and a screen behind which it hid to launch its war on Islam." [3]

Zawahiri also talks about the major shift in the direction that *Jihad,* struggle, against the enemies of Islam took as a result of the influence of Sayyid Qutb's *Milestones.* "The group rallying around Sayyid Qutb decided to deal blows to the existing government in its capacity as a regime that was hostile to Islam and which departed from the course of God and refused to apply the *Shariah.* The group's plan was simple. It did not aim to overthrow the regime or to create a vacuum of power, but to deal to the regime preventive, defensive, and retaliatory blows if it planned a new campaign of repression against Muslims. However, the meaning of this plan was more important than its material strength. The meaning was that the Islamic movement had begun a war against the regime in its capacity as an enemy of Islam. Before that, the Islamic movement's ethics and principles—and in which some believe until now—affirmed that the external enemy was the only enemy of Islam."[4]

At this point, we need to pause to review Zawahiri's comments regarding Qutb and the *Milestones*, attempt to comprehend their meaning and carefully analyze their significance in influencing present-time Islamic militant doctrines. Zawahiri praises Qutb for clearly defining the struggle of Islam not only as an ideological one, but one that stems from the very essence of the religion— Muslims unifying against the forces of *Jahiliyyah* (un-Islamic societal behavior, and a state of ignorance that Muslims believe existed before Prophet Mohammed). From Ibn Taymiyya to Osama bin Laden, all leaders of Islamic movements have methodically based their ideology and *Jihadist* activities on uncontroversial Quranic foundations, and have used detailed theological analysis that most Westerners would find it excessive and hugely unnecessary. This preoccupation with theological detail, however, provides us the first clue of how tightly woven is the ideology of Islamic militancy with public religion. Since the Quran—God's Word—cannot be challenged, any ideology, no matter how erroneous might be, that can be linked to a Quranic principle cannot be challenged either.

Next, "This affirmation greatly helped the Islamic movement to know and define its enemies", says Zawahiri. "Sayyid Qutb's call for loyalty to God's oneness and to acknowledge God's sole authority and sovereignty was the spark that ignited the Islamic revolution against the enemies of Islam at home and abroad. The bloody chapters of this revolution continue to unfold day after day."[5] Seven centuries ago, Ibn Taymiyya had declared *Jihad* against the Mongol invaders (an external enemy) on the basis of apostasy (heresy). Nobody since Ibn Taymiyya and till Sayyid Qutb had used apostasy as the basis of declaring a holy war against one's own Muslim government. El Banna and the Brotherhood had justified their early acts of violence in terms of specific political objectives.

Finally, Zawahiri's comments reveal how much Qutb and the *Milestones* influenced the movement in general and him, in specific, in terms of the strategy that would become the trademark of Islamic militants. El Banna founded the Brotherhood and became the architect of its organizational structure and social outreach programs. It was this genius that institutionalized the organization and ensured its sustainability. Sayyid Qutb established his ideological "milestones" for the faithful to use to "recognize the starting place, the nature, the responsibilities and the ultimate purpose of this long journey" [6] towards the creation of the Islamic nation. Moreover, he was the first to legitimize tyrannicide against Muslim rulers since Ibn Taymiyya did in the thirteenth century.

Al Azhar's Response to Qutb's *Milestones*

All Islamic scholars have disapproved of the ideology of the *Milestones*. To them, it was obvious that the book was a weapon of conspiracy against the government and the Nasserite regime. And as feared, the ideology of this book has dominated the ideas and actions of all of those who have conducted terrorist operations in the name of religion since Qutb. One response, however, is especially noteworthy as it presents the official *fatwa* (literally advice) of *Al Azhar*. Islam has no clergy but it has men of religion (*rijal al-din*) who are not ordained into their ministry but who receive a certificate that legally admits them as professional teachers of Islam. The most prestigious of educational institutions that grant such certificates is the Egyptian *Azhar* University in Cairo. *Al Azhar*, founded in the tenth century AD, is not only one of the oldest institutes of higher learning in the world, but the most authoritative voice of Islamic doctrine. Sheikh Mohamed Abdel Latif, head of *Fatwa* in *Al Azhar*, wrote his *fatwa* about *Milestones,* representing the opinion of the institute. The review went as follows:

"At first sight, the reader realizes that the subject of the book is a religious one. The style though is a provocative one. It surprises the reader with what agitates his religious feelings especially [the thought of] the simple young men who would rush without any consideration towards this new movement in the name of religion. As the call in the book takes the cover of religion, these young men would accept what it represents assuming that this was the call of truth and following it will lead them to the heavens.

"The author of the book denies the existence of the Islamic nation that existed centuries ago and that means that he denounces the glorious eras of Islam and all the masters of the religious sciences who lived throughout the centuries. According to him, they were all infidels living in what he calls *Jahiliyyah,* and had nothing to do with Islam until Sayyid Qutb arrived into this world.

"The book was an open invitation for the rising of some people to revive the Islam, because from his point of view, it does not exist anymore. The author was the one who made the effort to place the new milestones of this expected revival. Then after the revival of Islam in the lands of Islam, the movement will expand to cover the whole world. He wrote this book to guide these people who will be purifying the earth from the infidels. There is nothing stranger than this illusionary and destructive tendency that he calls 'the road to Islam.'

"The *Azhar* scholars asked if religion [has become a person] that is walking among people [asking them] to follow its governing and restrain from following their rulers. Or maybe the author thought he was God's representative on earth to rule, since he denies the existence of rulers and he is putting milestones for all people to rebel against their rulers.

"The Quran acknowledges the existence and role of the rulers and oblige us to obey them, and obliges the rulers to be fair and ask the citizens to cooperate with them. Islam never considered the rulers as being infallible, but that it is only human to make mistakes. It is very strange that someone or a group of people would rise and draw a crooked path and call it the only road to Islam. For life cannot be stable under any conditions or circumstances, without the existence of rulers who govern and derive laws. How can it be acceptable that a group of people wants to take the power and authority away from the rulers?

"The author attacks Islam and denies the existence of an Islamic society or system. He asks that laws should not be derived and legislated until the proper society, from his point of view, is established and it needs laws. The proper society is the one that he and his group will establish.

"In another illusionary vision of the author, he declared for himself the responsibility for the implementation of the Divine laws for organizing the life of people on earth. First, he suggests that we abolish all the existing systems, with no exceptions, and get rid of all the rulers. Then a new society is established and appropriate laws will be derived for it as needed.

"With his insane tendencies, the author contradicts Islam and pretends he is the only one who cares for this religion and for humanity. He tries to attract simple young people, especially men, in the name of God and in the name of *Jihad* for God. This is a big invitation to start wars on other peaceful people, and while the lands of Islam are also living in peace. It is obvious that the author wants nothing but clashes, destruction and evilness. Only God knows how far it may reach.

"He allowed himself to discuss the religion in a way that sounded that he is the savior of this religion and God's representative on earth. He elevated himself to the levels of the messengers and the prophets of God. Who is he to think that he could reach the rank of Prophet Mohamed? Is Sayyid Qutb, with his satanic intentions, he who is trying to lead the people into destruction to achieve his illusionary dreams?

"By reading this book, I only conclude that Qutb is a pessimistic human being who is looking at the world from behind some black glass and presents the world to the people in the same way he sees it. He allowed himself, in the name of religion, to provoke the feelings of the simple people, with what the religion refuses and denounces, in going after their leaders, as it will only result in bloodshed, destruction of civilization, massacres of innocent people, terrifying of societies, collapse of security, and stirring up riots in a very scary way that only God knows what the consequences will be."

I wonder if Sheikh Mohamed Abdel Latif had any idea how prophetic his statements about the destructive and evil consequences of the *Milestones* would become.

The End of the Sayyid Qutb Era

By mid-1964, Sayyid Qutb was pardoned because of health reasons and was released from jail, only to be arrested again on August 5th, 1965. His arrest came as a shock to his followers and students, especially because the Supreme Guide had delegated all authority to him. Shortly after, Hassan El Hodeiby, Supreme Guide, and Mohamed Hawash, Sayyid Qutb's deputy, were also arrested.

After several major arrests, the total number of leaders from this secret organization who went on trial was forty three. All of those arrested were accused for plotting to assassinate Abdel Nasser and overthrow the government. After major investigations, they confessed to certain accusations, and denied others. Although they all denied the fact that there was a conspiracy on the life of Abdel Nasser, they agreed that they had reestablished the new underground MB organization that aimed at overthrowing the government of Egypt. Additionally, they confessed that they received funds and weapons from MB organizations functioning outside of Egypt. The weapons included explosives, bombs, machine guns and artillery and they admitted that they had received training on how to use these weapons.

Members of this underground MB, who have graduated from science and engineering schools, had formed a group for scientific research that was responsible for manufacturing and assembling bombs. Additionally, they were able to obtain blue prints of major power stations and bridges across the country and studied their weak points to be able to explode them when needed.

Moreover, the Brotherhood had encouraged young students to infiltrate the different military academies, where they graduated and became army officers. These officers were responsible for collecting information about the different army divisions they were assigned to, and for the training of other MB member in the training camps that they had around the country—similar to the Al Qaeda training camps in Afghanistan. They had formed additional groups responsible for intelligence gathering and reporting it to their leaders; had developed manuals that they used to study the art and science of espionage and covert operations; used different names and identities for themselves to confuse the officials. They had members working in different sectors of the government who reported to them, and had even infiltrated the presidential offices and the cabinet of ministers.

In August 1966, Sayyid Qutb was sentenced to death, and executed eight days later, while Hassan El Hodeiby was sentenced to three years in prison. Other leaders were given sentences that varied from fifteen to twenty five years. Although Sayyid Qutb was executed and the organization was banned, his book *Milestones* was engraved forever in the hearts and minds of thousands of young people who eventually played and are still playing a key role in today's global terrorism. "The ideology of this revolution [Islamic movement] and the clarity of its course are getting firmer every day. They are strengthening the realization of the nature of the struggle and the problems on the road ahead—the road of the prophets and messengers and their followers until God Almighty inherits the earth and those who live on it", says Ayman Zawahiri in his recent book.[10] "The Nasserite regime thought that the Islamic movement received a deadly blow with the execution of Sayyid Qutb and his comrades and the arrest of thousands of Islamic movement members. But the apparent calm on the surface concealed under it an immediate interaction with Sayyid Qutb's ideas and calls and the beginning of the formation of the nucleus of the modern Islamic *Jihad* movement in Egypt" adds Zawahiri.

The Military Technical College Affair

Abdel Nasser's regime had crushed, at least in the public's eyes, the Brotherhood movement. Thousands of its members were detained and its leaders were either executed or in prison. But the reign of Abdel Nasser was also coming to an end. Nationalization of businesses, support of expensive military campaigns in Africa and Yemen, mismanagement of internal economy, and a false sense of military superiority, culminated with the poorly planned and, even worse, executed 1967 war with Israel, dealt Egypt a severe blow to its political and military image in the eyes of the international community. But nothing was worse than

Egypt's image of herself. The hopes of prosperity and independence that arrived with the expulsion of the British and the dawn of a popular social revolution had evaporated in six days. This was one of the darkest periods in the history of modern Egypt.

Again in Ayman Zawahiri's words, "The Nasserite regime received a deadly blow represented by the death of Gamal Abdel Nasser three years after the setback [the 1967 defeat to the Israelis], three years that he lived suffering from the consequences of the defeat. Thus, the myth of the Leader of the Arab nationalism who would throw Israel into the sea was destroyed." Zawahiri adds, "Anwar Sadat's assumption of power marked the beginning of a new political transformation in Egypt represented by the end of the Russian era and the start of the American era. Sadat began removing the protégés of the old regime. His strongest weapon in resisting those remaining protégés was his permission of some forms of freedom for the repressed people. As soon as some pressure was lifted from the Islamic movement, the giant [the Islamic movement] emerged from the bottle and the extensive influence of the Islamists among the masses became clear. Muslim youth won the overwhelming majority of the seats in university and schools student unions in a matter of few years. The Islamic movement began its march to control the trade unions." [11]

With chilling clarity, Zawahiri continues his description of this transitional and learning-from-mistakes period in Islamic resurgence. "A new phase of growth began for the Islamic movement. But this time there was no repetition of the past; rather the Islamic movement built on it, benefiting from previous experiences, lessons, and events. The Islamic movement began entering this phase of growth, spreading among its youth a deep awareness that the internal enemy was not less dangerous than the external enemy. This awareness began to strongly grow on the basis of clear legitimacy and bitter historical and practical experience."

But the Islamic movement was destined to receive another blow and temporary setback, and add to its archives of "lessons learned". These were the events of what became known in Egypt as the "Military Technical College" affair. In 1974, a group of cadets, including Karim Al-Anadoli, from the Egyptian

Military Academy attempted a coup d'état and an assassination of Sadat which failed. [12] The group's leader was Saleh Sirriya, a Palestinian born near Haifa, Israel, where he got involved with the underground Brotherhood and began to recruit young people, most of whom were university students in Cairo and Alexandria. His disciples lead normal lives as to not attract attention and their aim was to end the life of the "apostate prince" (Sadat). [13]

In his book, Zawahiri describes Saleh Sirriya as a mesmerizing speaker and a highly intellectual person, who received a doctorate in education from Ayn Shams University in Cairo. The group formed by Sirriya grew and was able to recruit a number of cadets from the Military Academy. "The youth began putting pressure on Sirriya to start the confrontation. Under their pressure, he agreed to carry out an attempt to overthrow the [Sadat] regime. A plan was prepared under which group members would silently overpower the policeman guarding the college gate, enter the college, and seize weapons and armored vehicles with the help of students acting as night supervisors. Then they would march toward the Arab Socialist Union headquarters to attack Al-Sadat and his government officials who were meeting there." [14]

Zawahiri adds: "The coup attempt failed because it did not take into consideration the objective conditions and the need to prepare well for it. The group who attacked the gate was untrained. The plan also met other difficulties during implementation. But the meaning that I would like to stress is that the Islamic movement after Abdel Nasser['s] successive blows to it proved that it was too big to be eradicated and too strong to be pushed into despair and frustration. This movement spawned a new generation after the 1967 defeat. This generation returned to the field of *Jihad*, brandishing its weapons against [the] ruling regime, which was hostile to Islam and which was allied with the United States this time. This operation [coup attempt] proved that the young mujahedeen did not differentiate between the old Nasserite-Russian era and the new Al-Sadat era; both eras were equally hostile [to Islam]." [15]

These testimonials by Ayman Zawahiri are of important historical significance and provide a rare insight into the revival of the Jihad movement in the mid-seventies, as these were the formative years of young Zawahiri as an Islamic activist. Moreover, they dispelled the speculation that the failed coup d'état was a plot organized by Libya. The government of Sadat eager to de-emphasize the public notion that Egyptian Islamic militants were behind the failed coup, promoted publicly the Libyan connection. Zawahiri not only does not refer to any outside influence, he remarks that the cadets of the Military Academy were the ones who were eager to attack, and convinced Sirriya to authorize the coup.

The Revival of Jihad Organizations and the 1981 Uprising

The establishment of the different *Jihad* groups within Egypt came after the discovery of the Military Academy group by the government. An acting prosecutor named Yehia Hashim established another *Jihadist* squad by the end of 1975. Ayman Zawahiri joined this new organization. Hashim's aim was to confront the government by waging a guerilla war against them. Zawahiri did not approve of this idea at all, and tried to convince Hashim that Egypt's terrain was not suitable for this type of warfare. The idea, however, continued to dominate Hashim and he planned to free Saleh Sirriya who was in prison for the Military Academy incident. Undercover agents discovered the plot, and Hashim, seeing this as an opportunity to launch his guerilla warfare, decided to escape to the mountainous region of Minia, in the South of Egypt, with his comrades. They bought weapons and took positions in the mountains of Minia under the cover of being a military unit. Their cover, however, was blown and the police stormed their hide out. Hashim was killed in the shootout and his comrades arrested. [16]

Several groups were organized between 1977 and 1979 and we will not detail all of their names nor those of their leaders. The ones of importance are Mohamed Abdel Salam Farag, an electrician and author of the book the *Neglected Duty*, and *Gamaa Islamiya* (The Islamic Group). Initially, the MB tried to adopt this group, but a difference in ideology between the MB and the *Gamaa Islamiya* became apparent. The *Gamaa Islamiya's* ideology was aligned more with *Jihad,* especially in the universities in Upper Egypt in the south. They started using violence to change the social conduct of the students that they saw as contrary to Islam.

In 1979, these young men from Upper Egypt joined other jihadist groups in Cairo, that were under the leadership of Mohamed Abdel Salam Farag and Abud Al Zomor. Although an umbrella organization was eventually formed under the name of *Gamaa Islamiya* and the leadership of Sheikh Abdel Rahman, who is now serving a life sentence in the US on charges of involvement in the 1993 World Trade Center bombing, the jihadists maintained their more violent and militaristic identity. Their common goal was to assassinate President Sadat and lead a coup d'état.

The most significant turning point in the Islamic political violence phenomena was associated with the *Tanzim Jihad* (the Egyptian jihadist organization) in 1981 that was responsible for the assassination of Sadat and the events of Asyut that were related to it. Zawahiri says in his book: "The events of the rebellion of October 1981 focused on two fronts: The first front was the attack on Sadat and the upper echelons of the regime during the military parade on 6 October and the attempt to kill the largest number of officials and seize the radio building [in Cairo]. Activity on this front succeeded in killing Anwar al-Sadat, but the upper echelons of the regime escaped and the attempt to seize the radio did not succeed. The second front was the armed uprising in Asyut and the attempt to seize the city. This attempt succeeded in seizing some police centers, but...was doomed to fail. It was an 'emotional' uprising that was poorly planned. The rebellion occurred two days after the assassination of Al-Sadat and was based on an unrealistic plan to seize Asyut and then advance northward toward Cairo. Thus, the [1981] uprising ended with a fundamental gain—the killing of Al-Sadat. The attempts that followed it were not successful because of poor planning and insufficient preparation." [17]

Zawahiri continues, by analyzing the events of the 1981 uprising and their aftereffects in a manner, that should be of considerable importance to the counter-terrorism intelligence organizations, typical of his clinically cold logic.

> However," adds Zawahiri, "the issue [the 1981 uprising] must not be viewed from the angle of these small

events. That uprising must be viewed from the angle of its aftereffects of these events and the facts that they proved:

1. The events showed the courage of the fundamentalists who attacked forces that were more experienced and larger in number and equipment.

2. The events showed the offensive nature of the fundamentalist movement, which decided to attack the regime in an attempt to kill its upper echelons among a large crowd of spectators.

3. The events showed that changing the regime, which had departed from Islam, became the central idea that preoccupied the Islamists, who rejected partial reform programs, patch-up jobs, and the attempts to beautify the ugly face of the regime with some reformatory measures.

4. The events proved that the phase of the unilateralism of the regime in attacking the Islamic movement had ended, and that the enemies of Islam in the White House and Tel Aviv and their agents in Cairo must expect a violent response to every repression campaign they carried out.

5. The events proved that the idea of work through martial laws, submission to the secular constitution imposed by referenda, and recognition of the legitimacy of the government had become worn-out ideas in the minds of the Islamists. Those Islamists decided to carry arms to defend the neglected creed, the banned Shariah, their violated honor, their homeland that was occupied by new international imperialism, and their sanctities that were sold in their agreements of surrender with Israel.

6. The events also showed the utter failure of the security services, which did not know that the country was charged with the Jihad current. This current was able to infiltrate the armed forces and to take from them some weapons and join the military parade forces, despite the tight security measures that were adopted to secure the parade. [18]

The above comments by Zawahiri demonstrate his brilliant communication and tactical skills. In masterfully worded and succinct statements, he sends messages of admiration and encouragement to the soldiers of the cause, clarifies the shift in the strategy of the movement, warns the enemies in Washington and Tel Aviv, and ridicules the security capabilities of the Egyptian government.

Jihad: The Neglected Duty

The assassination of President Sadat, head of an Islamic state and one who was a very popular figure with most of Egyptians, was a risky business in both a religious and political sense and required careful justification to the Egyptian public and Muslims in general. The justification, which was based on medieval theological doctrine that originated with Ibn Taymiyya, would become a recurring methodology in subsequent jihadist activities of the Islamic fundamentalists. Originally, it came in the form of a 55–page pamphlet that was titled *The Neglected Duty* and was produced by the Egyptian Islamic *Jihad* (*Tanzim Jihad*) and distributed most probably in the spring preceding the assassination of Sadat. Its author was Mohamed Abdel Salam Farag who, although an electrician by trade, became the most recent theoretician of the Jihadist movement and one who built upon the foundations of Ibn Taymiyya and Sayyid Qutb.

Understanding the meaning of the neglected duty and how it leads to the Quranic-based justification of *Jihad* against infidels and apostates is essential to anyone who desires to expand his knowledge of the motives that drive thousands of "soldiers" of *Jihad* to the battlefield and ultimately martyrdom. Before we go any further, however, let us review a couple of things regarding Islam and Muslims in as simple and un-theological terms as possible. The Quran is Islam's holy book that contains God's word as He revealed it to Prophet Mohamed. Between the Quran and the Prophet's Sayings, they contain everything that all Muslims must know about Islam and how to fulfill their individual and collective duties. Moreover, they are the undisputable and absolute references for all individual and societal behavior. In other words, to an American Christian they are the equivalent to the Bible and the Constitution. Even with this analogy we have not approached the level of blind obedience that the majority of Muslims have towards Islam and the Quran. There is nothing in Western religion or law that approximates the practice of Islam.

Given this brief insight into Islam, one begins to observe the connection of the careful, and often redundant and ambiguous justifications of everything Muslims do to the Quran. An eloquent writer or speaker with a strong religious base becomes a potent political weapon. From Hassan El Banna to the Al Qaeda operatives, the recitation of the Quran is a must. This is why the *Islamic Jihad* through Mohamed Farag published *The Neglected Duty* to justify Sadat's assassination. In the pamphlet, Farag argued that Jihad is an "armed action" is the heart of Islam and the neglect of this duty has caused the Muslims the current depressed state of Islam in the world. To make his argument uncontested, Farag raised violent Jihad to the status of a sixth pillar of Islam and accepted the traditions of the *Mahdi* (the Islamic version of messiah) who will reveal himself at the end of time and establish justice in the whole world. Muslims, however, should not become passive and complacent. It is their duty to actively fulfill God's original mandate of establishing a truly Islamic government, and restoring the caliphate in the world before the end of time and the appearance of the Mahdi.

There is a slight problem, though, with this justification in killing Sadat. Most Islamic authorities forbid rebellion against one's rulers when these rulers are Muslims. To get around this, Farag borrowed from Ibn Taymiyya and argued that such a mass resistance against an established government is not only justified, it is in fact a duty. In *The Neglected Duty*, Farag defines the current rulers of the Muslim world—as Sadat—as the primary enemies of Islam and apostates, and advocates their execution. Farag not only used Ibn Taymiyya's arguments regarding Jihad, he also built upon the foundations of Sayyid Qutb's fanatical theories. Professor Johannes J. G. Jansen says of Qutb: "Sayyid Qutb was the first author to argue convincingly in the eyes of many people that the world in reality was a *jahili* place. The designation as *jahili* doesn't sound very serious to Western ears, but to Muslim ears it does, because it implies apostasy from Islam and that is traditionally punishable by death. So if you can argue really convincingly to a Muslim public that the government is *jahili*, you have more or less sentenced the government to death."[19]

In his book *The Neglected Duty: The Creed of Sadat's Assassins and Islamic Resurgence in the Middle East*, Johannes J. G. Jansen translated and commented on Farag's book. He stated that the author of *The Neglected Duty* has severely shocked and deeply impressed the Egyptian Muslim readers with his writings. While Farag quoted the writings of Ibn Taymiyya, a medieval Islamic scholar who died in 1328, these writings of Ibn Taymiyya had their own historical context and his teachings cannot be mechanically transported to twentieth century circumstances.

"If the religious obligations of Islam cannot be carried out in their entirety without the support of an Islamic State, then the establishment of such a state is a religious obligation too. If such a state cannot be established without a war, then this war is a Muslim religious obligation as well", says Farag and in the text of *The Neglected Duty* argues that the rulers of the Muslims in this century "are in apostasy". They all (so we read) collaborate with Crusaderism, Communism, or Zionism. "They carry nothing from Islam but a name, even if they perform prayer ceremonies, or fast, or pretend to be Muslims." According to the author of *The Neglected Duty*, if Jihad is classified as an individual duty, together with praying and fasting, young individuals who consider converting to Islamic zealotry do not need to ask the permission of their parents when they want to join an activist cell. This echoes the message of Sayyid Qutb's Milestones calling the young Egyptian Muslims to rebel against their government by fulfilling their religious duty of Jihad.

But Dr. Mohammed Ammarah in his book *The Neglected duty: An Exposition, Dialogue and Evaluation* published in Cairo in 1982 states that the essential mistake in the theories expounded in *The Neglected Duty* is the similarity that Farag sees between the modern rulers and the Mongols of the days of Ibn Taymiyya, or in less diplomatic terms, to equate Sadat with Genghis Khan and his successors, and the Egyptian government and its bureaucracy with the Mongol hordes.

1. Gilles Kepel, *Jihad: The Trail of Political Islam,* pp 29-30
2. Ibid.
3. Ayman Zawahiri, *Knights Under the Prophet's Banner*, Part Three.
4. Ibid.
5. Ibid.
6. Sayyid Qutb, *Milestones*, pp 7- 13
7. Sayyid Qutb, *Milestones,* pp 53-76
8. Ibid.
9. Ibid.
10. Ayman Zawahiri, *Knights Under the Prophet's Banner*, Part Three.
11. Ibid.
12. Gilles Kepel, *Muslim Extremism in Egypt*, pp 70-78
13. Ibid.
14. Ayman Zawahiri, *Knights Under the Prophet's Banner*, Part Three
15. Ibid.
16. Ayman Zawahiri, *Knights Under the Prophet's Banner*, Part Three.
17. Ibid.
18. Ibid.
19. Interview with Professor Johannes J. G. Jensen About *The Neglected Duty* on 8 December 2001 by Jean-Francois Mayer. Obtained from www.religioscope.com.

The Jihadist movement needs an arena that would act like an incubator where its seeds would grow and where it would acquire practical experience in combat, politics, and organizational matters. The brother martyr—for this is how we think of him—Abu-Ubaydah al-Banshiri, may he rest in peace, used to say: 'It is as if 100 years have been added to my life when I came in Afghanistan.'

Ayman Zawahiri

Stage Five: Jihad against the External Enemies of Islam

September 11, 2001, Afghanistan

It was 05:00 in the evening, Afghanistan local time, 09:00 in the morning NY time, and somewhere in the harsh terrain mountains of Afghanistan, Osama Bin Laden, Ayman El Zawahiri and Mohamed Attef, his number one and two man respectively, most probably Refaie Ahmed Taha, and other lieutenants and colleagues were sitting on the floor around a radio and listening, with utmost concentration and anticipation, to the news. A few days earlier, they had received a cryptic message from their operatives in Germany with the date and time of the zero hour. Only Bin Laden and few men from his inner circle knew what was about to happen.

As the radio broadcasted the news of the first plane crashing into the North Tower, the group of men in the cave started crying, *Allah Akbar* (God is Great), a smiling Bin Laden raised one finger and motioned to them to be patient. With the news of the second plane crushing on the South Tower, Bin Laden raised a second finger and motioned again to be patient as it wasn't over yet. Finally with the crushing of the third plane on the Pentagon, Bin Laden raised one more finger, and the group cried, *Allah Akbar, Allah Akbar* and they all prayed. Elsewhere, the world was watching the same tragic events in shock, disbelief and horror wondering who was behind this despicable act of terrorism.

This was, by far, the most successful operation conducted by the International Islamic Front since it was formed in Febru ary 1998. The operation was so successful, even Bin Laden, who provided technical guidance on where the planes should hit the towers, didn't expect this outcome. He said, on one of the videos that were found by the Americans in one of the caves in Tora Bora, that from his previous experience in construction business, he expected that the damage of the World Trade Center (WTC) buildings would be limited to the floors above from the point of impact. The complete destruction of the two towers was beyond his wildest expectations.

But who is Osama bin Laden and Ayman Zawahiri and the rest of the group seating around the radio and rejoicing on the news of the most devastating attack on American soil? From where did they come, and what is the common bond that brought then to the caves of this remote corner of the earth? And, most importantly, what caused this type of hatred that turned humans into vicious and fearless machines of mass destructions? To answer these questions, one has to go back more than two decades to Egypt and Saudi Arabia and follow the road of religious fanaticism and immense hate for America and Israel that lead these two infamous Islamic leaders to the events of September 11 and beyond.

A Surgeon Turns Terrorist

Ayman El Zawahiri was born in Cairo, Egypt on June 19, 1951 to an upper class family. His father was a physician. One of his grandfathers was an ambassador, the other a noted Muslim cleric.[1] He was described as a quiet and studious child, and a very religious one who was keen to praying at the mosque. Being very intelligent, Zawahiri attended medical school, graduated as a doctor, and received his Master's in pediatric surgery. In the 1970's and in Cairo, Egypt, Ayman Zawahiri took the Hippocratic oath to save lives. In 1998 and in the caves of Afghanistan, along with Bin Laden he took another oath to kill Americans and Jews, and their allies, including civilians. This he saw as one of his most important duties as a Muslim consistent with his extremism Islamic ideology. It's quite a long way from the harsh terrain of Afghanistan to the upper class suburbs of Cairo, and the ideology of a physician and that of a fanatic terrorist couldn't be further apart, but this is the spatial and spiritual journey that Zawahiri has made in his illusion to reinstate the fallen Caliph and, thus, the Golden Age of Islamic intellectual and military supremacy.

Zawahiri was a teenager in 1968 when he joined a small cell of the outlawed Jihad group, also known as *Tanzim Jihad*, or Egyptian Islamic Jihad (EIJ), which aimed at overthrowing the secular government and establishing in its place a fundamentalist Islamic state.[2] It was not though till a few years later and during the "Military Technical College Affair", an event that was covered in the previous chapter, when young Zawahiri became more involved in the movement. It was Saleh Sirriya, the Palestinian-born activist who masterminded the attempted coup d'état, who impressed the young rebel. He described Sirriya as a "mesmerizing" speaker, as in his own words recalls the first time he heard the charismatic orator. "As soon as I heard the speech by this visitor, I realized that his words carried weight and meaning on the need to support Islam. I decided to meet this visitor but all my attempts were in vain."[3]

Security records in Egypt show he began his terrorist career in 1974 with a group led by Yehia Hashim. By the time the Islamic fundamentalist groups (EIJ and *Gamaa Islamiya*) were planning the assassination of Anwar Sadat and a military takeover of the Egyptian government, Zawahiri was a top commander of the movement. At this time and up until 1997, Zawahiri believed that the group should recruit army officers from inside the military, and carry out Jihad against the Egyptian government. His focus was still on the "domestic enemy". While other militant Islamic groups believed that their priority should be Jihad to liberate Palestine, Zawahiri believed that the road to liberate Jerusalem passes through Cairo.

To Zawahiri and his fundamentalist companions, the 1977 Camp David treaty between Egypt and Israel brought an outrage. As Sadat was eager to negotiate for peace, he became too closely associated with the Americans and the Israelis. While Egypt welcomed the peace treaty, Arabs elsewhere were against it and the fundamentalists saw this as a big betrayal of the Arab and Islamic world. The Arab League expelled Egypt and moved its headquarters to Tunis. It is worth noting that the driving force behind Egypt's expulsion was the Iraqi dictator, Saddam Hussein.[4] Islamic fundamentalists declared Sadat an apostate and traitor, and their religious scholars issued a *Fatwa* for his assassination.

His connection with the mujahedeen movement in Afghanistan came as a predestined event according to Zawahiri, who says: "My connection with Afghanistan began in the summer of 1980 by a twist of fate"[5] when he was asked if he would like to travel to Pakistan to help, as a surgeon, in the Afghan refugee camps. He immediately agreed as he saw this opportunity as a gift on a gold platter because he was always searching for a secure "base" for Jihadist activities in Egypt. After staying in Peshawar for four months where he confirmed how rich that region was for the Jihadist movement, Zawahiri returned to Egypt.

After Sadat's assassination in 1981, Zawahiri was arrested along with hundreds of other Islamic militants and was tried on conspiracy charges. The government was unable to prove he was directly involved in the assassination plot and he was acquitted of the conspiracy charges. In a second trial, he was convicted, however, on an unrelated weapons charge and spent 3 years in prison.[6] While Zawahiri was in prison, his charisma and knowledge of English language helped him emerge as an international spokesman for the Islamic activists that were imprisoned with him. "We are here, the real Islamic front. We are here the real Islamic opposition against Zionism, communism and imperialism."[7] thundered Zawahiri from his cell to a group of reporters. By the time he was released from jail three years later he had moved into the top ranks of Islamic militants.

The Millionaire Saudi becomes a Mujahed

Five years after the birth of Ayman Zawahiri in Cairo and in the heart of Saudi Arabia, Osama Bin Laden was born in 1956 in Riyadh. His father, originally a poor construction worker from the Hadramout region of Yemen, moved to Saudi Arabia where he established a large financial and industrial empire mainly because of his connections to the Saudi Royal family. His big business break came when he won contracts to renovate the three holiest mosques: The Al-Haram Al-Sherif in Mecca where the Ka'aba is located; the one in Medina where Prophet Mohamed is buried; and the Dome of the Rock in Jerusalem. "At one point, he [the father] used to pray at the three mosques in the same day", Bin Laden said in an interview with the Al-Jazeera satellite television in 1999.[8] Winning these lucrative contracts brought to the Bin Laden family wealth and prestige.

The 17th of fifty-two children, Bin Laden was raised in a very strict and religious way. Contradictions exist, however, about his upbringing. Was he the shy person who got married at a very young age to protect himself from moral corruption, or the wealthy playboy who used to spend his summers in cosmopolitan Beirut, Lebanon? No one will know for certain.

One thing is certain though about Bin Laden. He was greatly influenced by transformational leaders and monumental events. Wahhabism was running strong in Saudi Arabia during Bin Laden's formative years, the militant ideology of Sayyid Qutb's Jihad was flourishing in Egypt, and in 1967 the joint armies of Egypt, Syria and Jordan suffered a humiliating defeat by Israel. While he was studying economics at the King Abdel Aziz University in Jeddah he met Abdullah Azzam who was considered at the time as the Emir or Godfather of Jihad. Azzam studied Islamic law at Cairo's *Al Azhar* University where he met the family of Sayyid Qutb, before he went to Saudi Arabia to teach at the University of King Abdel Aziz. Azzam and Mohamed Qutb were both professors at the university at the time Bin Laden was studying there and they became very influential in shaping his future vision of Islam and Jihad. Azzam, a Palestinian who fought with the PLO in the 70's, sought Jihad as the path of Palestinian liberation, as he became disillusioned with the PLO leadership and its secular approach. Fate brought Azzam together with one of his students, Osama Bin Laden, in what perhaps will be considered as one of the critical stages in Bin Laden's transformation from a Saudi millionaire to one of Prophet Mohammed's most famous warriors.

The Soviet invasion and occupation of Afghanistan in 1979 provided Azzam the golden opportunity to practice his extreme Islamic ideals, and the perfect cause to unite the Muslims under the banner of the Prophet to a holy war against the infidel Soviets. One of his first recruits was Osama Bin Laden, and together they established a base in Peshawar, Pakistan, from where they recruited Arab revolutionaries, and where they housed and trained them to launch Jihad against the Soviets. Moreover, Azzam used this base to write and publish his books and magazines promoting his extreme brand of Islamism, and travel the world calling on Arabs to exercise their religious duty and join the "struggle". Bin Laden's future mujahedeen were taking bone and flesh at this remote corner of Pakistan thanks to the charisma of Azzam and Bin Laden's millions.[9]

Initially, Bin Laden's contributions to the Afghan cause were limited to providing the much needed logistical support—mostly cash and construction equipment—to the mujahedeen of Afghanistan. But the challenge and excitement of the battlefield proved irresistible to the young Saudi and he eventually joined the field operations and became one of the legendary leaders of the Afghan resistance. It was during this struggle against the Soviets that Bin Laden began creating his legend of invincibility. In the few interviews he has ever granted, he always recalled how his belief in God and the cause of his struggle have protected him in many dangerous situations. His favorite story is of a Soviet mortar shell that landed next to him and never blew up. "I saw a 120 mm mortar shell land in front of me, but it did not blow up. Four more bombs were dropped from a Russian plane on our headquarters, but did not explode." Bin Laden told *The Independent* during an interview in Sudan in 1993.[10] In a manner reminiscent of the early centuries-Islamic conquests through Byzantine territories, Northern Africa and Spain, such tales serve to confirm for Bin Laden and his followers that God is on their side and the ultimate victory will be theirs.

The Arab-Afghans

After the Soviet invasion of Afghanistan in 1979, the American intelligence set up a support program to help the Afghani mujahedeen with weapons and funds. The Americans also requested Egypt and other Arab countries to allow young Arabs who wished to join the mujahedeen to travel to Afghanistan. Members of the Jihad organization, responsible for the assassination of president Sadat, responded to this call to take arms not only because expelling the infidel Soviets from Arab lands was their Muslim duty, but also because they saw this as a golden opportunity to organize and hone their fighting skills away from the long shadow of Egyptian *Mokhabarat* (secret police). In one of the most serious miscalculations of its modern history, the Egyptian government was very eager to rid itself, or so it thought, of a major political headache and allowed members of the group to leave to Afghanistan. In fact not only the government of Egypt invited all Egyptian young people through newspaper advertisements to enlist, the Egyptian Defense Minister, Kamal Hassan Ali, announced that Egypt would provide training to the Afghani Mujahedeen in Egyptian army camps. Thousands of young Egyptian and Arab men were recruited, trained in Egypt and sent to Afghanistan. These men became known as Arab-Afghans.

One of the young Egyptian mujahedeen heading to Afghanistan for the second time was Ayman Zawahiri, who left for Saudi Arabia and from there to Afghanistan where he joined Bin Laden and soon he became his close friend, personal doctor and mentor. From Afghanistan they planned and directed their global terrorist organization united by the same background of being Arab-Afghans, and by their common ideology of defending, in their terms, their religion and liberating the Muslim lands not only from the infidels, but also from the enemy within, represented by the president Mubarak of Egypt and the Saudi Royal family. In their view, the Saudi and Egyptian regimes were assisting the Americans in the destruction of Islam and Muslims.

Egypt, however, was not the only Arab country to contribute to the evolution of Islamic fundamentalism and the eventual creation of a global Jihad army that the world will get to know after September 11 as Al Qaeda. Saudi Arabia, the birthplace of Wahhabism, had become an incubator of Islamic radicals long before the Afghan mujahedeen had become a force of resistance of Soviet occupation. * The royal family, eager to change its

* "The Saudi ministry of religious affairs printed and distributed millions of copies of the Quran free of charge, along with Wahhabite doctrinal texts, among the world's mosques including those that were built with money given by the Saudi government that are estimated to be more than 1500 built in the second half of the 20th century. The aim of the Saudi government was to produce new sympathizers for Wahhabism. This mass distribution by the conservative Riyadh regime did not always prevent more radical elements from using the texts of the faith to further their own objectives. The author most respected by the Wahhabites, Ibn Taymiyya, would be abundantly quoted to justify the assassination of Sadat in 1981 and even to condemn the Saudi leadership and call for its overthrow in the mid-90s. Yet, once Saudi Arabia had opted for the propagation of Islam as a tool of gaining influence abroad, it had no choice but to finance all those who claimed to belong to Sunni Islam, and to run the risk of underwriting revolutionary groups that were actively hostile to Riyadh." Gilles Kepel, *Jihad, The trial of political Islam*, pp. 72-73.

pro-western image in the eyes of conservative Arabs, saw the Afghanistan resistance as a golden opportunity to promote its Wahhabi ideals and neutralize internal unrest. Money and political support for the Afghan mujahedeen became a major objective of the kingdom during the 80's. In all fairness to the Saudis, however, it should be noted that while they supported the Wahhabi school of Islamic ideals and Jihad against the Soviets in Afghanistan, they did not advocate global Jihad against the west.

Pakistan was the other Muslim country that jumped quickly on the bandwagon of Jihad, as they recognized it as a potential effective weapon that could be used in their perennial territorial dispute with India over Kashmir. These miscalculations of Egyptian, Saudi and Pakistani governments greatly enhanced the capabilities of Islamic fundamentalists in the three countries and till the current time their citizens are paying the heavy price of being on-going targets of terrorist attacks.

Although eventually the Soviets were expelled from Afghanistan, the Arab-Afghans' assignment was not completed. One would have expected that once the Soviets were out of Afghanistan, the Arab mujahedeen would return to their countries and resume their former occupations. The long war in Afghanistan, however, had created among the Arab-Afghans a long-term "mentality of Jihad" that many found hard to abandon.[11] They started returning home only to face and cause troubles. Egypt, the birthplace of Muslim Brotherhood, Hassan el Banna, Sayyid Qutb, and Ayman Zawahiri, would be again the center stage of post-Soviet Afghanistan Islamic Fundamentalism. Zawahiri, the, by now, undisputed Emir of Egyptian Islamic Jihad, also returned to his former occupation being a terrorist. After the assassination of Azzam (something that some suspect Zawahiri had a hand in) in a car bomb in Peshawar in 1989, Zawahiri's hard line rhetoric began to prevail. The attractions that the Afghanistan natural environment provided, and the unification forces that the resistance against the Soviets had forged among Muslims were irresistible to him. He argued that the Jihad against the infidels should continue till total victory for the Nation of Islam was achieved. The following statements from his book *Knights under the Prophet's Banner* illustrate his strategic goals.

> That [Afghanistan] Jihad was a training course of the utmost importance to prepare Muslim mujahedeen to wage their awaited battle against the superpower that now has sole dominance over the globe, namely, the United States.
>
> The seriousness of the presence of Muslim, particularly Arab, young men in the arena of Jihad in Afghanistan consisted of turning the Afghan cause from a local, regional issue into a global Islamic issue in which the entire nation [of Islam] can participate.

And the armies of Muslim mujahedeen responded to the trumpet call of Zawahiri with vigor and newly-found confidence that was gained from their victorious war in Afghanistan against one of the world's superpowers. Their first target was the speaker of the Egyptian parliament, Refit El Mahout who was assassinated in September of 1990 †. Another major incident in Egypt was the massacre of 67 foreign tourists in Luxor, Egypt in 1997, where Zawahiri is believed to have helped *Gamaa Islamiya* in the planning. It was the first time that the Islamic militants targeted tourists, a pattern that became one of their strategic objectives in the next decade. Tourists were targeted for two reasons: the first one was to shake the stability of the government by hitting the economy, as tourism is one of the top sources of revenue of several fledging Islamic countries, and a big source of hard currency. The second reason, as was declared in a *fatwa* by Sheikh Omar Abdel Rahman who is currently in jail in the US in connection to the 1993 WTC bombings, was to rid the country of the Western influences as the tourists spread low morals in the society.

Some of the Arab-Afghans moved on, taking residence in more than 25 countries around the world and acquiring political asylum in the UK, Austria, Germany and Canada, often with the blessing of the intelligence agencies of the host countries. Others decided to stay in Afghanistan. Out of the 27 men on Egypt's most wanted list, 14 have obtained political asylum in Europe and Canada. Their location was not kept secret. Every

† I had just arrived in Egypt for the first time for an assignment and was staying at the Intercontinental Hotel in Cairo. The assassination took place outside by the main entrance of the hotel.

Arab journalist in London had their phone numbers, and various newspapers and TV stations frequently interviewed them. There are speculations that the number of persons from the Middle East seeking political asylum in Britain every year to be in the thousands. A large number of them were able to receive it. In pre- 9/11 Britain alone, there were more than fifteen groups working to overthrow the governments of Muslim countries. These groups stayed in contact and visited the same mosques and discussion groups. Government officials in London had made it clear that combating repressive dictatorships would still be allowed, as they referred to Britain as a free society and according to them someone who was yesterday's terrorist could be tomorrow's freedom fighter. Nelson Mandela was cited as an example of that.[12]

The Arab countries, thus, were not alone in miscalculating the true objectives of Islamic fundamentalists and underestimating their resilience and persistence. The U.S., Germany and especially England committed even more serious errors. Blinded by the effective propaganda of Islamists that they were political victims of oppressive dictatorial regimes, Europe and the U.S. provided a safe haven to these terrorist groups. September 11 was the wakeup call that changed their perception of Islamic fundamentalists, although till now one can still hear the voices of the human rights activists who erroneously believe the principal reason for terrorism is the undemocratic regimes prevalent in the Muslim world. Indeed these regimes greatly contribute to the popularity and strength of the Islamic fundamentalism movement, but they are far from the root of the problem.

Stage Six: The Birth of Al Qaeda

The war in Afghanistan ended with the defeat and withdrawal of the Soviets. Bin Laden returned home where he received a hero's welcome. He was the undisputed leader of the mujahedeen who had defeated a superpower. It was a great morale boost to the Arab ego and an even greater propaganda opportunity for the fundamentalists. Bin Laden seized the moment and engaged in a cross-country campaign to promote the ideals of Sayyid Qutb and Abdullah Azzam. His speeches at mosques were often recorded and distributed throughout the Middle East.

Then, on August 4, 1990 Saddam Hussein invaded Kuwait and Bin Laden saw this as a chance to promote himself as the new Caliph of a resurrected Islamic nation that would oust the apostate Saddam from Kuwait. He offered to the Saudi government to allow him to launch an attack against the Iraqis by activating his veteran mujahedeen. The Saudis wisely refused his help and chose instead to seek the help of Americans. While this decision of the Saudi government infuriated Bin Laden, it saved the Saudi royals from an almost certain civil war and potential coup d'état that very probably would have brought an end to their dynastic rule. The true motives of Bin Laden would become apparent a few years later when he openly engaged in Jihad to overthrow the house of Saud and used oil revenue and the holy lands of Saudi, as his base, in launching his battle against the infidels.

The end of the Gulf War ushered in a more visible and larger American military presence in Arabia. This contributed to Bin Laden's loathing of the Americans and provided him with a new platform for his war against the infidel West. His new message was now that the Americans had desecrated the Muslim holy lands and the apostate Saudi rulers had committed the ultimate sin by allowing the infidel soldiers remain in there.[13]

Bin Laden became very vocal in his opposition to the presence of US troops in Saudi soil. Given that he was known as a mujahedeen who fought the Soviets in Afghanistan and not as an Islamic scholar, Bin Laden begun to echo prominent Saudi religious scholars who advocated that the presence of Americans in the Gulf was part of a larger plan to dominate the Arab and Muslim world.[14]. This was quite possibly the beginning of Bin Laden's frequent future references to Islamic doctrine to support his Jihad against the West. He had discovered, as many of his predecessors from Ibn Taymiyya to Sayyid Qutb had, that Quranic references were a powerful and unchallenged tool in convincing the vast majority of Muslims to accept whatever the objective of their rhetoric might be.

The Saudi government eventually tired of Bin Laden's inflammatory rhetoric and placed him under house arrest limiting his movements to Jeddah. Bin Laden had, however, began planning his escape from Saudi to Sudan months earlier and was successful in doing so in April 1991, where he began a double life by investing heavily in banks and agricultural projects, and building a major highway, while he organized training camps for his Islamic militants. He was able to pursue both venues with almost unlimited freedom because of his special relationship with the Sudanese dictators, who were happy to provide him and his followers with new passports and identities in return for his investment capital.

More important than building and operating training camps for Islamic militants, however, Bin Laden was creating a formidable international network of terrorist operatives under the disguise of his multinational business operations. This accomplishment may be Bin Laden's greatest and a sign of his genius. He was able to conceive and apply traditional business practices in financing, managing and operating his terrorist network. To facilitate business, his corporations maintained accounts at banks in Cyprus, Malaysia, Hong Kong, Dubai, Vienna, and London. Moreover, his top operatives were able to travel freely throughout the globe to transact business and direct terrorist operations. Under the useful cover of his commercial operations, Bin Laden honed his skills as a political leader and planner of paramilitary operations against the Americans.

Another important task that strengthened the institutionalization of Al Qaeda was the development of the *Encyclopedia of Afghan Jihad* sometime between 1990 and 1993. The eight hundred pages Encyclopedia includes details of everything that was learned in the Jihad against the Soviets in Afghanistan, including how to use American Stinger missiles, and 250 pages of *how to* instructions in launching paramilitary attacks.

Pressures mounted on the Sudanese government by the US and Egypt, however, and in 1996 Bin Laden was expelled from Sudan to Afghanistan. Peter Bergen states that "Forcing Bin Laden to leave Sudan would turn out to be a little like the German High Command sending Lenin to Russia during World War I: while the policy might have resulted in short-term gains for the Germans, it set the stage for the creation of Germany's most implacable enemy."[15] There, in Afghanistan, Bin Laden would become a much greater threat to Americans and the world than he would ever have done from Sudan.

***

In Egypt, the principal staging area of Islamic militancy, we traced Ayman Zawahiri's footsteps to Afghanistan, and revealed his justification for choosing this land for his base (Al Qaeda). When Zawahiri was asked to travel to Pakistan to contribute as surgeon to the medical relief effort among the Afghan refugees, he immediately agreed, "because I saw this as an opportunity to get to know one of the arenas of Jihad that might be tributary and a base for Jihad in Egypt and the Arab region, the heart of the Islamic world, where the battle of Islam was being fought…The problem of finding a secure base for Jihad activity in Egypt used to occupy me a lot, in view of the pursuits to which we were subjected by the security forces and because of Egypt's flat terrain which made government control easy, for the River Nile runs in its narrow valley between two deserts that have no vegetation or water. Such a terrain made guerrilla warfare in Egypt impossible and, as a result, forced the inhabitants of this valley to submit to the central government and be exploited as workers and compelled them to be recruited in the army."[16] It is worth quoting below in its entirety how Zawahiri outlines the significance of using Afghanistan as the staging area for Jihad.

> For this reason this invitation [to participate in medical assistance to the Afghan refugees] came as a predestined event. I accepted the invitation out of an earnest wish to get to know the suitable arenas where I could establish a secure base for Jihadist action in Egypt, particu-

larly during the term of Anwar al-Sadat when the signs of a new crusade became apparent to everyone who had insightfulness and was obvious to everyone concerned about his nation's affairs.

When I came into contact with the arena of Afghan Jihad in 1980, I became aware of its rich potential and realized how much benefit it would bring to the Muslim nation in general, and the Jihadist movement in particular. I understood the importance of benefiting from this arena. Hence, after I stayed for four months there on my first visit, I returned in March 1981 and spent another two months there.

During my contacts and dealings with those who worked in that arena, several vitally important facts became clear to me and it is necessary to mention them here:

1. A Jihadist movement needs an arena that would act like an incubator where its seeds would grow and where it can acquire practical experience in combat, politics, and organizational matters.

2. The Muslim youths in Afghanistan waged the war to liberate Muslim land under purely Islamic slogans, a very vital matter, for many of the liberation battles in our Muslim world had used composite slogans that mixed nationalism with Islam and, indeed, sometimes caused Islam to intermingle with leftist, communist slogans. This produced a schism in the thinking of the Muslim young men between their Islamic Jihadist ideology that should rest on pure loyalty to God's religion, and its practical implementation… Another important issue is that these battles that were waged under non-Muslim banners or mixed banners caused the dividing lines between friends and enemies to become blurred. The Muslim youths began to have doubts about who was the enemy. Was it the foreign enemy that occupied Muslim territory, or was it the domestic enemy that prohibited government by Islamic Shariah, repressed the Muslims, and disseminated immorality under the slogans of progress, liberty, nationalism and liberation?

In Afghanistan the picture was perfectly clear: A Muslim nation carrying out Jihad under the banner of Islam, versus a foreign enemy that was an infidel aggressor backed by a corrupt, apostatic regime at home. In the case of this war, the application of the theory to the facts was manifestly clear. This clarity was also beneficial in refuting

> the ambiguities raised by many people professing to carry out Islamic work but who escaped from the arena of Jihad on the pretext that there was no arena in which the distinction between Muslims and their enemies was obvious.
>
> 3. Furthermore, the Afghan arena, especially after the Russians withdrew, became a practical example of Jihad against the renegade rulers who allied themselves with the foreign enemies of Islam.
>
> 4. A further significant point was that the Jihad battles in Afghanistan destroyed the myth of a [superpower] in the minds of the Muslim mujahedeen young men. The USSR, a superpower with the largest land army in the world, was destroyed and the remnant of its troops fled Afghanistan before the eyes of the Muslim youths and as a result of their actions.
>
> It also gave young Muslim mujahedeen—Arabs, Pakistanis, Turks, and Muslims from Central and East Asia—a great opportunity to get acquainted with each other on the land of Afghan Jihad through their comradeship-at-arms against the enemies of Islam. In this way, the mujahedeen young men and the Jihadist movements came to know each other closely, exchanged expertise, and learned to understand their brethren's problems.
>
> The Arab mujahedeen did not confine themselves to financing their own Jihad but also carried Muslim donations to the Afghan mujahedeen themselves. Osama Bin Laden has apprised me of the size of the popular Arab support for the Afghan mujahedeen that mounted, according to his sources, to $200 million in the form of military aid alone in 10 years. Through this unofficial popular support, the Arab mujahedeen established training centers and centers for the call to the faith. They formed fronts that trained and equipped thousands of Arab mujahedeen and provided them with living expenses, housing, travel, and organization.

This is how Al Qaeda was established in the rugged mountainous terrain of Afghanistan, a perfect setting chillingly reminiscent of the same environment chosen by the almost mythical "Old Man in the Mountain" leader of the "Assassins" eight centuries earlier. According to Zawahiri's methodical narrative presented above with amazing clarity, however, was not only Afghanistan's geography that made it attractive to him and Bin Laden. We must remind our readers at this point that it was not the concern for the wellbeing of the Afghan refugees and the provision of medical assistance to them that attracted Zawahiri to Afghanistan in the first place. It was his recognition of the potential that the Afghanistan arena provided to the Jihadist movement in Egypt, initially and to the global Jihadist movement eventually.

The Old Man in the Mountain

The notion of Bin Laden and Zawahiri hiding in the caves of the Hindu Kush mountains in the Afghanistan-Pakistan border, from where they directed a global network of terrorists, has attracted a lot of media attention and resulted into numerous articles and books covering an even larger number of theories and speculations about religious cults and descendants of medieval assassins. Not being totally immune from this temptation, we decided to look into the potential similarities between Al Qaeda (modern terrorists) and the medieval Assassins of Alamut, but from a very different perspective. To that end, we would like to present herein not what the connection of Al Qaeda to the sect might have been, but rather what Al Qaeda might have ended up being without the Iraq war and the Palestinian conflict.

The Assassins were part of a heretical Islamic sect whose roots can be traced back to Cairo around 1080 and during the reign of the Fatimids, which was a rival caliphate of the Baghdad-based Abbasids. The elite ruling class of the Fatimids was Shiite Muslims, while the majority of Egyptian population was Sunnis. This is the principal reason that Egyptians to this date are Sunnis rather than Shiites, as Iraqis, Syrians, and Iranians are. After the death of Prophet Mohammed, Islam was ruled in succession by four caliphs who were his relatives and close companions, named for that reason as the "Rightly-Guided" caliphs. The last of the four was Ali ibn Abu Talib, the Prophet's cousin and son-in-law married to his daughter Fatima. Ali's followers believed that Ali should have succeeded the Prophet by right and after that his sons and so on. Instead, Ali was the last of the four caliphs and after him the line of succession to his sons was broken. As a result of this, Ali's followers split from traditional Islam and formed the sect of Shiism, and eventually founded the Dynasty of the Fatimids, first in Northern Africa and then in Egypt, building and establishing Cairo as the capital of the caliphate.

But the conflicts among Muslim rulers did not end with the founding of the Shiite sect. The sixth Shiite ruler, Gafar al Sadiq, had two sons, Ismail, the eldest one, and Mousa. Gafar had named Ismail as his successor but tragically Ismail died before his father. Mousa was then named by Gafar to be the next Imam of Shiites. Ismail, however, had a son whom he had named to be his successor. Again, the faithful were split on the issue of succession and Ismail's followers went on to form yet another sect, that of the Ismailis.

In Fatimid-ruled Egypt, many of the ruling class and elites were Ismaili Shiites. Following the reign of Imam/Caliph Mustansir in the last decade of the eleventh century, the Shiites suffered another schism—this time was the Ismaili sect that was split. Mustansir had appointed his eldest son Nizar as successor. But his younger son, al-Mustali, conspired against his brother and he succeeded in usurping the throne from him. The followers of Nizar fled Egypt to avoid persecution and moved to Iran where the Ismailis had succeeded in establishing a state comprising of a defensive network of fortified settlements.

Among the principal followers of Nizar was a brilliant Persian who had converted to Ismailism. His name was Hassan-i-Sabbah who had gone to Cairo to study in the Al Azhar University, had been initiated into the higher ranks of Ismailis and was one of Nizar's followers. He fled Egypt with the rest of the Nizaris and later on he turned up in Persia as head of the revolutionary Nizari movement. Hassan-i-Sabbah managed to take control of the impregnable fortress of Alamut where he established his headquarters. In addition to the continuing wars among Muslims over issues of power and territory, the Nizaris were facing extra dangers as they were viewed as a strange cult and, thus, a potential danger to Islam. To protect their fortress and its tiny civilization, Hassan adopted assassination as a means of survival. Any ruler, political or religious leader who dared to threaten the Nizaris, risked death from the dagger of one of Hassan's fanatic assassins.

There are volumes written about how Hassan recruited, motivated, trained, and used his army of elite assassins, but most of it is speculation and wild theories. What is certain, however, is that for almost two hundred years—till the destruction of Alamut by the Mongols in 1258—the assassins from their fortress of Alamut and later on from Syria, as well, spread fear in the hearts of all of those who might otherwise attempt to attack them or persecute them. Whether Hassan-i-Sabbah and his successors, who became to be known as the "Old Man in the Mountain", used assassination as a tool of preserving their faith and secret society, or they allowed their soldiers to become professional killers and extortionists is up to speculation. It is known, though, that they were never involved in mass assassinations. The assassin had a specific target and he used only a dagger to accomplish his mission, knowing very well that he was committing suicide by doing so.

In reviewing the origin of the Assassins, their tactics and their impact on their world, and then try to draw parallels between them and the modern terrorists, one should not overlook an, not so obvious, observation. The Assassins although they never won any military victories and didn't gain or occupied any land, with the exception of the Alamut fortress, they terrorized the Islamic and part of the European world of crusaders for the large part of two hundred years with great success. And they accomplished all this even though they didn't have a political agenda or the broad public support that the recent Islamic fundamentalism movement is enjoying. The modern Assassins too without the issues of Palestine and Iraq would be just that—modern Assassins—without a loyal ecumenical following. Their radical ideology and militant tactics had not resonated that much in moderate Arab states, prior to the invasion of Afghanistan by the Soviets and the invasion of Lebanon by Israel. The aggressive Israeli policies towards Palestine, the increasing settlements in West bank and Gaza, the second Intifada, and, the "icing on the cake", the invasion against Iraq tipped the scales in favor of the Islamists and legitimized their "struggle" against the aggressor crusaders in the minds of even the most moderate Muslims.

Without this gift from America, the achievements of the modern Assassins would have not been much more than a footnote of political assassinations, much of the same as the targeted assassinations in the Islamic medieval world of the original Assassins. This is not to say that political assassinations are fine, don't cause much damage and should be ignored. There is a big difference, however, between targeted assassinations, mainly against unpopular Muslim military and political leaders branded as apostates and a full scale holy war between Islam and the West. The former is an important national issue for many Arab states that should be addressed by each Arab country for the sake of its own stability; the latter is a much more critical issue of global peace and stability.

Al Qaeda's Brain

Of the two men heading U.S.'s most wanted list, Ayman El Zawahiri, should be on the head of the list and not Bin Laden. Often referred as the "number two man of Al Qaeda", or "Bin Laden's right hand", Zawahiri was the former leader of the Islamic Jihad group until the year 2000. Zawahiri is a life-long Egyptian radical, who many believe to be perhaps the most influential leader of Al Qaeda. He has been called one of the masterminds and the real brains behind the organization and its operation. As a former head of the Egyptian Jihad, he has a long history of terror-related crimes and militant activities in Egypt and around the world, and his name has come up in nearly every case involving Muslim extremists since the 70s. Moreover, counter terrorism and Islamic militant experts regard Zawahiri to be more intelligent and more dangerous than Bin Laden. To Islamic fundamentalists, he is seen as the important ideological driving force behind the organization.

Some consider him to be the mastermind of the September 11 assaults on the WTC and the Pentagon. In mid-April of 2002, the Qatar's *Al Jazeera* TV showed portions of a videotape in which Zawahiri claimed credit for the attacks, referring to them as "this great victory'" and to the hijackers as "19 brothers." On the tape, Bin Laden is sitting beside him, shaking his head, speaking softly to himself and playing with his beard. Terrorism experts and Islamic militant analysts agree that Zawahiri's influence in reshaping Bin Laden's thinking and ideology is very profound. Zawahiri was able to convert him from a supporter of the Afghan's Jihad against the Soviets into a strong believer and exporter of the Jihad ideology and making him more violent and anti-West, especially anti-American. Analysts have described Zawahiri that to Bin Laden, he is what the brain is to the body. It was Zawahiri who convinced Bin Laden to establish Al Qaeda in 1988, thereby providing "The Base" for training, supplies and operations of militants from Egypt and elsewhere.

The Egyptian government, whose insistence for many years that Islamic terrorists had become global fell on deaf ears, had informed Western intelligence services several years prior to 9/11 that Zawahiri had traveled with French and Swiss passports in the name of Amin Osman. He is also understood to have had a Dutch passport in the name of Sami Mahmoud El Hifnawy in the early 1990s when he apparently traveled extensively in Western Europe, living at various times in Switzerland and Denmark. Jihad members testified during the 1999 trial in Egypt that he had entered the USA in 1995 using the alias Dr. Abdel Moez and while there raised funds used to finance the suicide bombing attack on the Egyptian embassy in Islamabad. According to London's Guardian newspaper, the US House of Representatives judiciary subcommittee on immigration was told by a counter terrorism expert in January 2000 that Zawahiri was one of several Islamic militants who had been granted green card status by the US Immigration Service. He seems to have had significantly greater experience in clandestine operations than Bin Laden.

According to terror analysts, Zawahiri, after settling in Afghanistan, worked to reestablish *Al Jihad* from where he controlled its activities by the Arab-Afghans in Egypt. He decided to widen its operational horizon to the international arena. That included a car bombing in Croatia in Sep. 1995, the assassination in Geneva of an Egyptian diplomat in Nov. 1995 who believed to have been an intelligence officer tasked with hunting down Islamic militants, and the bombing of the Egyptian embassy in Islamabad, a key base for Egyptian intelligence operations against terrorists like Zawahiri.

The Globalization of Islamic Fundamentalism

Seen by many counter terrorism and Islamic experts as the intellectual and ideological driving force behind the organization, Zawahiri's presence was vital in the formation of the coalition of the International Islamic Front (IIF). On February 1998, he merged his group, *Al Jihad*, with *Al Qaeda* to form IIF and Zawahiri was one of the five Islamic leaders who signed on to Bin Laden's declaration for the attacks against the US citizens. Zawahiri is believed to be the person who most influenced Bin Laden years ago to take up a worldwide struggle against perceived enemies of Islam. He had finally succeeded.

The statement of Jihad against the Jews and the Crusaders was signed on February 23, 1998. The statement had the names of Bin Laden, Zawahiri, who was referred to as the emir of the jihad group in Egypt, and Refaie Ahmed Taha of the Egyptian *Gamaa Islamiya*, who is said to have approved of the statement but never signed it. The statement also included two more names of leaders of groups in Pakistan and Bangladesh. This statement purports to be a *Fatwa*, religious ruling, requiring the killing of Americans, both civilians and militants. This statement is considered to be part of the evidence that links Al Qaeda to the September 11th attacks on NY and Washington. In this statement, they explained the reasons of their alliance in three points. In their own words, the first point was the occupation of the USA and the Arabian Peninsula, where they would turn the holy lands into a base from where they would spearhead their attacks against the neighboring Muslim countries. The second was American's continuing aggression against the Iraqi people, and the third point was the support of the Jews in the occupation of Jerusalem and the murder of the Muslims there.

After presenting these points, the statement continued that all these crimes and sins committed by the Americans are a clear declaration of war on Allah, his messenger and Muslims everywhere. And since the Muslim scholars throughout the Islamic history have agreed that Jihad is an individual duty if the enemy attacks Muslim countries, then on that basis, and in compliance with Allah's order, they issued the following *Fatwa* to all Muslims:

> The ruling to kill the Americans and their allies—civilians and militants—is an individual duty for every Muslim who can do it in any country in which it is possible to be done, in order to liberate the Al-Aqsa mosque and the holy mosque (Mecca) from their grip, and in order for their armies to move out of all the lands of Islam, defeated and unable to threaten any Muslim.
>
> We—with Allah's help—call on every Muslim who believes in Allah and wishes to be rewarded to comply with Allah's order to kill the Americans and plunder their money wherever and whenever they find it. We also call on Muslims ulema (clerics), leaders, youths, and soldiers to launch the raid on Satan's US troops and the devil's supporters allying with them, and to dispatch those who are behind them so that they may learn a lesson.

The message communicated by this *Fatwa* can be considered one of the most underestimated threats to Americans and the West in general, that continues to this day to be the core of the Islamic militants' recruiting propaganda and the principal justification of all attacks against the West. Its theme is simple: Americans and their allies are attacking Muslims in their lands causing much destruction and suffering. We must strike back and force them taste their own medicine.

If there has been any misunderstanding regarding this message and the goal of the Islamic movement in general, it should have been made crystal clear by Osama Bin Laden in a speech he addressed directly to the American people via a videotape aired by the Arabic TV network *Al Jazeera* on October 30, 2004 just four days before the US presidential election. The videotape, the first one from Bin Laden in nearly three years, not only clarified and amplified the message of Islamists; it erased any speculation about whether Bin Laden is alive and the status of his health, as he appeared looking well, composed, dressed in a princely garment, and without his usual AK-47 rifle and camouflage jacket. He spoke as an elder statesman representing the Islamic movement. Not that time or any other time has been a person or an organization, outside of the IIF umbrella, that has challenged his leadership and statements. He remained the undisputed political leader of the cause.

With chilling clarity and calmness, Bin Laden reminded the American people why the US was attacked.

> People of America, I talk to you today, about the best way to avoid another Manhattan and about war, its reasons and consequences. And in that regard, I say to you that security is an indispensable pillar of human life and that free men do not forfeit their security, contrary to [President George W.] Bush's claim that we hate freedom. If so, then let him explain to us why we don't strike, for example, Sweden? No, we fight because we are free men who don't sleep under oppression. We want to restore freedom to our nation. Just as you lay waste to our nation, we shall lay waste to yours.
>
> But I am amazed at you. Even though we are in the fourth year after the events of September 11, Bush is still engaged in distortion, deception and hiding from you the real causes. And thus, the reasons are still there for a repeat of what occurred.

In what may be the core message of Bin Laden's communication with the American people, he gives the reasons for all past attacks and futures ones, as well. And he reminds them that he told them about this before in his 1998 *Fatwa* and in his interviews with "Scott in Time Magazine in 1996, or with Peter Arnett on CNN in 1997, or my meeting with John Weiner in 1998."

> I say to you, Allah knows, that it had never occurred to us to strike the towers. But after it became unbearable to witness the oppression and tyranny of the American/Israeli coalition against the people in Palestine and Lebanon, it came to my mind. The events that affected my soul in a direct way started in 1982 when America permitted the Israelis to invade Lebanon and the American Sixth Fleet helped them in that. The bombardment began and many were killed and injured and others were terrorized and displaced… Destruction is freedom and democracy, while resistance is terrorism and intolerance?… So, with these images and their like as the background, the events of September 11 came as a reply to those great wrongs. Should a man be blamed for defending his sanctuary? Is

> defending oneself and punishing the aggressor in kind, objectionable terrorism? If it is such, then it is unavoidable for us.
>
> This is the message which I sought to communicate to you in word and deed, repeatedly, for years before September 11.

Without the usual poetic and Quranic references and threatening rhetoric that have characterized Bin Laden's past style, the "Sheikh" appeared to be reaching out for some type of dialogue. The reasoning of Islamic militants for waging war on America and the West may be warped, but in the messages, that Bin Laden and Zawahiri have been delivering for almost ten years now, the rationale for their terrorist activities is embedded.

The motives of Bin Laden's number two man, however, against America are not that clear. Some Egyptians believe Zawahiri's hatred towards the US peaked in 1998, when America pushed for twenty members of Al Jihad group to be extradited from Albania in July 1998 due to a foiled attack on an American installation in Tirana, and to stand trial in Egypt. On April 1999, Egypt tried Jihad members, who had been extradited from Albania, in one of the largest anti-terrorism trials in Egypt. The trial involved 107 Islamic fundamentalists, 63 of whom were tried in absentia. Most of them belonged to Al Jihad group and a large number of them were operating with Bin Laden. Zawahiri and one of his brothers, Mohamed, were tried in absentia and given death penalties. The name of the case was "Returnees from Albania".

On August 4, 1998, less than a month after the extradition of the Jihad members from Albania, the *Al Hyatt* newspaper office in Cairo received a fax from Al Jihad stating," We should like to inform the Americans that, in short, their message has been received and that they should read carefully the reply that, with God's help, will be written in the language that they understand." Three days later, the US embassies in Kenya and Tanzania in East Africa were bombed. Both Zawahiri and Bin Laden would be indicted by the US on charges of masterminding the bombing.

It was not until September 25, 2001, when Interpol finally issued an arrest warrant for Zawahiri at the request of the Egyptian police, which had given his name to the Interpol in 1996 and again in 1997 requesting his arrest and extradition. Egypt had accused Zawahiri to have masterminded several terrorist operations in Egypt as well as the suicide bombing of the Egyptian embassy in Islamabad on November 19, 1995 in which 17 people got killed.

Since September 11, Zawahiri has raised his public profile, appearing in videos obtained by the TV station *Al Jazeera* in which he delivers blistering denunciations of the US peppered with threats against US interests. *Al Hayat* reporter Mohamed Salah said that the videos represent a break from Zawahiri's former clandestine nature. His appearance was a message saying this is an alliance and Bin Laden is not alone and it's not only Al Qaeda, but there are other organizations, as well.

1. abcNews.com/WorldNewsTonight/October 3, 2001, "From Surgeon to Terrorist: the Second Most Wanted Man in the World" by Jim Wooten.
2. CNN/Programs/People in the News hosted by Paula Zahn/Ayman al-Zawahiri Profile.
3. Ayman Zawahiri, *Knights Under the Prophet's Banner*; Part Three, 2001
4. "Trapping the Extremists", *Al Ahram* newspaper (April 20, 2003, pg. 10, by Osama Sarraya).
5. Ayman Zawahiri, *Knights Under the Prophet's Banner*; Part Three, 2001
6. Jane's.com/JIR/Ayman Al-Zawahiri: attention turns to the other prime suspect, contributor Ed Blanche, 3 October 2001.
7. abcNews.com/WorldNewsTonight/October 3, 2001
8. "America's Most Wanted",The *Al Ahram* Weekly Online, Issue No. 552, , by Khaled Dawoud
9. BBC News Documentary, "The Roots of Jihad".
10. *The Al Ahram Weekly* Online, 2001, Issue no. 552, p 14.
11. BBC News Documentary, "The Roots of Jihad".
12. "London Calling", article from *Cairo Times.*
13. *Newsweek,* Sept. 24, 2001 p 45.
14. Peter Bergen, *Holy War, Inc.,* p 78.
15. Ibid, p 91.
16. Ayman Zawahiri, *Knights Under the Prophet's Banner*; Part Three, 2001, p 8.

Stage Seven: Post 9/11 Islamic Fundamentalism

To be able to deal with terrorism, its origin, its character, tactics and goals, in a post 9/11 world, the West needs to understand clearly who the "terrorists" are; the origins of Islamic fundamentalism; their goals; and what fuels and sustains their movement. This is a central issue which, although has been addressed extensively, hasn't been answered properly, with a few exceptions, either by American administrations or the news media. While Islamism Fundamentalism has been described in great detail in this section, it is appropriate to mention again that it is a religious and political movement—not an organization and definitely not just Al Qaeda. And its leadership is not just Bin Laden, Zawahiri and Zarqawi.

Diaa Rashwan, an Egyptian expert in Islamic militarism, further explains:

> The existence of this network connection of all affiliated [terrorist] groups, presents the wrong image which the media and security services sees Al Qaeda as a global organization with cells in each and every nation that are ready to act on orders issued from its leadership under the control of Bin Laden. More precisely, however, Al Qaeda now became a loose, wide-ranging organization framework containing two distinct levels. The leadership level, which possess a hierarchical internal structure, a unified intellectual and operative leadership, a theoretical framework and clear operating strategies. Its members appear to be centered in Afghanistan, Pakistan, parts of central Asia, India, the Arabian Peninsula and East Africa.
>
> The second level is what has been referred to as "the Al Qaeda network". This is a wide ranging network of organizations and individuals belonging to the Jihad movement or Islamic movement around the world. The way in which Washington declared its war on terror–making it seem very much like a war on Islam or the Islamic world—combined with the campaign against Iraq and the Israeli outrages against Palestinians, have come together to incite a number of these Islamist groups and individuals in different areas of the world against US and Israeli policy. As a result, sections of these groups have targeted American

> and Israeli interests around the world, using all the means at their disposal. This does not mean, however, that they are necessarily linked to Al Qaeda, except that all these organizations have a common enemy and agree on the use of violence against it. As a result, the US has expanded its definition of Al Qaeda to include a variety of diverse organizations and individuals without offering any real evidence of the link between them.

There are more critics of the Bush's administration failure to recognize the evolving nature of Al Qaeda. On November 7, 2004, New York Times reported in an interview with Michael Scheuer, the former chief of the CIA's Osama Bin Laden unit, that the government "doesn't respect the threat" because most officials still regard Al Qaeda as a terrorist organization that can be defeated by arresting or killing its operatives one at a time. Mr. Scheuer said that in addition to running its own core terrorist network, Al Qaeda was also providing support to regional Islamic rebellions around the world. Mr. Bin Laden is providing inspiration to Islamic extremists far beyond Al Qaeda's own membership, vastly complicating the task of combating the threat to the West. "The amount of punishment the CIA has delivered to Al Qaeda since 9/11 would have wiped out any other terrorist organization," Mr. Scheuer said. "But this is an insurgent organization. The difference between fighting a terrorist group and fighting an insurgency is one of size," he added. "Yet we still don't know how big it is. We still, today, don't know the order of battle of Al Qaeda."

The distinction that Michael Scheuer makes between terrorism and insurgency is an important one, as a misunderstanding of what the global Jihadist movement really is will certainly result in misguided strategies in combating terrorism. Moreover, it underscores the need for actions other than military strikes against the terrorists and their leaders (addressing the Israeli – Palestinian conflict), and points out a major flow in the US tactics. In a statement to European leaders shortly after the 2004 re-election of George W. Bush, British Prime Minister Tony Blair urged them to work with Bush on fighting terrorism and "resolving the conditions and causes on which terrorists prey." It is very tragic that two of the world's leading countries which have championed freedom and democracy around the world for the better part of the last century, to be so blindsided in their conclusions as to the real causes of terrorism. It is inevitable that the continuation of the conflict strengthens both sides of religious fundamentalists who entrench deeper and want to inflict more damage to each other. Also, it breeds a new generation of leaders and organizers who are younger, smarter, better educated, and who have been battle hardened and use more sophisticated and effective means of attacking the West and destabilizing its security and economy.

Outside the administration, however, analysts seem to have been more astute in debunking the myth of Al Qaeda mush earlier in the game. Back in May of 2002, Kimberly McCloud and Adam Dolnik of the Monterey Institute of International Studies said:

> By committing itself to eradicating terrorism, the Bush administration has put itself in a difficult position, especially if "Al Qaeda" begins popping up all over the map. While the US government must be diligent in protecting its citizens, it cannot try to extinguish every terrorist flame that appears without further encouraging the phenomenon as well as exhausting its resources. America must choose its battles wisely. Resisting immediate attribution of attacks to Al Qaeda is the first step in defusing the enemy. While the Bush administration has not necessarily been blaming all post-9/11 attacks on Al Qaeda, it has passively allowed others to claim themselves as Al Qaeda or to blame it.
>
> By allowing Al Qaeda to become the top brand of international terrorism, Washington has packaged the "enemy" into something with a structure, a leader, and a main area of operation. An invisible, amorphous enemy may be even more frightening. But we must be honest with the facts in order to construct a viable long-term strategy to combat terrorism.

The above analysis has proved to be very accurate and wise and makes one, once more, wonder how can all these armies of intelligence wizards in the US government be so wrong so often? The problem when you ask this type of question is that you open the doors into dark rooms where Machiavellian plotting and deceit are taking place. Perhaps our government needed to create an external enemy and one that serves well Washington's political philosophy and foreign policy.

Iraq War: Best Recruiter of Jihadists since Afghanistan

On January 4, 2004, the Arabic satellite channel *El Jazeera* broadcast an audio tape from Osama Bin Laden in which he urged the faithful everywhere to "continue the Jihad to check the conspiracies that are hatched against the Islamic nation." He said "The occupation of Iraq is the beginning of the full occupation of the other Gulf states... Gulf is the key for control of the world in the point of view of the big powers because of the presence of the biggest deposits of oil…My message is to incite you against the conspiracies, especially those uncovered by the occupation of the crusaders in Baghdad under the pretext of weapons of destruction, and also the situation in (Jerusalem) under the deceptions of the road map and the Geneva initiative."

Back in September 2003, on the eve of the second anniversary of the 9/11 attack, another Bin Laden audio tape praised the Iraqi resistance fighters and warned America that the battle was far from over and the United States has so far experienced "just the first skirmishes" and not yet begun to realize the true volume of its casualties. "Those fighters in Iraq, we greet them and salute them and support them and ask God to bless their efforts and their bravery in fighting the crusaders, and we tell them God is with you and the nation is supporting you, depend and rely on God and attack and devour the Americans and bury them in the graveyard of Iraq."

CNN reported that Secretary of Defense Rumsfeld in an interview with Jim Lehrer on *PBS' NewsHour* said the tape was just an attempt by the terrorist organization to prove to its followers that it's doing well and to solicit money from its financiers. Once more, the Washington elite failed to recognize or, perhaps, didn't want to, the true message in Bin Laden's statements. As they raise the threat level, our homeland security people become more vigilant; our local enforcement agencies become more strained and financially exhausted, as we all anxiously waiting for another attack against one of our cities. Not that our government should take these threats lightly. The error is that the attacks are not taking place in the US—there hasn't been any terrorist attacks on American soil since 9/11—but in Saudi Arabia, Pakistan, Indonesia, Great Britain, Spain, Afghanistan, Russia, India, and, yes, Iraq. Following this tape and during the month of November, 2003, Americans faced the worst insurgency violence in Iraq since the invasion and sustained the heaviest casualties of the war so far.

Zawahiri's propaganda—the West is attacking Islam, we must defend ourselves—reverberates throughout the Islamic world. Even moderate Muslims, who had distanced themselves further from the Islamic militants since 9/11, found themselves siding with and even actively supporting the mujahedeen. The Iraq war and the continued pro-Israel foreign US foreign policy have become the best recruiting tools that all the money in the world couldn't have bought for the Islamic fundamentalists. The occupation of Iraq has been a front-page story throughout the Muslim Arab world and has drawn wide sympathy and support from most European countries, as well.

Prominent Saudi religious scholars have called on Iraqis to support fighters battling US-led forces, saying fighting the presence of foreign troops is a duty, reported *Al Jazeera* in its website on November 6, 2004 as US troops were gearing up for a major assault on Fallujah. In an open letter addressed to the Iraqi people, twenty six scholars and religious preachers stressed that any armed attacked against the US-led coalition forces in Iraq by Muslims were "legitimate" resistance and a duty for all those who are able to do so. "It is a *Jihad* to push back the assailants."

These scholars went further than encouraging Muslims to fight a holy war against the crusaders occupying Iraq. They issued a *Fatwa* prohibiting Iraqis from offering any support to military operations carried out by US forces against resistance fighters. "Resistance is a legitimate right. A Muslim must not inflict harm on any resistance man or inform about them. Instead, they should be supported and protected," the *Fatwa* stated.

This latest *Fatwa* not only brought certain legitimacy to the Iraqi insurgency, it further illustrated the support that the resistance enjoys among Muslims. Moreover, it focused attention on the on-going conflict among Islamic moderates and clerics who promote radical views, especially in Saudi Arabia which has been hit by a series of deadly terrorist attacks since the Iraq invasion. This angered many in Saudi Arabia, the birthplace of Islam and home of its two holiest cities. Responding to the growing internal threat to the security of its people and, even more, to its fragile monarchy, the Saudi government launched a military campaign against anti-government fighters that started after three deadly attacks against residential compounds in Riyadh in May 2003. Several more attacks have followed and a number of westerners have been killed. The crackdown may also be viewed as a statement by the Saudis to their critics in the West, especially neo-con controlled Washington, that they are serious about reigning in terrorism.

The war against Iraq and the eventual occupation of another tragic Muslim country, has not only outraged Arabs and Westerners alike, it has alienated America from most of its traditional European allies, deeply divided Americans, dealt a severe blow to the financial stability of the US, it has also created challenges and dangers in several Arabic countries, particularly Saudi Arabia, Pakistan and Egypt—countries with serious domestic problems of their own. Saudi Arabia, the landowner and protector of the holy Islamic shrines and birthplace of the infamous Wahhabism, is facing, perhaps, the greatest challenge of them all. And its precarious condition poses a major potential threat to the West. Should the Islamic Fundamentalists—not terrorists, since not all fundamentalists are terrorists—take control of Saudi Arabia and its vast oil reserves, then what? Are we going to invade Saudi, regain control of the oil fields, and then march to Mecca and occupy it , as well, as some neo-cons in Washington have already suggested?

And what about Pakistan? Several assassination attempts have been made against the life of Pakistani President Musharraf . Torn between its commitment to the US to support its war against terrorism and a growing anti-Americanism in Pakistan fueled by the occupation of Iraq, Musharraf is walking a tight rope. And the conflict between Pakistanis and Indians over Kashmir is not helping the situation. What would happen if Pakistan becomes an Iran- or Afghanistan-like theocracy and its nuclear arsenal falls in the hands of Bin Laden and, worse, Zawahiri?

Then you have Egypt, the most populous Arab country and strongest US ally in the Middle East. Egypt is also the birthplace of Muslim Brotherhood, Hassan El Banna, Sayyid Qutb, Ayman Zawahiri and Mohammed Atta, and the first battleground of the resurrected Islamic Fundamentalism since the fifties. President Mubarak has not chosen a successor to his "throne" and his eventual departure from this world will very probably create a power vacuum and an opportunity for the fundamentalists who aided by the moderates, who are growing weary of the "dynastic" prospects of another Mubarak, might try to seize power by means of a referendum or election. If Egypt falls, Jordan will follow very quickly and what you have is a realization of Zawahiri's vision, as outlined in the *Knights under the Banner of the Prophet*, of an Islamic Nation, the resurrection of the Caliphate, stretching from Pakistan to the Red Sea and Mediterranean and controlling its vast oil fields and possessing nuclear weapons with long-range delivery capabilities.

If America and its coalition partners believe for a minute that they will bring freedom and democracy in the Middle East and Arab world by changing the current regimes, they are more naïve and dangerous than their toughest critics have led us believe. In countries where religion, and absolute obedience to Quran and Prophet Mohammed are their constitution, and Americanism and its brand of freedom and democracy are universally loathed, the best one can expect is an Iran-style theocracy and not an American-style democracy.

In the summer of 2004, another Islamic militant, Abu Musab Zarqawi, with alleged ties to Al Qaeda joined the pantheon of most wanted terrorists with a $25 million price for his capture or death. Before the Iraqi invasion by the US, the price on Zarqawi's head was $1 million. In October 2003, the price was raised to $5 million, then in February 2004 was doubled to $10 million and finally in the summer of 2004 it reached the $25 million mark. Who is this Zarqawi and what caused his meteoric rise to fame (infamy) in just a little over a year? News media all over the world have had a feeding frenzy during this period being provided with plenty of tasty morsels from the US administration and its "intelligence" agencies. Zarqawi's picture and description, as the one-legged Jordanian terrorist mastermind, became the typical opening news headline as the following samples that flooded the western media indicate:

"US Intelligence is Tracking New Terror Mastermind and his Network"
"A suspect emerges as key link in terror chain"
"The Zarqawi Node in the Terror Matrix"
"US Forces Facing Al-Qaeda Cell in Iraq?"
"Iraq's Bin Laden? Zarqawi's rise"

One has to wonder, however, whether Zarqawi really deserved all this notoriety, or his legend had been carefully and methodically created by the Bush administration for political reasons. There is plenty to feed this kind of speculation but one plausible hypothesis looms large. It is based on the knowledge that, in the absence of WMD in Iraq, the Bush administration became the subject of severe criticism abroad and in the US, even within his own conservative Republican party, for having invading another sovereign country under highly exaggerated threats. After the invasion and in the absence of any WMD, Bush's strategists replaced this major justification for going to war with Iraq with another one that still connects with the American public—terrorism and threat to homeland security. So, if terrorism was not found in Iraq, it had to be created and at a high enough scale as to justify such a preemptive action, as the invasion of a sovereign country, to the world and especially to the American people. But creating the "terrorism" connection would not be enough. Global terrorism is becoming increasingly an amorphous creature and the US needed to paint the image of someone and create its legend, that the American public and the world can "see" and demonize because of its barbaric behavior. At the same time, the Bush administration would strengthen its case that there was a link between Saddam and Al Qaeda prior to 9/11, and that the same terrorist cell continues to undermine Iraq's efforts for a peaceful and democratic future, by giving terrorism a face and a country. We see once again what it would prove to be Bush's standard practice—use the heavy guns of Machiavellian and Straussian strategies—if an external enemy does not exist, then create one.

One would expect that if Al Qaeda had an operation in Iraq, someone really "important" in the hierarchy of international terrorists would be leading this effort. The problem for the Bush administration, however, was that in the aftermath of the Iraqi invasion there were no well-known terrorists working in Iraq, and there must have been desperate to have a terrorist mastermind equal to Bin Laden and Zawahiri that was involved with the Iraqi terrorist activities. The best choice was Zarqawi, a third rate terrorist who prior to the war had a $1 million price on his head. By the, now well known, standards of western-movies bravado of George W. Bush, the bounty for Zarqawi had to be raised, gradually of course, to much higher levels. Zarqawi, who was competing with Bin Laden for prestige, funding and recruits, was more than happy to provide the reasons for having his bounty increased twenty-five-fold in less than a year—becoming more active and increasing his public profile. Moreover, the odds of catching Zarqawi were much greater than those of Bin Laden—and what gift would it be to the Bush re-election efforts if the US could snatch or kill Zarqawi? Americans like to measure things with $ signs; a high price for Zarqawi's head meant he was a "high value" target whose capture or "elimination" would mean a big political windfall for George W. Bush. So, in a world where deceptions and competition for power and control reign supreme, on both sides of the mirror, Zarqawi and Bush grinned at each other.

It was not till mid October 2004 when Zarqawi's *Tawhid* and *Jihad* group finally joined forces with *Al Qaeda* and Zarqawi pledged his allegiance to Bin Laden. This came as the US and coalition forces intensified their air strikes and ground assaults against Fallujah, believed to be Zarqawi's operational base and the insurgents' stronghold. The Bush administration welcomed the news as proof that their allegations about the collaboration between Bin Laden and Zarqawi had always been accurate. One wonders, however, whether the neo-cons are so much disconnected from reality or they truly believe that the American public, and the rest of the world for that matter, are so gullible to swallow this latest deception. Let's assume that the Bush foreign policy spin doctors are correct and Zarqawi and Bin Laden have been collaborating with each other before the invasion of Iraq. Why then, Zarqawi waited for more than nineteen months after the invasion to publicly pledge his allegiance to Bin Laden? And why was Al Qaeda so pleased with this decision that in a statement that appeared in their website they said: "That the leader of *Tawhid* and *Jihad* announced his allegiance to the sheikh of holy war, Abu Abdullah Osama Bin Laden, and holy warriors in our time is a good omen for victory"? In the same statement, Al Qaeda revealed that Zarqawi's *Tawhid* and *Jihad* group and Al Qaeda had been in communication eight months ago and viewpoints were exchanged till finally they agreed on the terms of the "merger". A statement like this clearly implies that there was no past relationship between the two groups and their agreement was not reached easily—as many people had asserted from the beginning that they were substantial differences between Zarqawi and Bin Laden. Of course, we have to thank George W. Bush that, by invading Iraq and elevating Zarqawi to mythic levels, he has also succeeded to close the deal between two terrorist organizations and strengthen them.

After two years the myth of Abu Musab Al Zarqawi came to a sudden end—almost as abrupt as his rise to power had been. On June 7, 2006 he was killed in a US air strike near Baqubah, north of Baghdad. This, however, did not end the violence in Iraq which not only continued but it intensified in the months ahead until changes in the Iraq strategy and the troop surge were implemented.

If the objective of the surge in Iraq was to reduce the death toll of Iraqis and US troops, then it was successful. If it was to deal a blow at the insurgency and Al Qaeda, then most likely it was a failure. The sectarian violence will escalate as soon as the Americans depart—no matter how long we stay there. And Al Qaeda will go "really" underground in Iraq and transfer most of its operations to Afghanistan, Pakistan, Syria, East Africa, South Africa and in places that the US intelligence hasn't even thought about. They will resurface where and when the conditions are ripe and when no one is looking at that direction. This has been the trademark tactic of the Islamic militants for more than six decades, and one would think that, by now, we should have figured this out.

PART TWO

THE MIRROR IMAGES OF EVIL

The Holy Wars of Christendom

When you live in a glass house, don't throw stones at others.
Popular proverb

In his first address to the nation after 9/11, President George W. Bush stated: "Our responsibility to history is already clear: To answer these attacks and to rid the world of evil …This will be a monumental struggle of good versus evil, but good will prevail." And to ensure that the meaning of his words was not lost, the president referred to America's response to this terrorist act as a crusade. "This crusade", he said, "this war on terrorism." According to Bob Woodward, in his book *Bush at War,* by making such statements "the president was casting his vision and that of the country in the grand vision of God's master plan." And with these statements, the president of the United States announced to the nation and the world, in what would become his coded religious language, that another crusade of

Christendom against the infidels was under way, just as Pope Urban II had done before him a little more than nine centuries ago.

It is safe to assume, however, that with the exception of the crusaders, waiting impatiently in their castles in the red states of the new world, and the evangelical faithful, president Bush's biblical references and his labeling of the war on terrorism as a crusade did not register with the vast majority of Americans. This was partly because the country was still in shock and partly because the words crusade and crusader have a very different meaning in the US than they do elsewhere in the world, especially in the Middle East and Mohammedom. So, it was not surprising that Bush's references to the struggle of the "good" against the "evil" and "crusade" made headlines in Europe and the Arab media and sent chills to the spine of every student of history, who has even a rudimentary knowledge of the crusades and their long lasting scars on the Holy Land and the Eastern Roman Empire (Byzantium).

Americans' knowledge of the crusades is a romanticized and sugar coated version of Hollywood-inspired Camelot and chivalry, with King Richard and his knights in their cross-bearing white robes riding on their white horses, singing hymns and marching to Jerusalem to expel the infidels from the holiest land of Christendom. History books and especially the epic movies of Hollywood have been sanitized from the brutalities and despicable acts of barbarism committed by the "knights of the cross" not only against the Muslim occupiers of the Holy Land, but, worse yet, against other Christians and Jews. Europeans, on the other hand, have a raw and unfiltered understanding of the Crusades and the Religious Wars of Christendom that followed the Crusades and ravaged the continent for almost two centuries. It is undoubtedly this burden of history that has unified the vast majority of Europeans against the latest of the US-led crusades of the West against the infidels of Iraq.

Although the word crusade hasn't been used again by President Bush in his public speeches—his staff and advisers have made sure of that—the fact that was used at all in the first place reveals the true feelings of this president and his faithful. And the issues that it raises go far beyond the obvious concerns that religious faith is hugely involved in both domestic and foreign policies and decision making of this administration, and that the line separating church and state is becoming less visible by the day. It begs all freethinking and responsible citizens of this country, and the world in general, to crack open the gate that leads to Armageddon—the long awaited eternal Kingdom for some and catastrophe of biblical proportions for the rest of us—and peek inside. And what one sees is the Mother of All Wars—a clash of religions—with all the destructive power that the toys of twenty-first century warfare make possible.

One of the most important axioms known to humans is the one that warns us that those who do not learn well the lessons of history, they are destined to repeat them. Unfortunately, almost without exception, it is also the axiom that is never followed. But I am an eternal optimist who believes that sooner or later we will learn to pay more attention to history and avoid making the same mistakes. It is in this spirit of optimism that I will attempt to present in this section of the book a *Readers Digest* condensed version of the death, destruction, suffering, manipulation, deceit, and geopolitical gains that are intricately linked with the Holy Wars of Christendom. And hope that knowledge, reason and the fear of an otherwise very predictable future will guide us in avoiding making the same mistakes once more.

Saintly Decree and Faustian Pact

The sun was setting over Ponte Milvio (Milvian Bridge) on this cold October day of 312 and Flavius Valerius Constantinus, alone and away from his Roman troops and officers, was calling on his father's God in earnest prayer to reveal to him who He was, and stretch forth His right hand to help him in his present difficulties.

> And while he was thus praying with fervent entreaty, a most marvelous sign appeared to him from heaven, the account of which it might have been hard to believe had it been related by any other person. But since the victorious emperor himself long afterwards declared it to the writer of this history... who would hesitate to accredit the relation, especially since the testimony of after-time has estab-

> lished its truth? ...he saw with his own eyes the trophy of a cross of light in the heavens, above the sun, and bearing the inscription "Εν τούτω νίκα", or "In this Conquer". At this sight he himself was struck with amazement, and his whole army also, which followed him on this expedition, and witnessed the miracle.

This was how Bishop Eusebius of Caesarea described the divine revelation to Constantine the Great, not yet sole emperor of the Romans, on the eve of a decisive battle between Constantine and his co-emperor Maxentius. The two men were engaged in a power struggle over the throne of Rome since the death of Constantine's father, emperor Constantius Chlorus, in 306 and finally they had gathered their armies to settle the dispute by force. Constantine's army was outnumbered by at least four to one and his chances of emerging victorious from the impeding battle were slim, short of a miracle. The vision that was revealed to Constantine, who was pagan at the time, was a sign that he would win this and other future battles if he would choose to fight under the banner of the new god of Christians.

> And while he continued to ponder and reason on its meaning, night suddenly came on; then in his sleep the Christ of God appeared to him with the same sign which he had seen in the heavens, and commanded him to make a likeness of that sign which he had seen in the heavens, and to use it as a safeguard in all engagements with his enemies.

Constantine ordered a new standard be made which would be known as a l*avaron* and be carried into this battle and all future battles by all his armies throughout the empire. This is an important benchmark in the history of Christianity and the world as it is the first time, and sadly not the last, that Christ was brought into the battlefield and soldiers fought and killed each other under His banner. Nothing could have been farther from his Word and Deeds. Although it was not identified as such at the time, historically the battle at the Milvian Bridge can be considered the very first Holy War fought more than three hundred years before Islam launched its first Jihad and one century before emperor Heraclius launched his Holy War on the Persian fire-worshipers who had stolen "The True Cross" from the Holy Sepulcher in Jerusalem.

The next day, the two armies clashed and Constantine emerged victorious against overwhelming odds. After winning another battle shortly afterwards by the Tiber River, Constantine entered Rome no longer as the junior emperor but as the undisputed ruler of the western half of the empire. He gradually consolidated his military superiority over his rivals in the crumbling Tetrarchy until 324, when he defeated the eastern ruler, Licinius, and became sole emperor. Constantine credited his victory at the Milvian Bridge to the god of Christians and, thus, decreed the end of any religious persecution within his vast empire. Now the sole ruler of the Romans, in 324 he rebuilt the ancient Greek city of Byzantium, naming it *Nea Roma*, providing it with a Senate and civic offices similar to the old Rome. The city gradually became the new capital of the empire and after his death it was renamed Constantinopolis or Constantinople.

Emperor Constantine I became known as Constantine the Great and he and his mother Helene are worshiped as saints in the Eastern Orthodox Church. Although his "greatness" and "sainthood" are most probably accredited to his military achievements and recognition of Christianity respectively, there are two other, hugely more significant, aspects of Constantine's genius and political astuteness that are undervalued, if not ignored. The first is his choice of the site of ancient Byzantium as the new capital of the empire, and the second his decision to emphasize the religious character of the imperial office above the military one.

Constantine was born in Naissus (today's city of Nis in Serbia and Montenegro) and he grew up away from the corrupting influence of Rome and the Senate. Reared and educated in this environment, he must have sensed that the future prosperity of the empire depended on developing its trade and that the growth potential was much greater in the East than in the West. Byzantium being located at the center of the Christian world, was also a gate to the Mediterranean Sea, and had the vast labor force and fertile lands of Anatolia at its back yard. As such, the new capital's location was ideal culturally, religiously and politically. By strengthening the natural fortification of the city with the longest and virtually impregnable wall of any city in the world, Constantine enhanced its military value and succeeded in keeping the capital of the empire out of the hands of the continually invading armies. In its eleven hundred years of reign, only twice "The City" fell in enemy hands. Without Constantinople, the Eastern Roman Empire would have perished considerably earlier than it did.

But Constantine's geopolitical coup of founding "The City" and making it the capital of his Christian empire, pales in comparison to the religious revolution he brought about in the imperial office. He considered himself an envoy of God, not divine as his predecessor pagan emperors, but sacred, who is anointed by God. He derived his authority as military chief from his status as *isapostolos* (equal to the apostles). Constantine, therefore, laid strong foundations for the merging of Church and State that shaped world history for more than a thousand years and continues to impact religion and politics to this day.

Another future development of the religiosity that Constantine instituted in the imperial office was the ritual of coronation of the emperor by the Patriarch of Constantinople. Emperor Leo I the Great (457-474) was the first one to have the patriarch carry out the ceremony of his coronation at the church of *Aghia Sophia* in the presence of the Senate, the Army, the representatives of the two parties, the Blues and the Greens, and of all the authorities of the empire. Patriarch and Emperor, thus, became the two halves of God: the Patriarch crowned the Emperor, but the former owes his nomination to the latter. The Emperor employed this formula to enthrone the Patriarch: "The Holy Trinity, who has entrusted me this Empire, confers upon you the function of Patriarch of New Rome." The Byzantine world thus had two heads—symbolized by the two-headed crowned eagle that remains till this day the symbol of Eastern Orthodox Church—the emperor and the patriarch. "To one the Creator entrusted the care of the souls, and to the other the governance of bodies and this totality had to be preserved intact and entire", said Emperor John Tzimiskes in the tenth century.

The significance of the coronation of the emperor by the patriarch becomes even clearer when we learn that the anointment of the emperor, and later on of the European Christian kings, was considered a Mystery or Sacrament by the Church. The Byzantine Emperor and later the Russian Tsar underlined this sacrosanct relationship to the Church by taking Holy Communion themselves, touching the Chalice with their own hands, during their coronation. This is why if one intended to assassinate a king or an emperor, one would have to do it prior to the coronation as to do it afterwards would bring the wrath of God down on oneself. One God, one empire and one religion, more specifically the Christian Orthodox faith, was the basic policy of the Byzantine Empire. This unprecedented union of earthly and spiritual authority in the person of a Christian monarch had profound and far-reaching implications. Caesaropapism was born, the Empire and the Holy Church flourished and they both exploded into the world. Christianity and the empire were thus founded and evolved together.

Constantine had many reasons for instituting the sacred image of an anointed representative of God on earth in his person. He had come to power through a bitter and long-fought struggle with his co-emperor. Moreover, not only he was an outsider to Rome's elites, he relocated the empire's capital from the eternal city to the unknown and obscure city of Byzantium. He needed legitimacy and protection for the right to rule the Romans. He found both in Christianity and the Church. By the end of the third century, Christian communities and their bishops had become a force to contend with. Christians were preferred for high government positions and churches like the Church of Nativity in Bethlehem and the Church of the Holy Sepulcher in Jerusalem were built. In the legions of the empire, however, Christianity did not enjoy the support of the soldiers who viewed it as womanish and the majority of them continued their pagan beliefs and rituals. Roman emperors had raised and remained to power through the support of the legions. Although this practice continued during most of the life of Byzantium as well, the emphasis of imperial legitimacy shifted from the Army to the Church, starting with Constantine I who obviously risked his throne on the potential success of the ecumenical power of Christianity.

Constantine and his Roman emperor successors' reaped the rewards of this gamble. The Byzantine Emperors with the blessing of the Patriarch would rule over their Christian subjects for eleven centuries—longer than anyone else before or after them. In reality, this union of church and state did not end with the fall of Constantinople in 1453. The Russian royalty became spiritual heirs of Byzantium and assumed the guardianship of Orthodox Christianity. Russia became the "third Rome" and her monarchs received the anointing of the Holy Spirit to maintain order and peace in the world. The Russian emperor adopted for his symbol the Byzantine two-headed eagle and his title "tsar" that is derived from the Roman "Caesar". The Christian monarchy of the Eastern Roman Empire thus lived for another four hundred and fifty years until the assassination of Tsar Nicolas II and his entire family during the Bolshevik revolution of 1918. In the West, all European monarchies are Christian too—heirs, in some way or another, of the Holy Roman Christian Empire.

The Christian Church benefited immensely from this symbiotic relationship as well. With over two billion believers, Christianity became the world's most populous religion and most importantly the "unofficial" religion of the West. Were it not for this strong union, Christian Europe would have succumbed to the invading armies of Islam on more than one occasion and the Western civilization, as we know it today, would almost certainly not have happened. This relationship (or should we call it a pact?) between Church and State has worked well for their individual survival for the past seventeen hundred years. But when one begins to trace the bloody path that Christianity and the nations of the West have traveled upon to reach the point where they are today, a question begs an answer: At what cost should this relationship continue?

The Religious Wars of Byzantium

Those who can make you believe absurdities, can make you commit atrocities.
Voltaire

It is tragically ironic that although religion was Byzantium's greatest strength, the empire's principal unifying force in defending herself against countless invading armies for eleventh centuries, and a huge source of inspiration to her outstanding art and architecture, it was also what tormented her soul the most, inflicted deep wounds to her once patrician body and eventually bled her to death. And it was her Christian character that led her to unprecedented victories with the expansion of land and Christianity, on one hand, and her ecclesiastical and theological disputes that led her to commit horrific atrocities against her own Christian populace, on the other.

Constantine the Great although was not the first Roman emperor to seek divine intervention in fighting his enemies, he was the first to take his armies into the battlefield under the *lavaron* (standard) of Christianity, a tradition that all future Byzantine emperors would honor till the fall of the empire in 1453. From Constantine on, Christianity and the Christian armies were on the move. But this fervor of Christianity would not be limited in the battlefield. Competing interests of primacy and apostolic succession that existed between the Eastern Roman Empire, centered in Constantinople, and the Western Roman Empire, centered in Rome, resulted into mutual resentment and mistrust that was fueled further by ethnic and political interests, but those would manifest principally in theological differences. Moreover, there were rivalries and animosities among the patriarchates of Constantinople, Alexandria, Jerusalem, and Antioch that frequently surfaced as major religious disputes over the issue of Christology. For centuries, the Orthodox Church and the entire Byzantine Empire, for that matter, were embroiled into several theological hair-splitting and nauseating squabbles over the nature of Christ that divided the Church and, sadly, had nothing to do with the real essence of Christianity. The two key disputes among Byzantine Christians that tore apart both the church and the empire were Monophysitism and Iconoclasm.

Monophysitism

The two chief antagonists of the Monophysitic heresy that still divides Orthodox Christians were Nestorius, Patriarch of Constantinople, and Cyril, Bishop of Alexandria. The dispute was whether Christ had one nature (either human or divine), or two (human and divine). In 428 and shortly after Nestorius became Patriarch of Constantinople he preached a series of sermons in which he challenged the devotionally popular attribution to Mary, Mother of Christ, of the title *Theotokos* (God-bearing). Instead of *Theotokos*, Nestorius offered the term *Christotokos* (Christ-bearing). The attribution of *Theotokos* to Mary implied the two natures of Christ--divine and human—while *Christotokos* implied one nature—divine or divine to human—and , thus, the origin of the term Monophysitism (from the Greek *mono* and *physis*), or belief that Christ had one nature. Cyril of Alexandria, a shrewd politician, vehemently opposed the Nestorian heresy and convinced Emperor Theodosius II, who had appointed Nestorius Patriarch of Constantinople, to convene a Council of Bishops in Ephesus in 431, which condemned Monophysitism as heretical, the title of *Theotoko*s was officially affirmed and orthodox doctrine on the nature of Christ clarified. Christ was pronounced true God and true man, as having two distinct natures in one person. This position was reaffirmed in 451 by the Council of Chalcedon. Cyril had won and Nestorius was deposed as bishop and sent to the monastery of Antioch and later on he was banished to Upper Egypt where he died around 451.

The Councils of Ephesus and Chalcedon, however, although they settled the official position of the imperial Orthodox Church, they neither settled nor ended the theological and political disputes that they ensued. In the west, the Popes accepted the Chalcedonian doctrine perhaps for being unable to fully understand the linguistic arguments expressed in the Greek documents. In the east, however, there was another story. For decades, both sides—the Orthodox and Monophysitic—continued their attacks against each other while trying, in vain, to explain and strengthen their position. It appears that Nestorius must have had strong support in Syria and Egypt where the decision of the Council of Chalcedon was largely rejected and Monophysitism grew rapidly, and with it a growing dislike and hostility towards the Empire. In his efforts to ease the tensions between the two sides, Emperor Zeno who came to power in 474 issued the *Enotikon* (union) law which was aimed, through skillful diplomacy, at bringing some type of reconciliation to the theologically-torn Empire. While Zeno's *Enotikon* brought temporarily relief to the dispute, various heretical views had become entrenched throughout the Eastern Empire by the time of his death in 491, and doctrinal infighting had become commonplace.

Emperor Justinian, who reigned from 527-565, is considered by many as one of the most important Roman emperors, if not the most important of them. But according to historian Procopius, perhaps the most important historian of the early Byzantine era, Justinian had also a dark side. While he is rightfully credited with many achievements—the issuance of the monumental new code of Roman law, the construction of many magnificent public buildings, fortifications, and churches in a style that came to represent Byzantine architecture (the great cathedral of *Aghia Sophia* in Constantinople was re-built by Justinian), and his efforts to regain territory in the western empire, contain the Slavs and Bulgarians and battle the Persians—he is also responsible for exhausting the imperial army and draining the treasury with his continuous campaigns east and west, and, worse of all, for his severe persecution of Monophysites and other heretics, and Jews.

Justinian decreed that heretics, including Monophysites, could not participate in political and administrative government service and they could no longer own property. He also intruded into the authority of the family, removing the father's authority over a son, should the son convert to Christianity and beheading the son who did not convert when the father did. He burned or demolished countless Greek, Roman and Egyptian temples and Jewish synagogues and built in their place churches. Even dissenting churches' properties were seized and turned into "Orthodox" churches. He even closed Plato's Academy in Athens, confiscated its land and converted it to church property.

Pagans were executed; heretics were persecuted and anathematized; Christians who returned to paganism faced death, exile and the loss of testamentary rights. Jews were systematically and progressively persecuted. A Jew could not testify against a Christian; could not own a Christian slave or convert any slave to Judaism; and could not will property and gifts to anyone, except a Christian, and an Orthodox one, for that matter. Jews were forbidden to celebrate Passover before Easter, or on Easter. Their scriptures were scrutinized and censored before they could be used in a Synagogue. His harsh religious persecutions brought considerable dissent and disorder. The greatest rebellion came to be known as the *Nika* Revolt during which the two factions of "blues" and "greens" and soldiers threatened his government in 532. The imperial army at Justinian's orders ended the rebellion by brutally slaughtering, some say, as many as more than 30,000 in the Hippodrome, which ironically was one of his grandest public works projects.

After the *Nika* Revolt, Justinian became less strict in dealing with the Monophysites and sought to reach a common ground between them and the Orthodox Christians. The Monophysite Church although greatly diminished during Justinian's rule, did not end. It has prevailed as the primary form of Christianity in Egypt and Syria and survives today in Iraq, Iran and other "oriental orthodox" Churches. Moreover, in the seventh century the continued Christological dispute between Monophysites and orthodox Christians gave birth to another heretical opinion, Monothelitism (one will). Emperor Heraclius seeking a compromise between Monophysitism and orthodoxy adopted Monothelitism in 622. This time, the latest Christian heresy drew fire from the pope in addition to the die-hard orthodox Christians, and although it had the support of three emperors, it died out in 680.

Iconoclasm

The Eastern Church underwent a period of relative theological calm for four decades—a welcomed reprieve for the exhausted empire as many dark clouds were gathering in the east and over Constantinople. Emperor Leo III was about to embark in another disastrous imperial campaign that would entangle church and crown for 125 years during the reign of twelve emperors. Leo began his crusade by first campaigning to baptize all the Jews and emboldened by the success of this endeavor, he proceeded to ban the use of all icons and in 830 ordered their destruction. This initiation of state sponsored *Iconoclasm* (icon-breaking) changed Byzantine culture forever. The pagan world had been full of images of all kinds of deities since the beginning of time. Christianity had done its utmost to wean it from these idolatrous practices but images proved to be deeply rooted in the human psyche, especially that of the Eastern Roman Empire. The early church recognized the need to replace the images with something "Christian" and religious artworks or icons of

Jesus, Mary, and saints started being used at Christian homes and churches.

Concerns, however, about the use of icons began to surface soon after as this practice, according to few bishops, bordered on idolatry, which was forbidden. In the eastern empire this concern grew more primarily for two reasons. The making of icons became an industry, with monasteries being the main producers, and this practice of *iconolatry* (icon-worshiping) brought a state of commercialism and profitability to the church that was uncharacteristic, at least at that stage of Christianity, of the teachings of Christ. The increasing wealth and influence of the church were becoming worrisome and potentially a threat to a strong and centralized Byzantine State. Moreover, Islam, which strictly prohibits the making, use, and worshiping of any images of Mohammed, was spreading in former lands of the Eastern Empire and had an influence on how her citizens, who tended to be more spiritualistic, saw icons as religious symbols. The issue of iconolatry was about to explode outside the walls of the church and throughout the empire.

During the third Council of Constantinople in 680 which convened mainly to deal with abolishing Monothelitism, the legitimacy of icons was affirmed by the church. This decision outraged many in Anatolia, an anti-icon sentiment began to grow and when Leo III came to power he saw this as an opportunity to increase his popular support and banned the use of icons. Germanus, the patriarch, strongly protested this imperial edict and appealed to the pope but accomplished nothing more than his removal, as a traitor, and replacement by another cleric, Anastasius. As mentioned previously, the relations between the eastern and western churches and between the pope and the emperor had never been good. The papacy used every opportunity to oppose the Constantinople-based rulers, and the controversy of iconoclasm was no exception, especially when there was genuine resentment to the destruction of images among the descendants of Romans, who had transferred their worshiping of Roman gods to the Christian icons. The pope, Gregory II, defended the use of icons and accused Leo for interference in ecclesiastical matters and persecution of image worshippers. The emperor replied that he, as a *basileus* and *iereu*s (emperor and priest) had every right to make decrees about such matters. The title of Emperor and Priest that the Church had conceded to the imperial rulers as a compliment for their zeal to protect the very faith that Leo was now attacking, had come to haunt her now. The Faustian pact between church and state that Constantine the Great had signed five centuries earlier was undergoing its first, and certainly not the last, major challenge.

In the East, most of the theologians and almost all the monks refused to accept the imperial edict. The fiercest resistance to iconoclasm broke out on the Greek mainland where a rebel leader, Cosmas, was named emperor. Leo crushed the revolt and Cosmas was beheaded. Angered from these events, he enforced iconoclasm with more fervor. Monasteries were destroyed, monks put to death, tortured, or banished. Iconoclasts were getting out of control, as shrines were broken open and bodies of saints buried in churches were burned. In the West, at Rome, Ravenna, and Naples, the people rose against the emperor's law. This anti-imperial movement marks the start of the schism between Italy and the old empire, the independence of the papacy, and the beginning of the Papal States.

The persecution of *Iconodules*—icon worshipers—continued with increasing intensity and zealotry for another fifty five years and through the reign of two more emperors. During this period, the emperors tried to abolish monasticism all together: monasteries were turned into barracks; the monastic habit was forbidden; and patriarchs supportive of the use of icons were deposed, tortured, and beheaded. They had to either support the imperial position or face severe consequences. Then in 780, Leo IV became ill and died leaving his wife Irene in charge of the empire, as she became Regent of her nine-year old son Constantine VI. Irene, who must have been a secret supporter of icons, took immediate steps to ease the oppression of the church and iconolatry. In 787, the second Council of Nicaea was convened, the icons were restored and Iconoclasm was repealed.

Twenty seven years after the Second Council of Nicaea and three emperors later, Iconoclasm surfaced again and the previous iconoclastic period was repeated with almost mathematical exactness. Again the icons were banned and destroyed, and their defenders fiercely persecuted. During the reign of three iconoclast emperors, the patriarchs played macabre musical chairs at the pleasure of the imperial whim; the papacy behaved exactly the same way; and one council rejected the icons, while another defended them. Finally, another empress, Theodora, Regent of her young son, Michael III, put an end to one of the stormiest and bloodiest periods of Christendom by restoring the icons in 843—this time permanently.

The Political Aspects of Religious Wars

The frequent conflicts, that existed within the church and between the church and the crown in Byzantium, are often perceived to be solely theological disputes, which without a doubt were, but many ignore the political conditions that existed and deal only with the theological aspects. Byzantine politics and religion were always closely linked since the emperor was the head of State as well as of the Church. Some emperors were not interested in religious matters and, wisely, left the clergy to deal with them. Others, as Justinian, although they did not initiate religious disputes—the Church was very eager and capable doing that on her own—chose to become the protectors and defenders of the imperial orthodox-version of Christianity and severely persecute any heretical—different—beliefs. Religious intolerance had become state policy in large scale for the first time. While Constantine the Great had decreed religious tolerance, by not making Christianity the official religion of the empire but by allowing Christians to worship their god without the fear of persecution, the pendulum had swung 180 degrees by Justinian's reign. Yet others, as Leo III and Leo V, chose to use their own beliefs in making Church policy, and their authority over the Church in enforcing it.

We have, thus, in Byzantium two major examples of conflict between Church and State resulting from their incestuous relationship. The first was Monophysitism where the State sided with the state-sanctioned "orthodox" religion and persecuted all other "heretical" religious institutions and faithful. The second was Iconoclasm which was used by the State to impose on the Church the imperial choice of icon ban, against the traditions of the "orthodox" clergy and majority of Christians. In examining these two events with the distinct advantage of hind sight, it is relatively safe to presume that Church interests were the major cause of the former conflict and political motives were involved in the latter one. The picture becomes, however, a great deal more fuzzy when one searches for political gains that might have materialized for either the Church or the Imperial Office. The expense to the imperial treasury in enforcing these edicts throughout the empire for centuries, the bloodshed and the political unrest that resulted against the Church and the Crown were much greater than any political or economic benefits that might have been gained in the short term.

So, what lessons can we learn from these two events of very long ago? The first one is that any union between church and state is bound to lead, sooner or later, to major conflicts among the people as any religion is not monolithic and matters of faith cannot be imposed upon the entire population of a state. Let the clergy debate the theological issues and allow the people to choose what satisfies their spiritual needs best. We cannot have freedom of religion and enforcement of laws and regulations, that stem from either theological doctrines, or their interpretation, at the same time. The second lesson is that there cannot be a true union—equal partnership—between church and state. Always one of the partners will be dominant of the other—usually the one who has the guns and the gold. This lesson in particular is the one that the clergy and the religious leaders are advised to heed. These unions are Faustian pacts that serve their institutional masters and are not in the best interest of the common people who become the helpless victims. And the third and final lesson is that religious intolerance leads to religious persecution, and religious persecution ultimately leads to disobedience, anarchy and rebellion.

The European Crusades and the Inquisition

We humbly ask forgiveness for the part which each of us has had in these evils by our own actions, thus helping to disfigure the face of the Church.
Pope John Pope II, 12 March 2000

Unlike the religious wars of Byzantium that are virtually unknown to western readers, the European Crusades, while they are a widely known and, to a great extent, revered, they are also hugely misrepresented and fictionalized in the west. It is the principal aim of this section, therefore, to present another side of this story that focuses on the potential motives of the crusades that are important in the context of current events, the geopolitical forces that contributed to their launching and those that emerged after the first crusades, and finally, and most tragically, on the mass slaughtering of not only Muslim soldiers, but also of innocent men, women, and children of Muslim, Jewish and, yes, Christian faith. And all this was done in the name of Jesus under the widely promoted and perpetuated, by the Church and western historians, guise of Holy wars that "God willed them" to expel the infidel from the Holy Land and return it to Christendom.

Although there were several crusades that originated in Europe against the Muslims in Palestine, we will examine the First and Fourth, as they are of particular importance to us. The broad historical outlines of the crusades are presented well in most history books and, thus, will not be addressed here. Moreover, much scholarship has been devoted to ascertain whether the true motives behind the crusading movement were spiritual or earthly and we will not be tempted to enter that debate either. We will offer an opinion on this subject, however, that is based on the actions of the principal knights during and after the First Crusade, rather than their presumed motives.

The First Crusade

At the onset of this virtual journey to 1095, it is important to state that there should be little doubt, if any, that the main goal of the papacy and of the majority of nobles and foot soldiers that participated in the First Crusade was to liberate the Holy Land from Muslim occupation. Because the Crusade, however, was not a monolithic movement and totally lacked cohesion of purpose and organization, it cannot be judged only on the merits of its intended goal and, moreover, cannot be viewed as a single occurrence. Quite often the behavior and actions of the multiple participants in its sub-crusades clashed, as what many sought was inconsistent with the stated papal objectives. Our focus, thus, will be to shed light on three key inconsistencies that cast a long and dark shadow on the proclaimed success of the First Crusade.

The first wave of the First Crusade, known as the People's Crusade, consisted mostly of peasants and lowly knights who gathered in huge and unexpected numbers and headed towards Jerusalem on their own and much earlier than it was planned. Their numbers swell close to 100,000 mostly unskilled fighters and included women and children against Pope Urban's instructions. About a quarter of them never made it to Constantinople—the crossing point to Asia Minor—and most of them were massacred by the experienced and superior fighting armies of Seljuks as soon as they entered their territories. The remaining few joined other waves of the First Crusade that followed later.

A closer examination of the People's Crusade strongly suggests that it was more than a mass migration of people seeking freedom from the daily oppression of their lives and a better future. While Pope Urban promised remission of sins to those who might die in this expedition, the earthly rewards that he mentioned might have been the strongest motivation for this first wave of "crusaders". France, Pope Urban said, was overcrowded and the land of Canaan was overflowing with milk and honey. The fact that many women and children participated in this crusade, facing, at best, an extremely long and difficult journey, and, at worst, death, supports the migration theory rather than a military undertaking. Moreover, the lack of central leadership and organization are typical of mass migrations.

The First Crusade did not end with the disaster of the People's Crusade. The Princes' Crusade followed in 1096 in a more organized manner and was led by nobles and knights from various regions of Europe. What was particular at the time of the Crusades was the Church's concern with the perpetual civil wars in Christian Europe. In particular, the entrenchment of the principal of primogeniture left large numbers of landless knights, younger sons who would not inherit, with nothing to do but wage war in hope of securing lands of their own. The Church may therefore have sought to divert the restless energies of these younger sons away from Christendom; if perpetual warfare was inevitable, better it should take place among the Mohammedans than in the heart of Christendom. Moreover, it is a common historiographical assumption that the Franks of northern France, the Provençals of southern France, and the Normans of Italy considered themselves separate "nations" and each wanted to increase its status.

We will follow the actions of the most significant of these movements, as they illustrate another element of the First Crusade—Expansionism. Alexius I, Byzantine emperor, who had sought the aid of European Christians through Pope Urban after the defeat of Byzantine armies by the Seljuk Turks in the disastrous battle of Manzikert in 1071, was so distrustful of the crusaders that he requested the leaders swear allegiance to him and promise to return to the Byzantine Empire any land recovered from the Turks. In return he would provide them with badly needed food as the princes had arrived with little provisions. Alexius was particular suspicious of Bohemund of Taranto, a Norman whose father—Robert Guiscard—was an old enemy of the Empire. The emperor's fears about Bohemund proved accurate. As the crusaders marched towards Jerusalem, they laid siege to the city of Antioch, which was the mid-point from Constantinople to the Holy Land, that lasted for eight months. As the city fell eventually to the crusaders, the princes began to argue about who would claim the city as his own principality. The squabbling over Antioch continued for months until the minor knights and soldiers, restless and tired, threatened to continue to Jerusalem without their leaders. Finally, at the beginning of 1099 the march was renewed, leaving Bohemund behind as the Prince of Antioch. This decision by Bohemund who never fulfilled his "crusade" to the Holy Land made clear his true intentions. He also proved that he was anything but an honorable knight as he broke his oath of allegiance to Alexius by usurping land that was Byzantine dominion prior to falling into Muslim hands.

Bohemund was not the first noble, however, to abandon the spiritual goals of the crusade for territorial gains. Before him, Baldwin of Boulogne, another important noble, abandoned the main body of the crusade in 1098 and set off on his own towards the Armenian lands around Euphrates. In Edessa he was adopted as heir by King Thoros, a Greek Orthodox ruler, who was disliked by his Armenian subjects. A short time after Baldwin's arrival, Thoros was assassinated and Baldwin became the new ruler, thus creating the County of Edessa, the first of the crusader states.

On July 15 1099 and three years after the first wave of the crusaders left Europe, Jerusalem changed masters once again as the remnants of the Princes' Crusaders entered the city. Over the course of that afternoon, evening and next morning, almost every inhabitant of Jerusalem—Muslims, Jews, and even eastern Christians, including women and children—was massacred. There were claims by anonymous writings that the slaughter was so great that the men waded in blood up to their ankles. Even if these claims aren't partially true, the massacre of Jerusalem's residents is one of the most abhorred events in Church history carried out by the "Knights of the Cross". In the days followed the massacre, Godfrey of Bouillon, another of the nobles of the Princes' Crusade, was made Protector of the Holy Sepulcher, refusing to be named king of the city where Christ had died. When Godfrey died in 1100, he was succeeded by his brother, Baldwin of Edessa, who took the title of "King of Jerusalem" and thus founded the third crusader state.

The Fourth Crusade

Although the motives of the nobles participating in the First Crusade are at least suspicious and the atrocities committed against Muslims, Jews and Christians shocking, the crusade was an unmitigated religious and military success as it expelled the Muslims from Jerusalem, established several crusader states in lands formerly occupied by Turks, and eased the pressure on the Byzantium by the Ottomans. The Fourth Crusade, however, not only it did not achieve its goal—recapturing Jerusalem from the Muslims—it wreaked violence on other Christians and caused geopolitical consequences of great importance, since the political space of the Byzantine Empire was fragmented into small states, Greek or Western, and was never again fully reunited.

The Forth Crusade, proclaimed by Pope Innocent III, was initially to be directed to Egypt first, because regaining Jerusalem would be easier once the crusaders had established a stronghold in Egypt. As the armies gathered in Venice, it became clear that there were not sufficient monies to pay the Venetians for the ships they had built for the European nobles. Enrico Dandolo, the Venetian Doge, offered that the crusaders could have their ships for assisting the Venetians to recapture the Venetian city of Zara that had recently fallen into the hands of the King of Hungary. The crusaders reluctantly agreed to Dandolo's proposal and in a few weeks the city of Zara was captured and sacked. But the Doge and the crusaders were not done. After conquering Zara, the crusaders diverted to Constantinople accompanied by the Venetian fleet led by Dandolo himself. A few of the knights disgusted with this decision sailed to Palestine alone, but the majority of the crusaders headed to the Byzantine capital intoxicated by the prospect of plundering the wealthiest and most famous city in the world.

In 1204 the joint Venetian and crusader armies sacked the weakened and unprepared city of Constantinople in what became one of the darkest periods of Christendom. The city was plundered of its wealth including the precious treasures of the Great Church (*Aghia Sophia*). Christian men were massacred and Christian women were raped. The conquering of the great Christian city ended the Fourth Crusade. The Empire was fragmented into four Latin states and the Byzantine imperial office and most of the Orthodox clergy moved to Nicaea where they remained for fifty years until the return of Constantinople into Byzantine control.

Although the fall of the Byzantine capital may be seen by many as another episode in nation warfare, "never, since the barbarian invasions some centuries before, had Europe witnessed such an orgy of brutality and vandalism," writes John Norwich in his book *Byzantium: The Decline and Fall.* "Never in history had so much beauty, so much superb craftsmanship, been wantonly destroyed in so short a space of time."

The Byzantine Empire never recovered its strength, or any considerable part of its lost dominion. Under firm and forceful leadership--which would not be lacking in the century to come--a strong and prosperous Byzantium, might have halted the Turkish advance while there was still time. Instead, the Empire was economically crippled, territorially truncated, powerless to defend itself against the Ottoman tide. There are a few greater ironies in history than the fact that the fate of Eastern Christendom should have been sealed—and half of Europe condemned to some five hundred years of Muslim rule—by men who fought under the banner of the Cross.‡

This brief examination of the Crusades and, especially of the reasons for undertaking them, provides sufficient support to the notion that migration, expansionism, and personal and state gains in wealth and power were among the main driving forces behind this extraordinary phenomenon that greatly impacted Christendom and the geopolitical balance of Europe and Middle East. Finally, if in an act of "catharsis" we were to seek indictments against the principal villains responsible for the "War Crimes" of the Crusades, the European princes and nobles, and especially the Venetians, should have been brought before a war crimes tribunal. The papacy, although it acted as the initial catalyst for the chain reaction of the Crusades, should be considered no more than an accomplice, and often it acted to prevent certain events, as was the case with Pope Innocent III and the Fourth Crusade.

The Albigensian Crusade

In Europe, the First Crusade ignited a long tradition of organized violence against non-Christians, especially Jews, which became a long tradition in European culture after the crusades. Although non-Christians suffered in the hands of "good Christians" throughout the Middle Ages, it should not be forgotten that "bad Christians" suffered just as much. One of the worst displays of organized atrocities committed by Christians against Christians in Europe is the genocide of Cathars in southern France during the twenty-year military campaign against them, known as the Albigensian Crusade. The Cathars, also known as Albigensians because of the presence in and around the city of Albi, were a Christian sect who doubted the biblical story of Creation, thought that Jesus was a Prophet instead of God, challenged the authority of Catholic Church and were outspoken critics of the corruption of the clergy. Of course, such free-thinking brand of Christianity could not be tolerated by the Church, especially the Medieval Catholic Church.

‡ John Julius Norwich, *Byzantium: The Decline and Fall*, p 182

The Catholic Church had always dealt swiftly with heresy, but till now heretics had not been seen as a major threat to the Church's dominance in Western Europe. The Cathars, however, were a mass movement that was spreading in Southern France. Most significantly, Cathars encouraged their converts to "think" and "question" already established Church doctrine and rejected the authority of the Catholic Church. Pope Innocent III emboldened by the perceived successes of the Crusades and the newly-founded influence that the Church could exert on the European nobility, was determined to suppress the Cathars. First he tried to convert them, and when this failed he declared a crusade against the nobles of Southern France—offering the lands of the heretics to any who would fight them and defeat them. This offer proved very effective, as it drew much of the nobility of the north of France against the nobles of the south, and thus revealed once more the true motives of those who eagerly participated in the Crusades.

The Albigensian Crusade lasted twenty years, 1209-1229, during which time thousands of Christians were either slaughtered or burned. The worst display of brutality was in the town of Beziers where its entire population—over 10,000 citizens—was massacred when the town was sacked by the crusaders. When Beziers fell, soldiers asked the papal legate Abbot Arnaus Amaury how to tell the faithful apart from the heretics and infidels. He uttered his infamous words: "Slay them all! God will know His own". It is believed that no more than 500 Cathars were in Beziers. The extermination of populations, cities and crops that ensued as a result of the Albigensian Crusade was so extensive as to constitute what might be called the first "genocide" in modern European history. The slaughter continued until 1229 when the Treaty of Paris ended, politically, the Albigensian Crusade. The independence of the princes in Southern France was squelched, but the Cathars were not extinguished. So, the Church invented another more effective and brutal tool to deal with religious dissent that was institutionalized in Christian Europe and used for almost six hundred years. It was The Inquisition.

Before we draw the curtain on the European Crusades, it is worth noting, though, that there is no other phenomenon in the history of Christianity and Western Civilization, than the Crusades, that has created such a historical memory of ill will—the memory of long onslaught of Muslims, Jews and Christians by Catholic Christians—in Jews, Muslims, and other Christians. And what is more tragic than the atrocities committed by the crusades is the almost total absence of their consequences in the historiography of the "Western Civilization".

The Inquisition

The Inquisition was a permanent institution of the Catholic Church responsible with the eradication of heresies that existed from the 12th century to the beginning of the 20th century. The hierarchical structure of the Catholic Church was ideal for directing and overseeing such an institution. It is ironic that while Emperor Constantine freed the Church from persecution, it was the Church that immediately launched its own persecution against anyone that was deemed to deviate from the "Orthodox" doctrine of the Church. Initially, these persecutions were not institutionalized by either the Church or the State and faded with each passing emperor or cleric. In the Middle Ages a permanent structure came into being to combat heresies. Beginning in the 12th century, Church Councils required secular rulers to prosecute heretics. There were more than religious interests, though, involved in the Inquisitions, especially the Spanish Inquisition, where the crown used religion to control the people, weaken political opposition and strengthen its own authority.

As in the case of the Crusades, there is a huge historiography devoted to the Inquisition and therefore we will not dwell in its gruesome details. It will suffice to note that the Inquisition, as the Crusades, is another prime example of where an incestuous relationship between Church and State can lead. Often, events unleashed for various reasons can take a life of their own and get completely out of control with disastrous consequences, i.e. Jewish Holocaust during World War II. Pope John Paul's II apology on 12 March 2000 for sins committed by the Catholic Church is an historic event of huge significance as it not only expressed regret and asked for forgiveness for past acts of the Church, but it also acknowledged that the Church has often made grave mistakes.

> We cannot fail to recognize the infidelities to the Gospel committed by some of our brethren, especially during the second millennium. Let us ask pardon for the divisions which occurred among Christians, for the violence some have used in the service of the truth and for the distrustful and hostile attitudes sometimes taken towards the followers of other religions...We humbly ask forgiveness for the part which each of us had in these evils by our own actions, thus helping to disfigure the face of the Church.

Although the sins were not specifically enumerated, by referring to the "violence some have used in the service of truth", the pope most certainly has subtly made reference to the atrocities committed during the Crusades and Inquisition. They were political acts by an institution of faith: the Crusades, The Inquisition, persecution of Jews, the forced conversion of Native Americans and Africans, acts to preserve the power and enrich the Church, acts committed in concert with secular rulers bound to the church by oath. More than a year later, on May 2001, and during a visit to Greece, Pope John Paul II made another dramatic apology to the Greek Orthodox Church by expressing regret for the "disastrous sack of the imperial city of Constantinople" by the Fourth Crusade. "For the occasions past and present when sons and daughters of the Catholic Church have sinned by action or omission against their Orthodox brothers and sisters, may the Lord grant us the forgiveness we beg of Him."

The historic apology issued by Pope John Paul II at the dawn of the new millennium was welcomed by Jews, and Orthodox and other Christians, although many felt it was too little and too late. While critics outside the Catholic Church did not think the pope's apology was specific enough or went as far as it should have, critics within the Church were not in agreement over the "appropriateness" of pope's apology for the crimes committed by the Church. The core arguments against the papal apology were based on the presumed infallibility of the Church, being a divine institution. This latter attitude illustrates that the roots of the causes for the Crusades and The Inquisition are indeed very deep in Christendom, and the danger of history repeating itself very real, although perhaps in different type of crusades.

The Crusades through a joint venture between the crown and the cross started a movement of expansionism for church and state that manifested in the Christianization and colonization of the Americas, Africa and Asia that lasted almost five hundred years, and became the defining event in the shaping of what we call Western Civilization. As a result of this movement, a set of religious, political, economic and social traditions grew out of the transformations created by the Crusades. While in Europe and the Americas the vast majority of colonized populations were converted to Christianity and assimilated in the Western culture, North Africa, the Middle East and Arabia remained Muslim and retained their ethnic identities. So, the impact of the Crusades on the colonized territories is measured by diametrically opposite standards—the Christian West has glorified them, while Mohammedom has vilified them.

The Religious Wars of Europe

There are a few regions, if any, on this planet which for so long have experienced the destructive forces of warfare as Europe. By the time the New World was discovered, Europe was still covered in the bloody cloak of the Inquisition that had torn apart the western regions of the continent for almost three centuries. But the worst was yet to come as the mid-sixteenth century brought about the most passionate and bloody chain of wars that Europe had ever experienced. The causes of wars are never simple or direct, but these military conflicts are a few examples of human warfare that largely can be linked to a religious struggle between Catholics and Protestants. Although the Peace of Westphalia in 1648 officially ended the armed conflict between Catholics and Protestants and the secular dominion of the Holy Roman Empire over the entire Christian world, it did not end religiously motivated wars. Since the end of the seventeenth century, most wars in Europe and elsewhere have been greatly influenced by religious differences, and it is particularly alarming to note that the twenty first century began with religiously-inspired conflicts.

We shall begin our unpleasant journey through the ravished landscape of the aging continent, by examining the geopolitical conditions that were prevalent in Western Europe in the mid-sixteenth century, in addition to the better known religious historiography of the Reformation. Politically, the House of Habsburg was the most prominent princely family in Europe in the 1550s. Philip II of the Spanish Habsburgs was the ruler of twelve separate European territories, a vast New World empire, and several North African outposts. His uncle, Ferdinand I of the Austrian Habsburgs, was the hereditary ruler of thirteen European territories, in addition to being the elected emperor of the Holy Roman Empire. The trade mark of the Habsburgs was that aimed more at family power and wealth than state power and national development. This pursuit of dynastic ambition resulted often to dynastic wars with no benefits to their subjects. These political problems were about to explode with the emergence of religious problems that were new and powerful. The early reformation launched by Martin Luther some forty years ago had been thus far remarkably free of bloodshed. Protestants were eventually split into further groups with Calvinists and Lutherans being the most powerful of them. The Catholics and Protestants each had firm control of certain territories, while many other principalities featured one powerful ruling majority and several rival minorities.

Religious differences eventually led to religious intolerance as each side proved unwilling to compromise and coexist with the other. The Catholic Church controlled vast political and economic resources and the rejection of her basic religious doctrines by the Protestants threatened not only its institutional fabric, but its power and wealth as well. Both Catholics and Protestants sought the aid of secular rulers to impose their particular interpretation of Christian faith on the other. And the secular authorities were more than happy to respond, as they realized that there were political and economic benefits to be gained from participating in this religious conflict. It was inevitable, therefore, that this growing division between the Christian princes would lead to a series of state and civil wars that would last for more than a century. Moreover, the vast majority of the population was exposed to famine and plague in addition to the endemic crime, disease, and wartime massacres. These social disasters contributed to the witchcraft hysteria that became the trade mark of the religious wars, as the rulers unable to find solutions to these problems had to invent scapegoats to divert the attention of the masses from the real problems. As we shall see in following sections, this technique has been used often in the past and has reared its ugly head again at the beginning of the twenty first century with the war against terrorism and Iraq.

After 1560, the rulers of Western Europe were no longer able to contain the revolutionary waves of this religious crisis. "Both Calvinists and militant Catholics began to rebel against the political status quo", writes Richard Dunn in *The Age of Religious Wars*. "They organized effective opposition against rulers who did not share their religious convictions. In the name of God they launched a wave of civil wars and rebellions against constituted authority." Two potent forces in this conflict, one on each side, were the Calvinists of John Calvin and, on the Catholic side, the Jesuits of St. Ignatius of Loyola. Although both were small in numbers, "working from diametrically opposite religious principles, Loyola and Calvin each built a select, cohesive, extroverted band of zealots."

The first set of these religious wars were the French civil wars that started in 1562, lasted for almost forty years and destroyed tens of thousands of innocent lives. The bloodiest incident in this immoral war was the slaughter of over 23,000 Huguenots (French Protestants) by Catholics on St. Bartholomew's Day in 1572 making it the worst systematic mass extermination of non-combatants in European history until World War II. The St. Bartholomew massacre was a turning point in both French history and European Christian history in general. Protestants would no longer view the Catholic Church as a misguided church, but as an evil one and Protestant movements would transform into militant movements fighting not for the reformation of the church, but for her survival.

The Thirty Years War

The French wars were followed by rebellions in Protestant Netherlands against the Spanish-Catholic-domination, and the war between Spain and England. The last and most destructive religious war was the Thirty Year War that started in 1618 and ended in 1648, and it was as much about politics as it was about religion, the self-preservation of the Habsburg dynasty being the central motive. This war, in addition to settling very little, had a peculiar feature. While it was fought on German soil, the central European territory of the Holy Roman Empire, it involved most of the major continental powers, as the chief warring factions were non-German. The religious nature of the Thirty Years War should not be under-emphasized, however. Since the Peace of Augsburg recognized Lutheranism but did not recognize Calvinism, a number of rulers and their subjects, who had become Calvinists, found themselves outside the religious protection of the treaty. This discontent fueled by the fanaticism of Calvinists and Jesuits finally broke into violence.

The opponents in the Thirty Years War were on one hand, the Austrian and Spanish Habsburgs and, on the other, France, Sweden, Denmark and the Netherlands. Spain was interested in the German states, because Philip II of Spain was a Habsburg and controlled the territories surrounding their western border; France was interested in the German states, because it wanted to suppress the growing power of the Habsburgs since they surrounded France's eastern border; Sweden and Denmark were interested in the northern German states bordering the Baltic Sea for economic reasons; and the Dutch had been battling the Spanish Habsburgs for independence since 1568. The inevitable war that ensued among them would surpass all other previous European wars in terms of extent and destructiveness. It was perhaps the first World War fought in Europe since nearly every major state in Europe became involved in the war in some way or another. The amount of human destruction alone made this war the bloodiest and most destructive war of European history before the nineteenth century.

The Peace of Westphalia

After thirty years of bloodshed, the war came to an end with the Peace of Westphalia in 1648. The treaty which simply reaffirmed the Treaty of Augsburg largely settled German affairs for the next century and a half. While the only important innovation of the treaty, in the context of the religious conflict, was the recognition of Calvinism, in geopolitical terms, with this treaty the balance of power in Europe had been radically changed. France was the big winner emerging as the major Western power, and states of the Holy Roman Empire, as Switzerland and the Netherlands, became sovereign states outside the empire, thus establishing a framework for a modern Europe. But more important than establishing fixed territorial boundaries for the newly created sovereign states, the treaty laid the foundations for what we consider today as the basic tenets of international law for the sovereign nation-states. It was agreed that the citizens of a respective nation were subject first and foremost to the laws of their own respective government rather than those of neighboring powers, be they religious or secular.

While France was the big winner of the religious wars, Germany and Spain were the big losers. While Spain was preoccupied with France during the French phase of the war, Portugal declared its independence from Spanish control. The war, however, had a devastating effect on the German people—more so than on any other warring state. Although the estimates of mass civilian casualties of up to thirty percent of the German population are treated now with caution, they had to be catastrophic by any measurement. The German economy did not fare any better. The European economy shifted westwards to the Atlantic states—Spain, France, England, and the Low Countries. Germany entered a period of economic stagnation that ended in the second half of the nineteenth century. This economic and political weakness is speculated to have been the long-term underlying cause of later German militarism that led to two World Wars.

There seems to be broad agreement among historians that the Peace of Westphalia is a major watershed of contact for the nation-states of Europe and the world, for that matter. There are those who consider it as the cornerstone of the League of Nations and UN. During the European religious wars anyone with an army felt empowered to invade some territory and force upon its people their brand of Christianity. The treaty, in its most simplified version, sought to end this practice, establish the sovereignty of nations—modern system of nation-states—and remove religion from the external affairs and disputes, including wars, of nation-states. Diplomacy was to replace faith.

We shall conclude the section on the religious wars of Europe with an excerpt from Richard Dunn's *The Age of Religious Wars:*

> In the years of religious conflict and political upheaval between 1559 and 1689, politicians of every stripe invoked God's will to suit their particular purposes. The aristocratic and bourgeois Calvinists found divine sanction for rebellion, constitutionalism, and limited government. The Jesuits found divine sanction for the deposition of heretical rulers and a return to papal suzerainty. The secular princes found divine sanction for absolute monarchy. Radicals found divine sanction even for republicanism, democracy, and communism. Such were the effects of religion on politics, and of politics on religion.

And so, the European religious wars of the sixteenth and seventeenth centuries—their causes and their consequences—give us a reason for pause and provide some serious food for thought in view of America's wars against terrorism and Iraq.

Crypto-theocracy in American Politics

Since the invasion of Afghanistan by the US, there have been many who have sounded an alarm that President George W. Bush is engaged in an ideological and religious crusade against those nations that his government considers to be part of a network of enemy states—meaning that he does not like their government—and aimed at changing these "regimes" by military intervention. Some go even farther and suggest that the United States has resurrected the religious wars that ravaged the European continent in the sixteenth and seventeenth centuries. In fact, so much has been written on this subject that if you Google George Bush and Religious Wars, you get 1,920,000 results; George Bush and Crusades, you get 102,000 results; and George Bush and Peace of Westphalia, 8,600 results. These huge numbers caught our attention and decided to look into this matter a bit closer..

The most compelling articles and books written on this subject are those that suggest that Bush and his Washington neo-cons with the support of the Evangelical Christians are replaying the European religious wars—a newer and improved version of them, anyway. We, respectfully, beg to differ with those suggestions, at least in part. We have to admit that there are similarities: the European religious wars had both an internal component—civil wars—and an external one—aggression against other states. The Bush crusades also have internal and external components. The European religious wars, although they were fanatical and brutal in every respect, they were refreshingly honest—if one could use that expression about any war—regarding what they were all about. The trade mark of the European religious wars was religious intolerance which was also their driving and sustaining force. The Calvinists were determined to either convert or exterminate the Catholics. And the Jesuits were even more determined to do the same to the Calvinists and other Protestants. Both sides made no attempts to camouflage their intent, and their conflict was crystal clear. The Bush crusades, on the other hand, although also fanatical and brutal, they are a lot more subtle and sophisticated.

The Bush religious wars, as mentioned above, have domestic and foreign policy components, and both moral and political agendas. The political and foreign policy agenda is derived from the neo-con ideology, and its domestic and moral agenda is derived from the Evangelicals—the extreme religious fanatics of Christianity—which we will refer to as the Christianists. We borrowed the term from an article that appeared in 11/8/2004 in http://www.dailykos.com and believe it should be rather illuminating for our readers to read some experts from this article.

> ...there is another movement in this nation, which I refer to as Christianism. The term is derived from "Islamist"—or those people who claimed to be followers of Islam, but are nothing more than terrorists who do not follow the principles of Islam. There are those "Christians" who do not seem to be following the principles of Christianity—thus the term "Christianist".
>
> Christianism uses Christianity in order to further its agenda, which can be quickly summed up in two goals:
>
> 1. The establishment of a state religion. This state religion, of course, is not to promote Christianity, but rather to consolidate power in order to achieve their second goal.
>
> 2. Legislation of their repressive moral agenda. The Christianists plan to destroy the system of checks and balances in the Constitution, and they plan to do this in the name of Christianity. The establishment of a state religion is critical to this.
>
> The Constitution is Christianism's biggest obstacle...there is normally no way that they would be able to secure the votes needed for a constitutional amendment. So they plan on legislating their way around it, by removing the system of checks and balances. We have seen this already in action—by proposing legislation that would prevent "activist judges" from "creating law" from the bench, which is really a way to keep judges from interpreting the law in a Constitutional manner, which would prevent them from pushing their moral agenda on the American people.

The "beef" of the European crusades and the Bush crusades was religious intolerance marinated in greed, and economic and political control. But while the European ones were direct and clear, the Bush moral wars are indirect and covert. His Christianists are effectively using wedge issues--gay marriages, abortion, Evolution—to galvanize the "faithful", and promote the changes they need in order to push their agenda. The national election of 2004 was a prime example of this Faustian pact. So, what we have in essence in the American government is a crypto-theocracy where our "divinely guided" secular leaders use Christianism to secure the support of the Christianists in order to solidify their political and military control over domestic and international goals, and the Christianists are happy to oblige in exchange for the right to exercise their "divine duty" to impose their brand of "moral values" on the rest of society.

The Rise of Neo-Conservatives: America at War

"Our people are coming to realize that in this country one crusade has led to another. After the first crusade we were not able to prevent the next war that was coming. We were not prepared for the war when we had to fight it. And twice we have not known how to settle the war when we had won it. Twice in one generation we have gone around this deadly cycle."
Walter Lippmann, 1952

Wilsonian Doctrine

"The Wilsonian thesis was, if I may put it in this way, that, since the world was no longer safe for the American democracy, the American people were called upon to conduct a crusade to make the world safe for the American democracy. In order to do this the principles of the American democracy would have to be made universal throughout the world. The Wilsonian ideology is American fundamentalism made into a universal doctrine." This is what Walter Lippmann said in 19521 regarding the Wilsonian doctrine that seems to have resurfaced, in its modified and improved latest edition, by the neo-cons in the 90s and adopted by George W. Bush during his presidency.

"The Wilsonian system of ideas does not recognize that America is one nation among many other nations with whom it must deal as rivals, as allies, as partners" continued Lippmann.

> The Wilsonian vision is a world in which there are no lasting rivalries, where there are no deep conflicts of interest, where no compromises of principle have to be made, where there are no separate spheres of influence, and no alliances. In this world there are no wars except universal war against criminal governments who rebel against the universal order. The Wilsonian ideology is a crusading doctrine, generating great fervor from the feeling that war is an intolerable criminal interference with the nature of things. The necessity of going to war is an outrage upon our privacy and upon our rights.
>
> Therefore, all wars are wars to end wars, all wars are crusades which can be concluded only when all the peoples have

> submitted to the only true political religion. There will be peace when all the peoples hold and observe the same self-evident principles. …in my view it is becoming increasingly plain that the Wilsonian ideology is an impossible foundation for the foreign policy of a nation, placed as we are and carrying the burden of our responsibilities. Our people are coming to realize that in this century one crusade has led to another. After the first crusade we were not able to prevent the next war that was coming. We were not prepared for the war when we had to fight it. And twice we have not known how to settle the war when we had won it. Twice in one generation we have gone around this deadly cycle.

In describing the Wilsonian ideology in an article written more than fifty five years ago, Walter Lippmann, who was perhaps the most important architect of that ideology, describes the Bush doctrine as well.

Neo-conservatives

In his April 26, 2003 U.S. Edition, The Economist under the Headline "The shadow men", said: "In 2000, a close-knit group of about 20 people took their places in the Bush administration, hoping to overthrow Saddam Hussein and spread American ideas of democracy throughout the Middle East. They called themselves 'neo-conservatives' and, for two years, no one paid them much notice".

As soon as the regime of Saddam Hussein collapsed, the US began to rattle its saber over Syria's head, and after more than a year from the invasion of Iraq, the US raised its threats against the other Muslim nation of its "axis of evil", Iran. At the same time, the US was dealing with North Korea, the third member of the "axis of evil" and the real threat to nuclear proliferation and world peace, with uncharacteristic soft diplomacy. This type of behavior from the Pentagon and State Department greatly concerns governments around the world who wonder what this group of neo-conservatives (neo-cons), who seem to have a stranglehold on the Bush administration, plan to do next. These concerns are serious enough and require further examination into who the neo-cons are, where their roots are, and what their ideology and goals are.

Leo Strauss and his Disciples

About the same time Walter Lippmann was discrediting the Wilsonian doctrine, a Jew refugee from Nazi Germany began his academic career in America teaching at several major American universities and finally settling at the University of Chicago. His name was Leo Strauss and his philosophy would influence US foreign policy as no other contemporary political philosopher has. In 1996, in an article *Time* magazine named him as one of the most influential and powerful figures in the nation's capital--quite an accomplishment for someone who has been dead for more than thirty years and who was not that influential and powerful when he was alive. The main reason that Straussian ideology still reverberates in the inner sancta of think tanks in the beltway is, perhaps, that he bred a small but potent group of conservative ideologists and academics who have quietly and gradually infiltrated and taken over first, political science departments, and, later, the US foreign policy. Strauss's disciples are known as the Straussians and his political philosophy as Staussianism.

Shadia Drury, professor at Calgary University and a leading scholarly critic of Strauss, explains that according to Straussian thinking there are three types of men: the wise, the gentlemen, and the vulgar.

> Like Plato, Strauss believed that the supreme political ideal is the rule of the wise. But the rule of the wise is unattainable in the real world. Now, according to conventional wisdom, Plato realized this, and settled for the rule of law. But Strauss did not endorse this solution entirely. Nor did he think that it was Plato's real solution.
>
> The real Platonic solution as understood by Strauss is the covert rule of the wise. This covert rule is facilitated by the overwhelming stupidity of the gentlemen. The more gullible and unperceptive they are, the easier it is for the wise to control and manipulate them

For Strauss, the rule of the wise is not about classic conservative values like order, stability, justice, or respect for authority. The rule of the wise is intended as an antidote to modernity. Modernity is the age in which the vulgar many have triumphed. It is the age in which they have come closest to having exactly what their hearts desire – wealth, pleasure, and endless entertainment. Nowhere is this state of affairs more advanced than in America. And the global reach of American culture threatens to trivialize life and turn it into entertainment. Only perpetual war can overturn the modern project, with its emphasis on self-preservation and "creature comforts." Life can be politicized once more, and man's humanity can be restored.

This terrifying vision fits perfectly well with the desire for honor and glory that the neo-conservative gentlemen covet. It also fits very well with the religious sensibilities of gentlemen. The combination of religion and nationalism is the elixir that Strauss advocates as the way to turn natural, relaxed, hedonistic men into devout nationalists willing to fight and die for their God and country.

I never imagined when I wrote my first book on Strauss that the unscrupulous elite that he elevates would ever come so close to political power, nor that the ominous tyranny of the wise would ever come so close to being realized in the political life of a great nation like the United States. But fear is the greatest ally of tyranny.

In all fairness to Leo Strauss, however, he was an academic, a political philosopher and was entitled to his opinions and ideologies. He was not a politician or a decision maker. If there is anything with which to fault Strauss, it may be that he was too persuasive with his students and ended up, intentionally or unintentionally, creating kind of a cult following. One cannot blame him for the disasters that have befallen upon the United States during the George W. Bush presidency as a result of the neo-cons control of Washington. Tragically for the nation, George W. Bush turned out to be one of Strauss' gullible gentlemen.

The original neo-cons were a small group of intellectuals, mostly Jewish, who started as liberals (Democrats) and moved to the right in the 60s and 70s as they became impatient with what they considered America's appeasement of the Soviet Union and reluctance to spent adequately on defense.[1] The label "neo" was given to them by the left and was considered to be an insult. It separated them, however, from the "real" conservatives as domestic issues were as much part of the neo-cons' agenda as were foreign policy issues. Many of the neo-cons cut their teeth working for or being involved with Democratic Senator Henry "Scoop" Jackson who was a hawk, a staunch anticommunist, and a severe critic of the appeasement policy of the 1970s towards the Soviets.

By the 1980s, the second generation of neo-cons had fewer Democrats, as most of them had become hard core Republicans. Ronald Reagan's aggressive approach of confronting the Soviets with sharp increases in defense spending was "manna" from the heavens for the neo-cons. The collapse of the Soviet Union strengthened their hand only temporarily as they found themselves "out of the loop" in the 90s during Bill Clinton's presidency. Despite being muted during this period, the neo-cons used the 1990s to sharpen their message and develop their blueprint for American global hegemony in the twenty-first century.

At first look, it seems that the neo-cons of the 90s revived the Wilsonian ideology. A closer examination, however, points out some differences between the two. Neo-con ideology tends to be more non-institutional and it is values-based. "It's a conservative Christian value base. Even though many conservatives are Jews, the sort of basic values that they are promoting are very much the sort of Protestant, Christian values that were dominant in 19th-century America." [10] Specifically, the neo-cons see a "unipolar world" in which there is good and evil. They believe America should use its military might to defeat the forces of darkness.

Principal neo-cons include Irving and William Kristol, Robert Kagan, Paul Wolfowitz, Abram Shulsky, Richard Perle, Michael Ledeen, Bill Bennet, and John Bolton. Dick Cheney and Donald Rumsfeld are recent neo-con converts during the Bush presidency and especially after 9/11 with Cheney becoming one of their staunchest supporters. George W. Bush did not support, or so it seemed, the neo-cons from the beginning of his presidency. In foreign affairs, he campaigned for a humble but strong policy and was very critical of nation building. His views in this area were strongly influenced by Condoleezza Rice and, to a lesser degree, by Colin Powell.

Then came September 11, 2001 and the world and George W. Bush changed. In the absence of other compelling and forceful ideologies, Bush turned to the neo-cons for advice, and they were more than eager to provide it. He embraced large parts of the neo-cons agenda, the most critical, as it turned out to be, of which was to invade Iraq and take out Saddam. Bush, however, went further with the neo-con ideology; he made it the centerpiece of his foreign policy and the focus of his reelection campaign in 2004.

"Most dramatically, he [President George W. Bush] and his closest advisers have undergone the policy equivalent of a born-again religious conversion. [They] have embraced an agenda so utopian as to make Woodrow Wilson look like a hard-bitten cynic. They seek nothing less than remaking Iraq in the Western image, thereby changing the political equation of the entire Middle East and beyond. The ultimate goal is not simply to make the world safe for democracy, but to make the entire world democratic." [2] In January 18, 2009 just before the inauguration of Barack Obama, Pat Buchanan speaking in Fareed Zakaria's GPS on CNN referred to Bush as "Wilson on steroids"—one of the best descriptions of Bush's ideology that I ever heard. The 2002 Bush National Security Strategy document provides further insight into Bush's ideology: "we must make use of every tool in our arsenal," to promote in "every corner of the world," the "single sustainable model for national success: freedom, democracy, and free enterprise," and to those ends, "the United States will, if necessary, act preemptively."

The challenge for Bush and his neo-cons is, however, as Cornelius Thomas put it, "how to implement democracy in a country that has no democratic culture; implant liberal secular values (on which democracy depends) where values are strictly religious, indeed Islamic; and plant a US-style market economy where the geography allows largely for a single commodity (oil) economy; and indeed how to sell Western culture (read Judeo-Christian culture) in the middle of a region where Islamic theocracy generally holds sway."

Noble Lies and Perpetual Wars

Terrorism is the ultimate misuse of fear for political ends. Indeed, its specific goal is to distort the political reality of a nation by creating fear in the general population that is hugely disproportionate to the actual danger that the terrorists are capable of posing.

Al Gore, Former Vice President of the U.S.

While one may question the direct influence that Straussian, Platonic, or Machiavellian political philosophy might have had on the neo-cons who occupy seats of great power in the George W. Bush administration, there is plenty of evidence to support the extensive use of deception, religion and aggressive nationalism—the roots of which can be traced to Strauss and Machiavelli—by the neo-cons in their war against "evil" and the establishment of the PAX Americana as the sole and undisputed global military and economic power. To that end, we will examine the chain of deceptions that have been used by the neo-cons and will start with "Exhibit A", the demonizing of the Soviet Union during the Cold War years in a post-Watergate and post-Viet Nam America.

From Cold War to Holy War

We will not be driven by fear into an age of unreason, if we dig deep into our history and our doctrine and remember that we are not descended from fearful men, not men who feared to write, to speak, to associate, and to defend causes which were for the moment unpopular.

Edward Murrow, 9 March 1954

"In the past, politicians promised to create a better world…those dreams failed…But now, they have discovered a new role that restores their power and authority. Instead of delivering dreams, politicians now promise to protect us from nightmares. They say that will rescue us from dreadful dangers that we cannot see and do not understand. And the greatest danger of all is international terrorism. A powerful and sinister network, with sleeper cells in countries across the world. A threat that needs to be fought by a war on terror. But much of this threat is a fantasy, which has been exaggerated and distorted by politicians. It's a dark illusion that has spread unquestioned through the governments around the world, the security services, and the international media." And so began the BBC controversial documentary series—"The Power of Nightmares"—that aired in January 2005 and stirred up quite a storm on the other side of the Atlantic but went almost unnoticed by the American mass media and public. On the contrary, we were fascinated with it and found it hugely encouraging to our efforts, because while the documentary brings to light many unknown (at least to us) events of deceit and manipulation—mostly during the cold war years—it traced the lives, political philosophies, and tactics of the same protagonists—Islamic fundamentalists and neo-conservatives—on both sides of the Atlantic as we had done, and most importantly reached almost the same conclusions as we have.

Although we have covered the neo-conservatives (neo-cons) in the previous section of this book and will not attempt to repeat it here. The Godfather of neo-cons was Leo Strauss, a professor and political philosopher who believed that the prosperous liberal society of post WWII America with its selfish values would lead the country to self-destruction. He, as the hero of "Gunsmoke", was going to protect America from evil. While Matt Dillon used all the virtues of an honorable lawman of the Western frontier, Strauss believed that politicians should use powerful and inspiring myths—religion and nation—that everyone could believe in to battle the forces of evil throughout the world. Many of Srauss' students, like Paul Wolfowitz, would become the disciples of his political philosophy and with others, who studied his theories elsewhere, like Irving Kristol and his son William, would form a group that would become known as the neo-conservatives. Their aim was to stop the social disintegration, so they set out to recreate Strauss' "myth of America as a unique nation whose destiny was to battle against evil in the world. And in this project, the source of evil would be America's Cold War enemy: the Soviet Union." And the US, according to the Straussians, by acting on these myths would not only rid the world of the "evil empire" but it would be able to overcome the fundamental weaknesses that plagued the American society.

There was an obstacle, however, in the way of this neo-con ideological war against the Soviets. It was Secretary of State

Henry Kissinger who believed in global interdependence and who, with President Nixon, commenced the thawing out of the Cold War era with their policy of détente. In 1972, the US and the Soviet Union signed a treaty limiting their nuclear arms arsenal. "...we witnessed the beginning of the end of that era which began in 1945. With this step, we have enhanced the security of both nations. We have begun to reduce the level of fear, by reducing the causes of fear—for our two peoples, and for the peoples in the world." said President Nixon.

But a world without fear was the last thing the neo-cons wanted. Fear is a very ancient and universal emotion in man and is defined as the sensation that we are in danger, that something bad is about to happen. Dreams have disturbed the primitive mind, but nightmares have terrorized the early men driving them into willing and earnest association with each other for mutual protection against the vague and unseen imaginary dangers of the nightmares. Once you instill fear in the minds of the people about a particular danger, then you can convince them of anything, and do just about anything that is supposed to protect them from this "danger". The use of fear has been and continuous to be the core component that justifies the existence of religious and military—defense—institutions, as without fear they will go out of business. Historically, this fear, however, has not been totally baseless—it has relied on real potential dangers—societal insecurities stemming from disease and hunger, attacks by hostile neighbors and other tribes, and spiritual concerns about after life—but it has been greatly exaggerated and manipulated for a specific gain. The salvation of one's soul, the protection of one's earthly possessions and wellbeing are what Church and Governments are using to keep us constantly afraid and very obedient.

The neo-cons had to attack and destroy Kissinger's vision of détente and that opportunity came with the American defeat in Vietnam and the resignation of President Nixon over Watergate. They seized their moment as they allied themselves with two hawks in the administration of Gerald Ford—Donald Rumsfeld, the new Secretary of Defense, and Dick Cheney, Ford's Chief of Staff. Rumsfeld began the campaign of fear by saying that the Soviets were ignoring the treaty and secretly building up their weapons, with the intention of attacking America. Here is Rumsfeld in a 1976 speech: (BBC, "The Power of Nightmares", 2005)[§]

> The Soviet Union has been busy. They've been busy in terms of their level of effort; they've been busy in terms of the actual weapons they've been producing; they've been busy in terms of expanding production rates; they've been busy in terms of expanding their institutional capability to produce additional weapons at additional rates…Year after year after year, they've been demonstrating that they have steadiness of purpose. They are purposeful about what they're doing. Now, your question is, what ought one to be doing about that?

But Rumsfeld's allegations were pure fiction. The systematic deceit of the American public by the neo-cons had begun. According to the BBC documentary, the neo-cons through Rumsfeld convinced Ford to appoint an "independent" inquiry. The inquiry was called Team B, its chairman was a well-known critic of the Soviet Union and the other leading member was Paul Wolfowitz, a charter member of the neo-con fraternity. Team B examined closely all the CIA data on the Soviet Union and no matter how closely they looked, they were unable to find any evidence of the weapons that Rumsfeld had alleged they possessed. Team B, however, instead of declaring that they had found no weapons, they assumed that the systems the Soviets had developed were so sophisticated they were undetectable. "For example, they could find no evidence that the Soviet fleet had an acoustic defense system. What this meant, Team B said, was that the Soviets had actually invented a new non-acoustic system, which was impossible to detect. And this meant that the whole of the American submarine fleet was at risk from an invisible threat that was there, even though there was no evidence for it."

So, the manipulators at Team B were going to deceive the President and the American public that the "fact that the weapon doesn't exist…it doesn't mean that it doesn't exist. It just means that we haven't found it." Now, anyone around the

[§] All quotes and excerpts that appear in this section are from the BBC documentary "The power of Nightmares", 2005 unless otherwise referenced.

world with the faintest of pulse would recognize that this conclusion sounds almost identical to the statements made in the months leading to the invasion of Iraq by exactly the same neo-cons—Rumsfeld, Cheney, Wolfowitz—regarding the existence of WMDs in Iraq. Given this pattern of deceitful rhetoric by Rumsfeld, Cheney and Wolfowitz, one wonders, why didn't someone in the media, or in the government or intelligence community say, "Hold on! Haven't we heard exactly the same bull before? Like 26 years ago?" Oh, how much we miss you Ed Murrow!

To the credit of CIA, the agency accused Team B of moving into a fantasy world. The neo-cons, however, had their agenda. They set up a group called the Committee on the Present Danger—just in case someone missed the implied danger—to publicize the findings of Team B. One of the politicians who joined the Committee was presidential hopeful, Ronald Reagan. Through films and television, the Committee proceeded to convince Americans that their country was in grave danger from unseen and sinister forces and it was their duty to act before the young men of America had to fall defending the borders of their country.

> This dramatic battle between good and evil was precisely the kind of myth that Leo Strauss had taught his students would be necessary to rescue the country from moral decay. It might not be true, but it was necessary, to re-engage the public in a grand vision of America's destiny, that would give meaning and purpose to their lives. The neo-conservatives were succeeding in creating a simplistic fiction—a vision of the Soviet Union as the center of an evil in the world, and America as the only country that would rescue the world. And this nightmarish vision was beginning to give the neo-conservatives great power and influence.

In 1981, the neo-cons got their first big break when Ronald Reagan took control of the White House with the help of the religious fundamentalists who went to polls in large numbers for the first time. Until then, they were a politically active group but they were working mostly from the fringes of power and never from within. Reagan as a member of the Committee on the Present Danger had become acquainted with the neo-cons and when he set up his new administration, many neo-cons were part of it. Paul Wolfowitz became head of the State Department policy staff, his close friend Richard Perle became the Assistant Secretary of Defense, and the head of Team B, Richard Pipes, became one of Reagan's chief advisers. The neo-cons believed that "they now had the chance to implement their vision of America's revolutionary destiny—to use the country's power aggressively as a force for good in the world, in an epic battle to defeat the Soviet Union. It was a vision that they shared with millions of their new religious allies." But the neo-cons faced strong opposition from the government bureaucracies, Congress, and President Reagan, who although believed that the Soviet Union was an evil empire, he also believed that he could negotiate nuclear disarmament and a treaty that could end the Cold War.

To persuade Reagan, the neo-cons set out to prove that the Soviet Union was a much greater threat than anyone had previously thought, including even Team B. Their goal was to demonstrate that all terrorist groups, from the PLO to the Baader-Meinholf and the Provisional IRA were part of a coordinated strategy of terror run by the Soviet Union. I believe that this is the first time, at least in modern history, that state-sponsored terrorism was used as a serious global threat. The main proponent of this theory was Michael Ledeen, a leading neo-conservative and a special assistant to the Secretary of State. The CIA, at least initially, completely disagreed with Ledeen's premise that terrorism was not the fragmented phenomenon that it appeared to be. They argued that Ledeen's theory was just another neo-con fantasy. But if you cannot make the CIA analysts agree with your theories, you just change the leadership of the agency. And that's what happened with Reagan's appointment of William Casey, a powerful ally of the neo-cons, as the new head of the CIA. Casey not only believed in Ledeen's fantasy, but being angry at his experts on terrorism for coming up with little evidence linking the Soviet Union to terror groups, ordered them to read Claire Sterling's famous book *The Terror Network*—the source of Ledeen's theory. They did and found that virtually all of the examples she cited turned out to be CIA disinformation—false stories planted in the foreign press that she unwittingly used in good faith. Casey was told about this even by the CIA operations people, but he had made up his mind. He believed the Soviets were involved in terrorism and there was nothing anyone could tell him to dissuade him. Lies became reality.

Casey was successful in convincing Reagan to take steps against this imaginary threat and in 1983 the foundations of American foreign policy were cracked—sadly that would not be the last time as twenty years later American foreign policy changed even more dramatically with the pre-emptive war against Iraq—as the US President signed a secret document that authorized the funding of covert wars to push back the hidden Soviet threat around the world.

> It was a triumph for the neo-conservatives. America was now setting out to do battle against the forces of evil in the world. But what had started out as the kind of myth that Leo Strauss had said was necessary for the American people, increasingly came to be seen as the truth by the neo-conservatives. They began to believe their own fiction. They had become what they called "democratic revolutionaries," who were going to use force to change the world. "LEDEEN: We are aiming for an expansion of the zone of freedom in the world. And in part that had to do with fighting communism, and in part that had to do with fighting other kind of tyrannies. But that's what we were about, and that's what we're still about."

By the time Reagan authorized covert operations against the Soviets, the Afghan mujahedeen resistance—assisted by Muslim fighters from most of the Arab countries—had been fighting the Soviet invasion, and provided the perfect opportunity for the Reagan White House neo-cons to achieve their vision of transforming the world. The Reagan Doctrine was born and the mujahedeen—the same type of resistance that the US is fighting in Iraq and now calls insurgency—were freedom fighters, who could bring down the Soviet Union and help spread democracy around the world. Supporting the freedom fighters in Afghanistan became the premier cause for the entire conservative movement during the Reagan years.[**].

> American money and weapons now began to pour across the Pakistan border into Afghanistan. CIA agents trained the mujahedeen in the techniques of assassination and terror, including car bombings. And they gave them satellite images of Russian troops to help in their attacks. At the same time, another group began to arrive in Afghanistan to fight alongside the mujahedeen. They were Arabs from across the Middle East, who had been told by their religious leaders that their duty was to go and free Muslim lands from the Soviet invader.

In 1987, the new leader of Soviet Union Mikhail Gorbachev decided that Russia must withdraw the Russian troops from Afghanistan, as he believed that the whole Soviet system was facing an imminent collapse. He also believed that he could save it through political reform, and this meant reversing the policies of his predecessors, including occupation of Afghanistan. According to BBC, Gorbachev tried to negotiate with the Americans a gradual and face-saving withdrawal from Afghanistan warning the US that any sudden departure from the highly unstable country would result not in peace but rather would throw the government into the hands of the hardline militant Islamists that the US at that time, of course, called freedom fighters.

The Soviet Union collapsed. This collapse, however, was not caused by Mikhail Gorbachev, or Ronald Reagan, or by any action that the US government took. "I think probably one of the greatest myths in America…is that actions of the American government were responsible for the collapse of the Soviet Union. The Soviet Union collapsed like a house of cards because it was a house of cards. It rotted away from within." So says Mel-

---

[**] In Part Three of the book we detail the rise to power and the ideologies of two groups: the neo-cons and the Islamic fundamentalists. Reagan's Doctrine makes it possible for these two groups to unite in Afghanistan in their fight against the Soviet invasion of that country. Both believed that that could defeat the evil empire and that they had the power to transform the world as well.

vin Goodman, Head of Office of Soviet Affairs, CIA, 1976-1987 in the BBC documentary. For the neo-cons, however, the collapse of the Soviet Union was a triumph.

> And out of that triumph [there] was going to come the central myth that still inspires them today: that through the aggressive use of American power, they could transform the world and spread democracy. But in reality, their victory was an illusion. They had conquered a phantom enemy, an exaggerated and distorted fantasy they had created in their own minds. The real reason the Soviet Union collapsed was because it was a decrepit system, decaying from within

Believing that they had brought down the Soviet Union and that it is their destiny to defeat other regimes and liberate the world and spread democracy, the neo-cons set their sights on Saddam Hussein. Although Saddam was one of America's closest allies in the 1980s, his invasion of Kuwait in 1990 changed that, and it provided the neo-cons with an opportunity to renew their pursuit of transforming a post-Soviet Union world. Neo-cons like Paul Wolfowitz, who was undersecretary of Defense, wanted to oust Saddam and begin their transformation of the Middle East and fulfill America's destiny to defeat evil in the world. President George Bush (senior) liberated Kuwait but stopped short of invading Baghdad and ordered the fighting to stop. He believed that America's role was to create stability in the world, not to try to change it. In a 1996 interview, Brent Scowcroft, National Security Advisor to President George Bush, said "Saddam Hussein is not a threat to his neighbors. He's a nuisance; he's an annoyance; but he's not a threat. That we achieved. It was never our objective to get Saddam Hussein. Indeed had we tried, we still might be occupying Baghdad. That would have turned a great success into a very messy probably defeat."

In 1992 Bill Clinton defeated George H.W. Bush and for the next eight years the neo-cons found themselves, for the first time in twelve years, hugely distanced from the seat of power. But the neo-cons were determined to regain power. "And to do this, they were going to do to Bill Clinton what they had done to the Soviet Union: they would transform the President of the

United States into a fantasy enemy, and image of evil that would make people realize the truth of the liberal corruption of America." Whitewater and Monica Lewinsky provided them with the ammunition, and for eight years they practiced political terrorism. The neo-cons came close to bringing Clinton down and they might have succeeded were it not for the American public which approved Clinton's performance as President, even during the darkest hours of the proceedings of his impeachment.

Then on 9/11 came the attacks on America that shocked the world. And the attacks had another dramatic effect: they brought the neo-cons back to power in America. A small group formed that began to shape America's response to the attacks. "At its heart were Donald Rumsfeld and Paul Wolfowitz, along with the vice-president, Dick Cheney, and Richard Perle, who was a senior advisor to the Pentagon. The last time these men had been in power together was 20 years before, under President Reagan. Back then, they had taken on and, as they saw it, defeated a source of evil that wanted to take over America: the Soviet Union. And now they saw this new war on terror in the same epic terms." The neo-cons had come around a full circle. They started with the Cold War and now they saw an opportunity to complete their mission with a Holy War—the Iraq War—which is "Exhibit B" of this citizen's case against the US president.

The Iraq War

I don't oppose all wars. What I am opposed to is a dumb war. What I am opposed to is a rash war. What I am opposed to is the cynical attempt by Richard Perle and Paul Wolfowitz and other armchair, weekend warriors in this administration to shove their own ideological agenda down our throats, irrespective of the costs in lives lost and in hardships borne.

President Barack Obama in October 2002, then an Illinois state senator

"The war in Iraq is not going as advertised. It is a flawed policy wrapped in illusion. The American public is way ahead of us." With these words, Rep. John Murtha (D-Pa) started his press conference on the Capitol Hill on Thursday, November 17,

2005 and it ended by calling for the immediate and complete withdrawal of US troops from Iraq. His comments send shock waves in Washington at a time when the debate about the justifications for going to war in Iraq had been re-opened and heating up. Rep. John Murtha's comments, however, couldn't be dismissed by the White House as being made by another of these liberal democrats "who have adopted a policy of cut and run." Rep. Murtha a retired colonel who served 37 years in the Marine Corps, is a Vietnam veteran with two purple hearts, and the senior democrat on the defense subcommittee of the House Appropriations Committee and known for his pro-defense stands. So, his call for withdrawal could have a significant impact on the debate over the future of the Iraq War.

But before the debate on when and how we should withdraw from Iraq heats up anymore, the Congress needs to answer to the American people how they got us there in the first place. Considering how much time, money and effort was devoted by the Congress and the mass media investigating Clinton's Monica-gate, I think our men and women in uniform, the American public and our allies deserve to know exactly how the leaders of this great country—who wrapped with the American flag threaten to label anyone who questions their actions as unpatriotic—betrayed the trust of the very same people they were elected to protect; and how they used fear and deception systematically and repeatedly to lead them to an unjust and dangerous war.

It is not a secret—although the mass media and the Washington politicians seem to ignore it—that the neo-cons had Iraq and Saddam Hussein in their sights more than three and a half years before 9/11. In January 26, 1998 in a letter to then President Bill Clinton they urged him "to enunciate a new strategy [that] should aim, above all, at the removal of Saddam Hussein's regime from power... That now needs to become the aim of American foreign policy...American policy cannot continue to be crippled by a misguided insistence on unanimity in the UN Security Council." What prevented them from implementing that strategy were a "wrong president" and the lack of a justification that could be "bought" by the American public. Moreover, fighting a war against Saddam had been the focus of the Bush administration, particularly of Vice President Cheney, from the onset of Bush's presidency. Before 9/11, however, there was no substantial reason to justify such a war. Saddam and his regime were contained after the first Gulf war in 1991. President Clinton followed on the footsteps of former President Bush and carried on the policies of the economic sanctions and the disarmament of Iraq. Saddam was not a threat to his neighbors anymore, and by no means was he a "grave and imminent threat" to the US.

The perfect opportunity for the neo-cons came with the attacks of 9/11. Now with the new administration, they had many allies in the White House and Pentagon who were sympathetic to their "war cries", and the fear of a new external enemy had gripped America. The Bush administration was quick to include Saddam in their list of external threats and make him a symbol of terrorism along with Bin Laden. In his 2002 State of the Union Address, Bush referred to Iraq as one of the members of the "axis of evil." About the same time, and less than two months after US forces attacked Afghanistan, he secretly ordered a war plan drawn up against Iraq. "I knew what would happen if people thought we were developing war plan for Iraq," Bush is quoted as telling Bob Woodward. Bush feared that if news got out about the Iraq plan as US forces were fighting another conflict, people would think he was too eager for war, journalist Bob Woodward writes in Plan of Attack, a behind-the –scenes account of the 16 months leading to the Iraq invasion. The most recent, and most dangerous yet, neo-con strategy of noble lies for perpetual wars had begun. Larry Johnson, a former CIA intelligent analyst and State Department counter-terrorism official, referring to the events that led to the invasion of Iraq says, "…the Bush administration organized and executed a classic 'covert action' program against the citizens of the United States" and goes on to define what is covert action.

> Covert action refers to behind-the-scenes efforts by US intelligence agencies to plant stories, manipulate information and shape public opinion. In other words, you write stories that reporters will publish as their own, you create media events that tout a particular theme, and you demonize your opponent.

It is understandable that some may disagree with Johnson's assertion and to that end we will try to show that, even though it might be very difficult to proof beyond any doubt that there was a White House covert action against the American citizens, there is otherwise irrefutable evidence that shows that all assertions made by the Bush administration to justify the Iraq War were flatly false.[††] Bush justified the war on Iraq on the grounds of combating global terrorism and protecting America's homeland security.

Although a connection was never found between Bin Laden and Saddam's regime, the administration used this alleged connection as one of two principal reasons to go to war with Iraq. Moreover, Bush and Blair for months lobbied the UN and European leaders to convince them that Saddam possessed Weapons of Mass Distraction (WMD) such as the ones he had used in the past against his own people in Northern Iraq. These WMD, that he allegedly possessed, would become an imminent threat to the homeland security if he made them available to terrorist organizations. These justifications were accepted by the American public and Congress—but not by the UN—who were made to believe that that there was some underground cooperation between Saddam and Bin Laden and Iraq was somehow involved in 9/11, and that Iraq possessed WMD and intended to use them against the US. We will carefully examine both of these assertions based on publicly available information and determine their validity.

Assertion One: Iraq possesses chemical and biological weapons and either has or will soon have the capability to develop nuclear weapons. In his 2003 State of the Union Address less than two months before the Iraq invasion, the Presi-

---

[††]"In all my years around Washington as an observer and as a member of several administrations, I have rarely witnessed an event as bizarre as President Bush's farewell press conference yesterday (1/12/09)...How can you reflect on going to war, *a war of choice*, and argue that "not finding weapons of mass destruction was a significant disappointment", as President Bush did yesterday? And putting the "not finding the weapons" in the same breath as "we shouldn't have hung the sign, *Mission Accomplished*!" Ed Collins is a CNN contributor and a Republican who served President Reagan as political director.

dent of the United States of America had this to say about Iraq, Saddam, and their alleged WMD.

> A brutal dictator, with a history of reckless aggression, with ties to terrorism, with great potential wealth, will not be permitted to dominate a vital region and threaten the United States…Twelve years ago, Saddam Hussein faced the prospect of being the last casualty in a war he had started and lost. To spare himself, he agreed to disarm of all weapons of mass destruction. For the next 12 years, he systematically violated that agreement. He pursued chemical, biological, and nuclear weapons, even while inspectors were in his country. Nothing to date has restrained him from his pursuit of these weapons—not economic sanctions, not isolation from the civilized world, not even cruise missile strikes on his military facilities.

Information relating to the above statements made by President Bush and publicly known months before the Iraq War shows that in all accounts he misled the American people and the United States Congress. According to Hans Blix, UN weapons inspector, the inspections worked and the sanctions restrained Iraq's weapons development program. "More weapons of mass destruction were destroyed under [the disarmament process] than were destroyed during the [first] Gulf War" stated Blix. Also, many of Saddam's attempts to acquire prohibited technologies were blocked by international sanctions. According to a September 2002 British government report, Iraq's Weapons of Mass Destruction, "UN sanctions on Iraq were hindering the import of crucial goods for the production of fissile material." According to the same report, "Iraq would not be able to produce a nuclear weapon" as long as the sanctions remained effective. It can be safely concluded, that the Bush administration chose to use highly questionable intelligence while overlooking more reliable information that pointed to diametrically opposite conclusions.

Here is again President Bush with more allegations he made in his 2002 State of the Union Address.

> Iraq continues to flaunt its hostility toward America and to support terror. The Iraqi regime has plotted to develop

> anthrax, and nerve gas, and nuclear weapons for over a decade... This is a regime that agreed to international inspections -- then kicked out the inspectors. This is a regime that has something to hide from the civilized world...The United Nations concluded in 1999 that Saddam Hussein had biological weapons sufficient to produce over 25,000 liters of anthrax -- enough doses to kill several million people...The United Nations concluded that Saddam Hussein had materials sufficient to produce more than 38,000 liters of botulinum toxin -- enough to subject millions of people to death by respiratory failure...Our intelligence officials estimate that Saddam Hussein had the materials to produce as much as 500 tons of sarin, mustard and VX nerve agent. In such quantities, these chemical agents could also kill untold thousands. He's not accounted for these materials. He has given no evidence that he has destroyed them...From three Iraqi defectors we know that Iraq, in the late 1990s, had several mobile biological weapons labs. These are designed to produce germ warfare agents, and can be moved from place to place to evade inspectors. Saddam Hussein has not disclosed these facilities. He's given no evidence that he has destroyed them.

For several months prior to Iraq's invasion, Saddam allowed the monitors to have complete freedom of movement, and access to all sites—including his palaces which were previously off limits—in the renewed UN inspections. Both Hans Blix and IAEA director El Baradei reported that Iraqis provided access consistently without delays and without conditions. Also, no weapons were found by either the UN inspectors or the US military, which, with absolute freedom of movements and access to all sites in Iraq, has found nothing whatsoever after more than thirty three months of occupation. Perhaps, President Bush should have listened more to the UN inspectors and Iraqi officials than to the hawks in his own administration. Moreover, there has been no evidence of any Iraqi nuclear weapons activity. The allegation made by the president that "the British government has learned that Saddam Hussein recently sought significant quantities of uranium from Africa. Our intelligence sources tell us that he has attempted to purchase high-strength aluminum tubes suitable for nuclear weapons production." has also proved to be false. Finally after the war, US investigators found no evidence of mobile biological weapons laboratories, and during the 1990s UN inspectors also found no such evidence after extensive searches.

Conclusion: Assertion One has been found to be totally false.

Assertion Two: There was a link between Osama bin Laden and Saddam Hussein prior to the Iraq War. The existence of a link between Bin Laden and Saddam was the cornerstone of the argument for going to war against Saddam Hussein. The existence of WMD in Iraq alone, although a legitimate concern for Iraq's neighbors and Israel should not have been a sufficient enough justification for invading another sovereign country, unless there was a clear connection between Saddam and Al Qaeda in pre-war Iraq. There are other countries that possess nuclear weapons and which are not too friendly with the US, i.e. North Korea, which, correctly, we are not attacking nor invading because they are not collaborating with the terrorists and are not posing a "grave and imminent threat to our home land security." President Bush, Vice President Cheney, Defense Secretary Rumsfeld, and Secretary of State Powel—to mention only the main characters of this well organized, yet disgraceful disinformation campaign—said time and time again that there was a link between the terrorists responsible for the 9/11 attacks and Baghdad.

> In Iraq, a dictator is building and hiding weapons that could enable him to dominate the Middle East and intimidate the civilized world—and we will not allow it. This same tyrant has close ties to terrorist organizations, and could supply them with the terrible means to strike this country—and America will not permit it. The danger posed by Saddam Hussein and his weapons cannot be ignored or wished away. The danger must be confronted. *President Bush in his 2003 State of the Union address.*
>
> If we are successful in Iraq...then we will have struck a major blow right at the heart of the base, if you will, the geographic base of the terrorists who had us under assault now for many years, but most especially on 9/11. *Vice President Cheney in September 2003.*

> There are Al Qaeda in Iraq…Saddam Hussein is harboring Al Qaeda operatives who fled the US military dragnet in Afghanistan. *Donald Rumsfeld in August 2002.*

If such a link could be established beyond the shadow of a doubt, then going to war against Iraq might have been justified. After all, going to war against anyone should be a matter that should require the utmost consideration, especially by the country that possesses the most powerful war machine that the world has ever known. So, was there a link or not? This is the sole question that the Congress of the United States of America should have deliberated on before the war and this is the question the American public should be asking now the President of the United States—its Commander in Chief—and holding him accountable to his decision. So, in view of this, let us examine again publicly available information before the war and classified information made available after the war and determine the merits of the Bush administration's principal justification for the war.

Months of investigations have found that no such links ever existed. In fact, it is well known in the Arab world that Bin Laden was no friend of Saddam, whose secular government was far from the theocratic, Taliban-style of government that serves Bin Laden's global Islamic expansionism well. The only terrorists that were found in Iraq after the American invasion were the mujahedeen that had crossed the borders from neighboring countries to fight the infidels. Iraq had not ever been engaged in any terrorist activities against the US prior to the war. None of the nineteen hijackers of 9/11 were Iraqi citizens. As early as August 2002, Alex Standish, editor of Britain's top military journal said, "They are trying to convince us of something that is highly unlikely…if they really believe that Saddam is feeding and sustaining bin Laden's men, then they can't possibly understand the fundamental difference between Iraq and Al Qaeda." Standish continues, "I can't see any reason why Saddam, coming from an Arab nationalist, fairly secular background, would have any interest in supporting or promoting an extremist and militant religious ideology that would ultimately be opposed to everything he has ever stood for." The distinction that Standish makes between Al Qaeda and Saddam is crucial and one that there is no way that the British and American intelligence communities would have missed. In fact, back in 2001 and 2002, the State Department, the CIA, the FBI, and other agencies reported that there was no link between Saddam Hussein and Al Qaeda, and that Iraq did not engage in terrorist attacks against the US. In June 2004, in its final report the 9/11 commission reported that found no "credible evidence" of a "collaborative relationship" between Iraq and Al Qaeda, punching some big holes into the key justification of President Bush's administration for going to war against Iraq.

Moreover, British intelligence sources have disputed Powel's claim of a Baghdad-Al Qaeda connection. A report written by the British Ministry of Defense intelligence in January 2003 which was leaked to BBC said: "While there have been contacts between Al Qaeda and the [Baghdad] regime in the past, it is assessed that any fledging relationship foundered due to mistrust and incompatible ideology." Later on in February 2003, British Foreign Secretary Straw admitted that he had not seen any intelligence that Saddam was harboring Al Qaeda operatives as had been reported by Don Rumsfeld.

Even after all this evidence showing that the purported link between Baghdad and Al Qaeda was nothing more than a ploy by the Bush administration to create an external enemy which the US was justified to destroy, President Bush and Vice President Cheney in their, by now well-known, arrogant, hubristic, and "earth-is-flat" style continued to stick to their claim that there was a link. "The reason I keep insisting that there was a relationship between Iraq and Saddam and Al Qaeda [is] because there was a relationship between Iraq and Al Qaeda" said President Bush the day the report was released. A few days earlier, Cheney had said that Hussein "had long-established ties with Al Qaeda." The only one that seemed, although momentarily, to acknowledge—after the invasion of Iraq, of course—that there was not any link between Saddam and Al Qaeda was Don Rumsfeld, who when asked in October 2004 about such a connection, he said "To my knowledge, I have not seen any strong, hard evidence that links the two." There you have it, from a cold calculated war monger who no longer has a reason to continue lying after his objectives were met.

Conclusion: Assertion Two has been found to be totally false.

There seems to be broad agreement that there was a meltdown of the intelligence and national security agencies both before 9/11 and again before the Iraq War. But government cannot depend entirely on intelligence—no punt intended here. There are decision makers, surrounded with cadres of strategists and policy experts, whose job is to make the "right" decisions for all of their constituents. Hiding behind the failure of intelligence assessments is not an acceptable excuse—as no excuse is acceptable for this type of failure—and the political interpretation of such data raises serious doubts about the quality of the policy-making process of the Bush administration that led to the disasters of 9/11 attacks and the Iraq War.

If the intelligence, however, was more correct than not—as much information revealed after the Iraq War suggests—then this raises serious questions about the integrity of a government in a democratic society. Perhaps we ceased to be a democratic society some time ago. Back in 2002 the Bush National Security Strategy document made public what the neo-cons have been planning for decades: "We must make use of every tool in our arsenal," to promote in "every corner of the world," the "single sustainable model for national success: freedom, democracy, and free enterprise," and to those ends, "the United States will, if necessary, act preemptively. " When a nation decides to act preemptively against another for no legitimate reasons, it has already lost its right to speak of freedom and democracy as the whole foundation of freedom and democracy rests on integrity and sound judgment and not deceit and manipulation. The words of Senator Robert Byrd resonate louder today than did in February 2003 when he delivered his landmark speech on the floor of the US Senate in an effort to avert the Iraq War.

> ...And war must always be a last resort, not a first choice. I truly must question the judgment of any President who can say that a massive unprovoked military attack on a nation which is over 50% children is "in the highest moral traditions of our country". This war is not necessary at this time... Our mistake was to put our-

> selves in a corner so quickly. Our challenge is to now find a graceful way out of a box of our own making.

It appears that the Bush administration had a predetermined plan to go to war, some say, since it came to office, and the WMD that Iraq allegedly owned and the link between Saddam and Al Qaeda were used as a political manipulation to secure the support of the American public and international community. While the UN inspectors were still conducting their investigations, the US went to the UN and asked, basically, for a green light to attack Iraq. Given that no WMD have been found in Iraq, it is obvious that Bush didn't want the inspections to be completed as they would have revealed that no WMD were present in Iraq, and, thus, the justification for attacking Iraq would have been significantly weakened. "The president [George W. Bush] has adopted a policy of 'anticipatory self-defense' that is alarmingly similar to the policy that imperial Japan employed at Pearl Harbor, on a date, which as an earlier American president said it would, live in infamy. Franklin D. Roosevelt was right, but today it is we Americans who live in infamy" said Arthur Schlesinger as the invasion of Iraq began.

Not only the Bush administration decided to go to war against Iraq unilaterally with only Britain as a major ally, they did so against the will of the UN assembly, the UN Security Council, most of the American citizens and the world community. President of Egypt Mubarak warned that a war against Iraq would breed one hundred more Bin Ladens. Mubarak's words turned out to be very prophetic. After invading Iraq, the US became the most hated and mistrusted country in the Middle East. Moreover, the war on Iraq demonstrated the failure of diplomacy and undermined the UN as an international organization with legitimacy in the eyes of the world. American soldiers were taken into a bloody conflict by their president and his neo-cons and Iraq was transformed into another Vietnam.

Afghanistan, on the other hand, was and continues to be the hotbed of terrorism. The masterminds of Al Qaeda are most likely still hiding and operating in the mountainous ranges between Afghanistan and Pakistan, and probably planning for the next major attack against the US and its interests around the world. The Bush administration rather than concentrating its efforts on Afghanistan and finishing the job there first, has shifted its focus and resources to yet another war that was claimed to be against terrorism. Afghanistan was replaced with Iraq and Bin Laden was replaced with Saddam. By December 2003, while only less than 11,000 American soldiers were in Afghanistan looking for Bin Laden, Zawahiri, and, let us not forget, Mullah Omar that are still at large, 130,000 soldiers were in Iraq. The worse Bush can label Saddam, even in the heat of the 2004 election political rhetoric, is a brutal dictator to his people, and he is awaiting Iraqi justice in a prison cell in Iraq. Was this reason sufficient enough for the thousands of American soldiers dead or disabled for life and the hundreds of billions of dollars price tag of the War on Iraq? And worse yet, was this worth the lies and deceptions that the Bush administration used against the American people and the international community? How can the United States of America, the cradle of modern Democracy, and the world's only remaining super-power be trusted again?

The war against Iraq, however, is not only an indictment against the Bush administration because of the immorality of the war and the deceptions that were used to justify it; it is an indictment as well against the major information media, especially the TV networks, for relinquishing their duty to question, investigate, and criticize the actions of the government when criticism was necessary. Unfortunately, electronic media have become tools of corporate America and a platform of government propaganda. The printed media is somewhat better, but unfortunately a small percentage of Americans still read newspapers and magazines. And the American public should be found as nothing less than co-indictors as they share a great deal of this responsibility too. The questions that gnaws me is this; is the American public really so disengaged from the political process that it is easily fooled and manipulated, or is it that it is ideologically aligned with the imperialistic motives of this administration? I guess we will never know for certain, but either case is an alarming and frightening prospect to be happening in any society, especially one that espouses to be democratic.

A final thought on this immoral and largely unpopular war. I wonder if in 2003 there was a draft in place and the sons and daughters of the senators and congressmen who decided to take this country to war, of the neo-cons who plotted to deceive us, and of the privileged class who doesn't have to join a professional army to make a living had to fight and perish in a far away and hostile land, would this war had ever happened? And I wonder if Bush, Cheney and Rumsfeld had served in the armed forces of this country, fought in a war themselves and witnessed the horrors of war, would they even contemplate placing thousands of husbands, wives, sons, daughters, sisters and brothers in harm's way in the battlefield against another sovereign nation, that not in the least threatened the national security of these United States of America.

The Need to Have an External Threat

The Fear of the Other

The whole foundation of neo-con strategy rests on the existence of a constant enemy (external or internal), the danger that this enemy poses, and the fear of what this enemy could do to us. This concept is not really new; it was articulated initially by Machiavelli, recycled by Leo Strauss and perfected by the neo-cons in the Reagan and Bush administrations. It is very ingenious and effective strategy and one that we deemed important to expose and expand on it a bit more. To that end, we have selected Edward Said's concept of *Oriental Other* to help us place it in the proper contemporary context.

Orient Express, Aladdin, Ali Baba and the 40 thieves, Sinbad the Sailor—this is what comes to mind when an Occidental thinks of the Orient. At first impression, the term Orient projects romantic and exotic images of flying carpets, warriors, and sultans in their mythical palaces, but a deeper look into the origin of the term Orient reveals a very different image—one that is a carefully crafted and demeaning, one of something inferior, less civilized and most importantly, different than "our" world. No one—more fairly, almost no one—associates sciences, literature, architecture, philosophy, highly accomplished individuals—such as Ahmed Zewail, Naghib Mahfouz, Harun Al-Rashid, Ibn Rushd—and the Umayyad and Abbasid Dynasties with the Orient. To understand better the meanings of Orient and Occident (West), their origin and the way they have impacted colonization and geopolitical events in the past two centuries and continue to do so till this date, we will venture briefly into the complex and highly thought-provoking concepts of the Occident and the Other of Edward Said, being fully aware that this attempt to condense the 300 plus pages of *Orientalism* in a few pages is indeed a risky business.

Edward Said, in his highly acclaimed classic *Orientalism*, contends that the Orient is almost a European invention (British and French) that includes India and the Bible lands. Moreover, Said asserts that all the West knows about the Orient comes from writings of mostly British and French diplomats, soldiers, businessmen and painters (orientalists) who had the opportunity to travel to and live for a short periods of time in the Orient during the peak of colonialism in the late eighteenth and nineteenth centuries. These orientalists, who very well might had a good knowledge of the particular field of their profession but only a limited and superficial knowledge of the Orient, through their writings and paintings created a stereotypical image of the Orient as the "Other", a homogeneous creature which was diametrically opposite of "Us".

> Orientalism…[is] a created body of theory and practice in which, for many generations, there has been a considerable material investment. Continued investment made Orientalism, as a system of knowledge about the Orient, an accepted grid for filtering through the Orient into Western consciousness.

Said argues that this information about Orient was collected and used by the colonial powers of Britain and France initially and the United States after WWII to justify their imperialistic interests. He draws on Antonio Gramsci's concept of hegemony to support this notion.

> In any society not totalitarian certain cultural forms predominate over others, just as certain ideas are more influential than others; the form of this cultural leadership is what Gramsci has identified as hegemony, an indispensable concept for any understanding of cultural life in the in-

> dustrial West...it can be argued that the major component in European culture is precisely what made that culture hegemonic both in and outside Europe; the idea of European identity as a superior one in comparison with all the non-European peoples and cultures. There is in addition the hegemony of European ideas about the Orient, themselves reiterating European superiority over Oriental backwardness, usually overriding the possibility that a more independent, or more skeptical, thinker might have a different view on the matter.

One of the most important theories that Said presents in *Orientalism* is the distinction between pure and political knowledge and how this distinction affects the information we receive and the knowledge we attain about almost everything. Based on that theory, Said argues that knowledge about Shakespeare, for example, is not political whereas knowledge about contemporary China or the Soviet Union, and one could add in today's world knowledge about the countries that comprise President Bush's "Axis of Evil", is. "One reason for saying that a humanist who writes about Wordsworth, or an editor whose specialty is Keats, is not involved in anything political is that what he does seems to have no direct political effect upon reality in the everyday sense" points out Said.

> ...the determining impingement on most knowledge produced in the contemporary West (and here I speak mainly about the United States) is that it be nonpolitical, that is, scholarly, academic, impartial, above partisan or small-minded doctrinal belief. One can have no quarrel with such an ambition in theory, perhaps, but in practice the reality is much more problematic. No one has ever devised a method for detaching the scholar from the circumstances of life, from the fact of his involvement (conscious or unconscious) with a class, a set of beliefs, a social position, or from the mere activity of being a member of a society. These continue to bear on what he does professionally.

Said continues by asserting that the imperial interests of Britain, France and, of late, the United States trigger their political societies to infuse their civil societies with a sense of political urgency that is aimed at promoting and protecting these imperial interests. " I doubt" Said says "that is controversial to say that an Englishman in India or Egypt in the later nineteenth century took an interest in those countries that was never far from their status in his mind as British colonies. To say this may seem quite different from saying that all academic knowledge about India and Egypt is somehow tinged and impressed with, violated by, the gross political fact—and yet that is what I am saying." Said contends moreover, that an American or a European when come up against the Orient they will act as an American or a European first, and as an individual second. And this reaction is neither casual nor accidental. It happens because of the engrained belief that one belongs to a power with definite interests in the Orient, and one who occupies the part of the earth which has had a very long and malevolent historical involvement in the Orient since the time of Homer.

Edward Said's Orientalism was first published in 1977 shortly after the break out of the Lebanese Civil War in 1975. The book's first page opens with a description from that war that ended in 1990, but "the violence and ugly shedding of human blood continues up to this minute" wrote Said in his May 2004 preface to the same book. It is tragic that as I am writing this section in the fall of 2005, Lebanon is again in the news with the UN report on the appalling assassination of its former Prime Minister Rafik Hariri. *Orientalism*, says Said, is very much tied to the tumultuous dynamics of contemporary history and it is in this context that we have chosen to use it as the introductory piece to this section.

> I emphasize that neither the term Orient nor the concept of the West has any ontological stability; each is made up of human effort, partly affirmation, partly identification of the Other. These supreme fictions lend themselves easily to manipulation and the organization of collective passion has never been more evident than in our time, when the mobilizations of fear, hatred, disgust, and resurgent self-pride and arrogance—much of it having to do with Islam and the Arabs on one side, "we" Westerners on the other—are very large-scale enterprises.

If we examine closely how the "war against terrorism" and the "Iraq War" have been sold to the American people and international community by the Bush administration, we will see rather clearly how the concept of the "Oriental Other" has conveniently and effectively been used by the recent American and British neo-imperialists to exploit the horror of 9/11 for political and corporate gain, and how the war against terrorism has, in fact, become a war for empire building. Once more, Edward Said delivering one of his most powerful diatribes:

> Even with all its terrible failings and its appalling dictator (who was partly created by U.S. policy two decades ago), were Iraq to have been the world's largest exporter of bananas or oranges, surely there would have been no war, no hysteria over mysteriously vanished weapons of mass destruction, no transporting of an enormous army, navy, and air force 7000 miles away to destroy a country scarcely known even to the educated American, all in the name of "freedom." Without a well-organized sense that these people over there were not like "us" and didn't appreciate "our" values—the very core of traditional Orientalist dogma...—there would have been no war.

Creating an external enemy, however, is not limited to the Oriental Other as the Cold War chronicles remind us. A recent reminder of that era was the movie "Good Night, And Good Luck" which was released in the US in October 2005. The movie, which takes place during the early days of broadcast journalism in 1950s America, it chronicled the real-life conflict between the legendary television newsman Edward R. Murrow and Senator Joseph McCarthy and the House Un-American Activities Committee. These were the dark years of McCarthyism at the peak of the Cold War and of an America crippled by the fear that communists infiltrating every aspect of American life—a huge threat to the security of the country and to the American dream. With a desire to report the facts and enlighten the public, Ed Murrow and his staff defied corporate and sponsorship pressures to examine the lies and scare tactics perpetrated by McCarthy during his communist witch-hunts. Murrow and CBS prevailed at the end with McCarthy being discredited and censored by the US Senate in 1954. Murrow was the first and last journalist who decided not to be silenced by the fear of being considered un-American for standing up for civil liberties and the truth. Murrow, in his closing remarks in his historic 9 March 1954 broadcast, said:

> It is no time for men who oppose Senator McCarthy's methods to keep silent. We can deny our heritage and our history, but we cannot escape responsibility for the result.

"Good Night, And Good Luck" is much more than a movie about Ed Murrow and his courageous and legendary battle with Joe McCarthy and those who supported him and appeased him. It is a movie whose clear message resonates today more than it did fifty years ago. There could not be any debate whether McCarthy was an evil man whose acts showed an unmatched malice, but without treating him more leniently than he deserves, one could see that he was as much a victim of the Cold War paranoia that had seeped deep into the American psyche. And what he did was not much more than one misguided and evil man's crusade against the imaginary threats of a faraway enemy. Today, we are again confronted with a similar threat of an imaginary and far away enemy, but this time the perpetrator of fear and deceit is not just a man, but the entire US government led by an evil group of ideologues with a clear and purposeful strategy. And worse yet, there are no Ed Murrows around nowadays, not even by a long stretch. On the contrary, the mass media today have become very obedient and useful tools for the politicians and corporations. And that is a very sad and discouraging situation, indeed.

While McCarthy and his Un-American Activities Committee did not send their victims to the guillotine as Robespierre and the Committee of Public Safety and their Revolutionary Tribunal did in France in 1793-1794, they did terrorize many Americans in the early 1950s. The attacks of 9/11 brought into the forefront a different enemy—one that is different than us, culturally and religiously, and fits well into the Said's model of the Oriental Other--and one that we Occidentals would have no hesitation to declare a war against. While the enemy was different, the techniques used were the same as in the Cold War scare.

But how can we win a war against terrorism? Who is the enemy, and how do we know when we have won? Thus, this is the dilemma in which the Bush administration finds itself with the Iraq War. At first examination, one might conclude that the US made a serious mistake by declaring war on terrorism immediately after 9/11. A closer look, however, reveals a much different picture—a masterful move that was aimed at inducing a sense of primal fear to America. And that strategy has served the neo-cons, the religious right and the Bush administration exceptionally well. The brilliance of the move was to use the words "War on Terror". If we look up the definition of the word terror, we will see that it refers to an intense state of fear, where someone becomes overwhelmed with a sense of immediate danger. Our noble leaders had succeeded to create a very menacing external enemy against which they had the duty to protect the American people, and, for good measure, our principles of freedom and democracy. And they have kept this enemy very much alive and growing. In vintage "external-threat" rhetoric used liberally in his 2003 State of the Union address, our president and commander-in-chief reminded us of this danger as our military was finalizing its attack plans against Iraq.

> Today, the gravest danger in the war on terror, the gravest danger facing America and the world, is outlaw regimes that seek and possess nuclear, chemical, and biological weapons. These regimes could use such weapons for blackmail, terror, and mass murder. They could also give or sell those weapons to terrorist allies, who would use them without the least hesitation.
>
> This threat is new; America's duty is familiar. Throughout the 20th century, small groups of men seized control of great nations, built armies and arsenals, and set out to dominate the weak and intimidate the world. In each case, their ambitions of cruelty and murder had no limit. In each case, the ambitions of Hitlerism, militarism, and communism were defeated by the will of free peoples, by the strength of great alliances, and by the might of the United States of America.
>
> Now, in this century, the ideology of power and domination has appeared again, and seeks to gain the ultimate weapons of terror. Once again, this nation and all our

friends are all that stand between a world at peace, and a world of chaos and constant alarm. Once again, we are called to defend the safety of our people, and the hopes of all mankind. And we accept this responsibility.

1. "Bush's place in the pantheon" David M. Kennedy, Christian Science Monitor, January 20, 2004
2. "Empire Builders: Neo-conservatives and their blueprint for US power. Neo-con 101. The Christian Science Monitor.
3. Brief biography of Walter Lippmann.
4. "The American Mongols" by Hussain Haqqani, Foreign Policy magazine, May/June 2003.
5. "Bush secretly Ordered Iraq War Plan, Book Says" by Calvin Woodward and Siobhan McDonough, AP, 14 April 2004.
6. Ibid.
7. "A Turning Point in the Iraqi Mess" Christian Science Monitor, November 21, 2003.
8. "Iraq Insurgent Force May Number 20,000: Guerrillas Led by Sunnis, Not Foreigners Hoping to Build Islamic State", Jim Krane, AP, 7/9/04.
9. A new Vietnam" by Ahmed Amrawi, Sunday, 10 August 2003.
10. "Q&A: Neo-cons' niche in American history, Christian Science Monitor interview with Walter Russel Mead, Jan. 15, 2004

Knights under the Banner of the Prophet

Liberating the Muslim nation, confronting the enemies of Islam, and launching Jihad against them require a Muslim authority, established on a Muslim land, that raises the banner of Jihad and rallies the Muslims around it. Without achieving this goal our actions will mean nothing more than mere and repeated disturbances that will not lead to the aspired goal, which is the restoration of the caliphate and the dismissal of the invaders from the land of Islam. This goal must remain the basic objective of the Islamic Jihad movement, regardless of the sacrifices and the time involved.

Ayman El Zawahiri

Is Jihad—terrorist activities—launched by the Islamic Fundamentalists against the US, Europe and several Muslim countries a religious duty of every Muslim that is inspired by the Quran and the sayings of Prophet Mohammed? This question has sparked considerable debate both among Muslims and Islamic scholars, on one hand, and Western media, politicians and academics, on the other. Although recent events, even prior to 9/11, point to a violent image of Islam that infuriates moderate Muslims and rallies the Holy Warriors of the West, it is vitally important to examine this issue carefully and separate myth from reality. We shall avoid, however, seeking an answer to this question by using Quranic references and interpretations. There is a vast chasm that separates the diametrically opposite views of Islamic scholars on this subject, and attempting to take a position will lead us to a very steep and slippery slope. Instead, we shall address the realities of Arabic and Muslim actions during the past thirteen centuries. An entire section has been devoted to this subject in the Part One of the book titled "Islamic Empires" and we hope our readers were patient as they followed our journey through one of the most fascinating periods in human history—the early years of Islamic empires, their rise and fall until the collapse of the Ottoman Empire in the beginning of the twentieth century. Only a brief summary of that segment, aimed at properly framing the issues of Jihad and imperial expansionism, is presented below.

Islamic Conquests

The seventh century saw the birth of a new religion and an unprecedented military expansion by the, so far, unknown Arabian tribes. By 642 Persia and Egypt, two of the richest regions in the world guarded by two of the mightiest armies of the time, had been taken over by Muslims. The founder of Islam had been dead for only ten years and already the world's borders had been considerably redrawn, and although these lands would change hands again and again during the next 1300 years, they would remain Muslim till this date. The Islamic tide continued its march to Northern Africa, after pausing for a few years while they launched their first—of many unsuccessful—attacks against the mighty Byzantine capital of Constantinople, then to Iberia where they easily conquered Spain which became one of the flourishing Islamic empires—the Umayyad Dynasty—that lasted for seven hundred years and changed the character of the Iberia peninsula forever.

From Spain the Umayyads advanced towards France in an apparent effort to expand their imperial dominion on the rest of the continent. Their plans had to be postponed for several centuries, however, as the Umayyads suffered a crushing defeat in France at the Battle of Poitiers. In 718 they besieged Constantinople for the second time in forty years and this time because of poor planning and bad weather the Islamic armies were completely annihilated. Despite these setbacks, by the year 743 the Arabic empire was at its glory. In Europe, it was controlling the south of France and the Iberian Peninsula. In the Mediterranean Sea, the Arabs were controlling the Islands of Majorca, Minorca, Efeikia, Corsica, Sardinia, Crete, Rhodes, Cyprus, a part of Sicily and several islands in the Aegean Sea. In Africa, they were controlling the lands from Gibraltar to the Gulf of Suez and in Asia, from Mount Sinai to the hills of Mongolia.

The defeats of Muslims in Poitiers and Constantinople took the wind out of the sails of the soldiers of Mohamed, at least for the time being. The world took a deep breath as it was shown in the battlefields of France and in the straits of Bosporus that the Muslim armies were not invincible. It would be hundreds of years before Islam would pose again a serious threat to Europe and the Byzantine capital. The caliph was facing, however, more serious problems in the heartland of Islam. The Umayyad dynasty had begun fracturing internally. Many of the non-Arab Muslims became increasingly unhappy with the discrimination shown towards them by the Umayyads. The opposition unified under the leadership of the descendants of Mohamed's uncle, Abbas, and after several military conflicts between the two groups it succeeded in overthrowing the Umayyads and bringing to an end an empire that in ninety years had dramatically changed the world map. After the fall of the Umayyad Dynasty, the capital of the Islamic empire moved from Damascus to Baghdad and the Abbasids began their five hundred-year reign.

The early years of the Abbasid dynasty were marked with unfulfilled expectations, on the part of the non-Arab subjects of the empire that were instrumental in securing the overthrow of the Umayyads, and the systematic, almost barbaric, extermination of the Umayyad clan throughout the empire. There were no more military conquests and territorial expansions of Islam of any significance, with the exception of Sicily's surrender in 902, during the Abbasid dynasty, as Islam began a period of looking inwards and focusing on stabilizing its own internal affairs. The territorial gain of Sicily was miniscule when compared with the vast land expansion of the early Arab conquests, but its capture by the Muslims was noteworthy for its strategic significance. Moreover, it would become the last real land addition to the Arab-Muslim caliphates, the disintegration of which had already begun.

In the meantime another power was rising from the East. The Seljuk Turks, who had migrated from the Punjab region in Central Asia, accepted Islam in the tenth century and established themselves in the Transoxamia region under their khan, Seljuk. In 1055 their khan, Tugrol Bay, advanced to Baghdad, occupied the capital and became the de facto ruler of the Abbasid Empire. The caliph had no choice but to recognize Tugrol as sultan (temporal ruler) of Persia and Mesopotamia, and later of Syria. The Arabs were removed from the administration of the Tugrol and the Great Seljuk Sultanate was established. Although the caliph of Baghdad had ceased being the effective temporal ruler of Islam for some time now, the recognition of the Turkish sultan ended officially the reign of the caliphs, who till the fall of the Ottoman Empire in 1924 remained only as the spiritual leaders of Islam.

Soon the Seljuks became the controlling power over Asia. When the Sultan died, his nephew Alp Arslan came to power and the caliph made him the Sultan. Arslan was able to capture Armenia but his main objective was the rival caliphate of the Fatimids in Egypt. The Seljuks had become staunch supporters of the Sunnis and the Fatimids, being Shiites, were both a military target and a religious adversary. Alp Arslan began preparing for a major military campaign against the Fatimids and in the spring of 1071 started his march towards Cairo. Fate, however, took him to a different battlefield near the garrison town of Manzikert in what was destined to become one of the most significant battles in history and one that changed the course and destiny of the Byzantine Empire, and consequently the history of all Balkan nations.

The Byzantine army suffered one of the worst defeats in the long and proud history of the empire. The emperor was captured alive and the once invincible Byzantine army melted away in the Anatolian wilderness. The migration of ghazi tribesmen into Anatolia and Persia continued and, aided by their huge land gains in Anatolia at the expense of the Byzantine Empire, contributed to the creation of a number of independent states under the suzerainty of Baghdad. The strongest and most significant of these states was the sultanate of Rum which was located in Asia Minor and comprised mostly of the territory won from the Byzantines. Although the sultanate of Rum was the longest lived of all Seljuk states, it too was destined to decline, as so many other great states in history had done before it.

The decline of the Seljuks coincided with the rise of another tribal power, the Mongols, whose great conquests culminated during the reign of Genghis Khan or Universal Ruler, as he took the Mongols to China and Crimea. By 1225 he controlled everything between the Caspian Sea and Korea. The Mongols believed that Genghis Khan was immortal and they were destined to rule the world--not unlike the Islamic belief of creating the Dar al-Islam (nation of Islam). It would not be long before these two mighty tribal powers would clash for world dominance.

The Mongols' principal targets were Baghdad and Damascus—the seats of Muslim power at that time outside of Andalusia. Hulagu, the Mongol khan, marched west towards Baghdad and demanded from the last Abbasid caliph the complete surrender of the city, which he refused. What followed was not merely the collapse of once proud city and glorious dynasty, but an event of much greater historical significance to Baghdad and Muslims the effects of which are felt to this day. Hulagu laid siege to the capital which unable to defend itself against a much stronger Mongol invasion force fell in 1258. The caliph and all male members of his family were executed thus officially bringing to an end the Abbasid Caliphate. Baghdad was utterly destroyed and tens of thousands, perhaps one hundred thousand, were massacred in one of history's worst pillages that lasted almost a month.

Berke, Khan of the Golden Horde and Hulagu's cousin, was appalled with the destruction of Baghdad, a famous Islamic city, and the execution of the caliph himself. Although Hulagu was his cousin and a fellow Mongol, the Abbasids were Muslims after all. The resulting animosity between the two leaders led to several wars, the first to pit Mongol armies against each other. Hulagu concerned about Berke's anger over the treatment of the Abbasid caliph and the sacking of Baghdad, decided to head north toward Russia with part of his army and send one of his generals to deal with the Egyptians who were his next target. In 1260, the Mamluks, who were the de facto rulers of Egypt, aided purportedly by the Mongols of the Golden Horde were able to deal Hulagu's Mongols a decisive defeat, the first ever suffered by the Mongols.

The sacking of Baghdad and the defeat of the Mongols by the Mamluks changed the dynamics in the Middle East dramatically. Eventually the Mongols were assimilated into the Islamic Turkish culture of the south, rather than the Christian Russian culture of the north. The young Mamluk sultanate was now the leading power in the region, and it was this power that would lead the final offensive against Europe. Since the collapse of the Abbasid Caliphate, the house of the Caliph moved from Baghdad to Cairo which became the capital of the Caliph. The Mamluks retained control of Egypt until the Ottoman conquest in

1517 when the house of the Caliph moved from Cairo to the new Ottoman capital of Istanbul (Constantinople).

Of all the Ottoman conquests, the military campaigns of Suleiman the Magnificent may be viewed both as a continuation of the Islamic conquests and a response to an aggressively expanding Europe. Like most other non-Europeans, Suleiman fully understood the consequences of European expansion and saw Europe as the principal threat to Islam. After succeeding his father, Suleiman began a series of military conquests into the European heartland that ended with the unsuccessful siege of Vienna in 1529. Moreover, the naval strength of the Ottomans became formidable during the reign of Suleiman with the help and under the leadership of Barbarossa, the most famous of the Barbary pirates, whom Suleiman appointed Grant Admiral of the Ottoman fleet. Until his death in 1544, Barbarossa ravaged the coasts of Mediterranean. The combined naval forces of Spain, Venice and the Pope, however, dealt a crushing defeat to the Ottomans in 1571 in the battle of Lepanto off the Western coast of Greece. This was the first major victory of any European army or navy against the Ottoman Empire and as such it had great psychological importance to both sides.

The general decline of the Ottomans that started with their defeat in Lepanto continued and it halted any significant future conquests. The tide had turned against them and it culminated in the defeat they suffered in the Battle of Vienna in 1683. The Turks retreated into Hungary never again to threaten central Europe. In 1699, the Ottomans signed the Peace of Karlowitz by which they handed over to Austria the provinces of Hungary and Transylvania, leaving only the Balkans under Ottoman control. The age of Ottoman conquests had come to an end and the once mighty empire had started its decline.

What one should take away from this tidal wave of Islamic conquests should be the recognition that there was nothing Holly about them. There were nothing more than bloody acts of land grabbing and unparalleled human and material pillaging just the same as in all other military conquests before and after them.

Nation of Islam vs. Nation of War

Sayyid Qutb shaped the modern revival of Islam and laid the foundation of terrorism by his redefinition of the word Jihad and how it is used today. Jihad as translated from Arabic means holy war, or struggle, strife, fight, or battle. The term originated in the seventh century when Muslims fled from their lands in Arabia fearing for their lives after they had converted to Islam. After they grew in number and power, they waged holy war against the non-Muslims of Arabia until they were able to return back to their lands. These wars or struggles became known as Jihad. The wars carried out by Arabs after the death of Mohamed, however, were anything but holy wars and correctly are referred by Islamic scholars as Islamic conquests or Islamic invasions. These conquests resulted in the expansion of the Islamic lands as the Arabs conquered the northern parts of Arabia, Egypt, North Africa, Spain, and eventually minor Asia and Persia. Recognizing this territorial expansion of Muslim rulers is an important step in recognizing also that the lands the Muslims claim as their own today (including Jerusalem) are nothing more than conquered lands as the result of their territorial expansion. Having territorial ambitions and being victorious in battle does not make Muslims, however, any more oppressive nor more violent than the Persians, Greeks, Romans, Byzantines, Spaniards, Dutch, or Brits who have behaved similarly throughout history. Below is a sample of the vitriolic propaganda that has existed for a long time but which has reached epidemic levels since 9/11.

> Islam is as malignant now as it was 500 years ago. The difference is that then Christians understood it better... Muslims oppress, murder, violate, and destroy non-Muslim peoples. This is incontrovertibly so and such actions are supported by Islamic clergy everywhere. It is important to remember that this violence is religiously embedded within Islam and existed from its origin.

The above quotation is from an article by Arthur M. Hippler, Ph.D. titled "On the Difficulties with Islam" that appeared on catholicculture.org../../../Downloads/www.catholicculture.org

February 7, 2002 and it illustrates the venomous rhetoric that has been poisoning the American perception of Islam and Muslims since 9/11. What makes this article particularly noteworthy is that it is featured in a "Christian" website, and is well written by an academic who has presented, with a few exceptions, accurately the historical and religious background of Islam, and analyzed the reasons of "Why does Islam hate us?" in an excellent manner. In fact, it is the most comprehensive answer of that question I have come across in the past several years. But the article is also full of carefully implanted vitriolic statements against Muslims and Islam and apparently ignores its own assessment of the reasons why Islam hates us. Here is how the article concludes:

> Thus for a complex set of reasons, some of which are political and some of which are historical, but all of which are deeply embedded in their religion and for that reason are very difficult to change, Islam is an enemy of all of us and if it has its way, you and I and our children either will convert to Islam, or we will die. Islam, as now constituted in its popular form, is in fact the enemy of civilization. Our task is to understand this, to recognize that it is difficult to state it openly, and to know that we must strive over the next generation to destroy its terrorist elements, encourage its reasonable ones, and work toward a fundamental change of Islam itself. Admittedly this is a difficult task and will take great determination and there is a real question whether we have the will for it. If we do not, we shall perish.

This type of propaganda is not uncommon and as such it poses a real danger since it sidesteps the real causes of the conflict and throws more fuel to an already ravaging inferno. It also hurl us in the middle of the debate of whether the nature, teachings and practice of Islam are indeed violent and threaten our existence, and, thus, our own survival dictates the destruction of Islam and its followers. But we cannot even attempt to demystify the causes of the allegedly impending "clash of civilizations" without examining the two important concepts in the history of Islamic warfare—the medieval distinction between *Dar el Islam* (the House of Islam) and *Dar el Harb* (the House of war)—and the concept of Jihad. Perhaps there are no other concepts that are as important for the West to clearly and fully understand as these, and ironically these are the concepts that have been more misunderstood, more exploited, and more misinterpreted and misrepresented than anything else.

So what are *Dar el Islam* and *Dar el Harb*? While there are those who trace the origin of these two concepts to Quran and Prophet Mohammed, some of the most credible opinions (Christian Science Monitor, "Morality and War", October 11, 2001) seem to support that around the tenth century Islamic jurists in the Abbasid period defined the concepts of *Dar el Islam* as the realm of Islamic society or nations under Islamic control, and *Dar el Harb* as the territories outside the Islamic state with which there were no treaties and, thus, a state of warfare existed. On the other hand, there are those, as Dr. Hippler whose aim is to demonize Islam, that have argued that aggression and world dominance are embedded in both the teachings and practices of Islam and have led to violent Jihad. History, however, is not on Dr. Hippler's side. Muslims initially were persecuted by the non-Muslims of Arabia and Prophet Mohammed and his followers fled from their lands in Arabia fearing for their lives after they had converted to Islam. Muslims' faith in Islam and their desire to spread it to all corners of the earth may have contributed to the unprecedented and rapid expansion of Islam in the first century of its existence, but trying to read more into these military campaigns is indeed preposterous. To conclude that Muslim territorial ambitions were driven by the teachings of Islam is no different than to conclude that the conquest of the New World and the forced conversion of Native Americans to Christianity by Catholic Spain were inspired by the teachings of Christ!

The Islamic empires that existed in the Middle Ages were not a monolithic entity with the single goal of conquering the infidel lands and converting their peoples into Islam. On the contrary, several rival emirates and, sometimes, rival caliphates existed that competed with each other and with which they were often at war. Moreover, these Islamic empires had to compete with and defend themselves against other mighty contemporary empires as the Byzantine and Persian Empires. They were all vying for vast territorial gains and global dominance. In other words, they were all imperialistic and Islam was neither more nor less imperialistic than the rest of them, and a lot more benevolent in its actions toward those it occupied than the Christians were against Muslims and Jews.

Another argument that the anti-Islamic propagandists have been making is that if Islam were to prevail in the world, all non-Muslims should either convert to Islam or die. Again, history is against them as the following principal example illustrates. Muslims occupied Iberia (Spain) for 700 years until 1492. Although some of those occupied converted to Islam, the majority—Christians and Jews mainly—did not and they were not massacred. On the contrary, the *Dar el Islam* included not only Muslims but also non-Muslims who came under the protection of Pax Islamica. They were protected against internal insecurity and external aggression. However, when Spain defeated the Muslims and re-conquered its land, Jews and Muslims were either expelled or killed. Ironically, the majority of the Jews who fled the persecution of Christian Spain were welcomed in Salonika and Istanbul (Constantinople) by Beyazid II, Sultan of the Ottoman Empire, and there they were allowed to reach high levels of prosperity and achievement. The European Christians, on the other hand, during the sixteenth and seventeenth centuries turned viciously against each other because of religious intolerance. It is highly hypocritical of anyone, especially the Christian Catholics, to stigmatize Islam as an aggressive and violent religion. History proves them wrong.

Islamic Fundamentalists' *Great Game*

So far the debate over the true nature of Islam seems to be between those who consider the religion as the root cause of terrorism and those who reject that notion and proclaim Islam a religion that promotes peace. Neither side has been able or willing to venture out of these deeply drawn lines. It is important, therefore, to distinguish between the teachings and practices of Islam and the teachings and practices of Islamic fundamentalists and terrorists, as they are not one and the same. The mutant strain of Islam that is represented by the terrorists, and with which the West is mostly familiar, is deeply unrepresentative of

Islam's past and not shared by the vast majority of Muslims. But it certainly represents a part of Islam—a radical, fundamentalist part—that simply cannot be ignored or denied. And the seeds of this radical form of Islam were sown more than seven and a half centuries ago; the reason was the sacking of Baghdad by the Mongols. Today, the seeds have given life to many healthy weeds difficult to eradicate; the core reason is the invasion of Baghdad by the US. Who said history does not repeat itself?

It's hard to convince Westerners and non-Muslims, however, that Islam is a religion of peace, when, at least in the last twenty five years, all the actions being done in the name of Islam have been bloody. The borders of Islam are bloody, says Huntington in *Clash of Civilizations* and Abdel Rahman al-Rashed, head of the *Al-Arabiya* TV network, in one of his commentaries said, "Not all Muslims are terrorists, but it is exceptionally painful that almost all terrorists are Muslims. What a pathetic record. What an abominable achievement. Does this tell us anything about ourselves, our societies and our culture?" This is a pretty serious indictment of Muslims, especially when it comes from an Arab-Muslim, and it certainly fuels the anti-Islamic sentiments that have grown considerably in the West and particularly in the US since 9/11. But, at the same time, it is not an unfair statement and as such it begs some further examination.

Five years after the sacking of Baghdad a child was born in Persia to an Islamic scholar. His father escaped to Syria for fear of the Mongols that occupied his land. The child proved to be a brilliant student, followed in the footsteps of his father, was able to complete his studies at age 19, and became a professor of Islamic studies himself. Well versed in Quranic studies and theology the young man started issuing fatwas (religious decrees) without following any of the traditional legal or religious schools. His radical views made him a target of the traditional Orthodox Islamic schools that consequently were able to imprison him. The young rebel, however, would make his imprint in Islamic history not because of his rather heretical interpretations of the Quran, but rather because of his unprecedented declaration of Jihad against another Muslim.

This energetic Islamic activist was Ibn Taymiyya and would become the most prolific Islamic writer of all time, with the exception of Ibn Rushd. Ibn Taymiyya declared that a ruler who fails to strictly enforce the Shariah (Islamic law), including the performance of Jihad, forfeits his right to rule. He became a strong advocate and participant of Jihad against the Crusaders and Mongols who occupied parts of what he considered *Dar al-Islam.* He directed Jihad against rulers he considered as apostates because they did not follow the true faith. Ibn Taymiyya greatly influenced the modern history of Islam as he laid the foundation of terrorism by redefining the word Jihad then and today. He became the conservative voice of Islamic thought in the Middle Ages and his thinking inspired the late eighteenth century Wahhabi school of thought as well as many twentieth century Islamic revivalist movements, including The Islamic Jihad that was responsible for the assassination of the late Egyptian President Anwar Sadat in 1981.

Since the hold of religion on Muslims is very powerful—and very difficult for westerners to comprehend—Islam has been exploited throughout the centuries from Ibn Taymiyya to Osama Bin Laden to justify the actions of radical Muslims against Muslims and non-Muslims alike. Islam, thus, has become the inspiration and Jihad the instrument for the Islamic conquests of yesteryear and today's terrorism. The means, however, that certain radical groups are using against civilians in this struggle are fundamentally against the teachings of Islam. So, what is it that this group of Muslim revivalists wants to accomplish?

Muslim revivalists basically want to proceed from where their civilization ended, as if they are living in a vacuum. There have been several radical Islamic movements in the long history of Islam with the most recent revival taking place shortly after the fall of the Ottoman Empire. It all started with the birth of the Muslim Brotherhood movement in 1928 which began as a religious reform movement. Its purpose was to restore Islamic law as a counterweight to the secular ideas of the West that were seen as the reason for the decay of the Islamic societies at that time. Western culture was seen as equivalent to *Jahiliyyah* (a term referring to the paganism and barbarism that existed before Islam). Led by its founder, Hassan El Banna, the group announced its ideological program in 1935 with the Quran being the law of God and Prophet Mohamed God's last messenger, and it required all Muslims to lead the same path of the Prophet in their everyday life. It was every Muslim's duty to revive the glory of Islam in the form of the *Dar el Islam*—Nation of Islam—that unites all the Muslim countries. Muslims would have to teach their children the true faith and for this reason, the Muslim Brotherhood had to form an Islamic government that implements the rules and laws of Islam.

The Muslim Brotherhood adopted the slogan "Islam is the solution." This saying consists of three concepts that have guided the general direction of the group over the years since it was founded. The first concept deals with the proper Islamic teaching and behavior of the Muslims. The second concept deals with the reestablishment of the Islamic nation on the basis of the Islamic Caliphate system that ruled and united the Muslims for several centuries until it was abolished in 1924, with the collapse of the Ottoman Empire. The third concept is the implementation of the Islamic law—Shariah—which becomes the ruling law of the country and which is done gradually. The reason for this was that the ruling of a totally "corrupt" society after overthrowing its secular government would have been a great risk. Society should be prepared for such a change and preparation would be achieved through methodic plans of spreading this "pure" form of Islam throughout Mohammedom. The Muslim Brotherhood claims that they do not demand the rule for themselves. They welcome any leader who would accept and implement Shariah and they pledge their support to that end. Until this day, 81 years after the formation of the Muslim Brotherhood, the successors of the ideology of Hassan El Banna still believe they can achieve the reform he was seeking.

Hassan El Banna's Muslim Brotherhood was a peaceful and non-political movement, at least initially, concerned with religious and moral issues. By the time the state of Israel was founded on lands that were Palestinian, the movement had become more political without losing, however, its religious character. When Egyptian President Camel Abdel Nasser refused to grant them the Islamic state they were expecting, they became violent and they attempted to, unsuccessfully, assassinate him.

What followed is best described in Zawahiri's own words in his book *Knights under the Prophet's Banner*.

> The Jihad movement in Egypt began its current march against the government in the mid-1960s when the Nasserite regime began its famous campaign against the Muslim Brotherhood (MB) group in 1965. Some 17,000 members of the MB were put in prison and Sayyid Qutb (one of the most prominent MB thinkers) and two of his comrades were executed. The authorities thought that they had eradicated the Islamic movement in Egypt once and for all. But God willed that those events were the spark that ignited the Jihad movement in Egypt against the government.

Sayyid Qutb became the intellectual grandfather of radical Islamists and was followed by Zawahiri and Bin Laden. He revived the notion of *Jahiliyyah* after an educational trip to the US in 1949. "As he traveled across the country, Qutb had become increasingly disenchanted with America. The very things that, on the surface, made the country look prosperous and happy, Qutb saw as signs of an inner corruption and decay. [1] To Qutb, "American society was not going forwards; it was taking people backwards. They were becoming isolated beings, driven by primitive animal forces. Such creatures, Qutb believed, could corrode the very bonds that held society together. And he became determined to prevent this culture of selfish individualism taking over his own country."

After Sayyid Qutb, Islamic fundamentalism mutated again to a more radical and resistant strain as Zawahiri and El Farag took center stage. They became the "neo-fundamentalists" of the Islamic movement. While El Banna's and Qutb's ideologies were driven by a strict, although twisted, interpretation of Islam, Zawahiri and his followers became more political activists and revolutionaries than religious zealots. They would use the religious and moral teachings of Ibn Taymiyya, El Banna, and Qutb for political gain and regime change within their own society. But this was a risky preposition both from a military and religious point of view. Militarily, they could not take on the powerful Egyptian regime, and Islam forbids Muslims to take arms against other Muslims unless they are declared apostates, and then it is the duty of every Muslim to kill them. Even then, there is a grave religious risk, as falsely accusing one as apostate is even a greater sin in Islam. By the end of 1980, Zawahiri with a number of Sayyid Qutb's followers formed Islamic Jihad, an organization which may be considered as the militant wing of MB from which Zawahiri was distancing himself.

Zawahiri, although a wealthy and well educated aristocrat from Cairo, was an angry young man with militant tendencies. He interpreted Qutb's ideologies to mean that the corruption that he warned against "included the Western system of democracy. Democracy, Zawahiri believed, encouraged politicians to set themselves up as the source of all authority, and by doing this, they were rejecting the higher authority of the Quran. This meant that they were no longer true Muslims, and so they, and those who supported them, could legitimately be killed. The terror this created, he said, would shock the masses into seeing the truth behind the corrupt façade of democracy." [2] So what had started as an "external" enemy—the threat of Western materialism, corruption and modernity—was now defined as an "internal" enemy, as well, in the faces of the rulers who allowed and even supported the corrupt policies of the West—reading America.

Islamic Jihad succeeded to assassinate President Sadat in 1981. Thousands of members of Muslim Brotherhood and Islamic Jihad were imprisoned, Abdel Salam Farag was executed and Zawahiri was imprisoned on a lesser charge and tortured. But what horrified Zawahiri more than torture was the realization that Sadat's assassination did not shock the people, not in the manner that he hoped, or mobilized them against their government. They remained relatively apathetic and under the spell of American ideology. So, while in prison he started looking for new strategies and a new "base" of operation, as the Egyptian geography and topography had proved less than optimal for the guerilla warfare they had started employing. Being a medical doctor, Zawahiri received an invitation in 1980 to go to Afghanistan to provide medical assistance to the thousands of wounded mujahedeen. He recalls this opportunity as a predestined event, as it took him to place that he found ideal for establishing a secure base for Jihadist action in Egypt, especially during the term of President Sadat. After serving his prison term, Zawahiri returned to Afghanistan with the clear goal to establish "The Base"—Al Qaeda, Arabic for base—for the Islamic Jihad in the mountainous terrain of Hindu Kush. There, he would meet a young Saudi millionaire-turned Mujahed named Osama Bin Laden.

> A Jihadist movement needs an arena that would act like an incubator where its seeds would grow and where it can acquire practical experience in combat, politics, and organizational matters… Furthermore, the Afghan arena, especially after the Russians withdrew, became a practical example of Jihad against the renegade rulers who allied themselves with the foreign enemies of Islam… A further significant point was that the Jihad battles in Afghanistan destroyed the myth of a [superpower] in the minds of the Muslim mujahedeen young men. The USSR, a superpower with the largest land army in the world, was destroyed and the remnants of its troops fled Afghanistan before the eyes of the Muslim youths and as a result of their actions. That Jihad was a training course of the utmost importance to prepare Muslim mujahedeen to wage their awaited battle against the superpower that has sole dominance over the globe, namely, the United States… The seriousness of the presence of Muslim, particularly Arab, young men in the arena of Jihad in Afghanistan consisted of turning the Afghan cause from a local, regional issue into a global Islamic issue in which the entire [Islamic] nation can participate.

One can see the genius of Zawahiri coming through, as he recollects, in the *Knights under the Prophet's Banner*, the strategic significance of Al Qaeda—the Afghan arena—as a training ground, the victory of Mujahedeen as the symbolic rebirth of Islamic might, and the globalization of the Jihadist movement as the necessary means for achieving the ultimate goal—the establishing of the *Dar el Islam* (Nation of Islam).

> The regime [Egyptian government] had no choice but to turn the battle against the Mujahed Islamic movement into an international battle, particularly when the United States became convinced that the regime could not survive alone in the face of this fundamentalist campaign. It was

> also convinced that this spirit of Jihad would most likely turn things upside down in the region and force the United States out of it. This would be followed by the earth-shattering event, which the west trembles at the mere thought of it, which is the establishment of an Islamic caliphate in Egypt. If God wills it, such a state in Egypt, with all its weight in the heart of the Islamic world, could lead the Islamic world in a Jihad against the West. It could also rally the world [of] Muslims around it. Then history would make a new turn, God willing, in the opposite direction against the empire of the United States and the world's Jewish government.

The above statements from Zawahiri's own pen reveal in linear logic the real goal of Islamic Jihad which is to force the United States—only remaining superpower—to remove its protection of Egypt, which would allow the establishment of an Islamic caliphate in Egypt and the eventual destruction of the United States and the state of Israel. Whether Zawahiri's true intentions were to launch a global Jihad against the crusaders of the America and the Zionists are certainly questionable. This kind of rhetoric, though, sells very well in Arab Street nowadays and indeed greatly helps the neo-fundamentalists' recruitment and fund-raising efforts. What is certain, however, is that his main goal was to overthrow the Egyptian government and establish an Islamic republic in Egypt, similar to the ones in Iran and Taliban-Afghanistan. We can guess who the caliph of this new Islamic nation might have been.

In the 1800s Afghanistan became the arena upon which two imperialistic powers—the British Empire and Czarist Russia—competed for land and power and greatly intervened in the internal affairs of the country. It was part of the "Great Game" played by the European "great" powers at the expense of weak and poor nations struggling to survive in the Middle East and the Indian sub-continent. In an ironic twist of history, two hundred years later two Islamic leaders—Zawahiri and Bin Laden—were planning their own version of the "Great Game" at the expense again of weak and poor nations. Following is another excerpt from Zawahiri's book that takes us once more inside the mind of this brilliant chess grand master.

In the 1990s the US confronted a new phenomenon that represented a fierce challenge to its dominance and arrogance, namely the emergence of two Islamic states that liberated their territory under the slogan of Jihad in the cause of God against the infidel occupiers of Muslim lands. Those two countries were Afghanistan and Chechnya. The matter did not stop there, for these two emerging countries became the safe haven and destination of emigrants and mujahedeen from various parts of the world or what the US describes as Arab Afghans, fundamentalists, terrorists, and so on.

The Chechen mujahedeen's defiance of Russia, their insistence on liberating the Muslim Caucasus, and their determination to complete the Jihad begun by Imam Shamil [Basayev] against the Czarist Russia posed a great threat to the influence and interests of the United States, for the Caucasus floats on a sea of petroleum whose estimated reserves are no less than the oil reserves in the Arabian Gulf, especially as the US influence in Central Asia is increasing and taking the form of military bases, spy stations, oil companies, and joint maneuvers.

The liberation of the Caucasus would constitute a hotbed of Jihad (or fundamentalism as the US describes it) and that region would become the shelter for thousands of Muslim mujahedeen from various parts of the Islamic world, particularly Arab parts. This poses a direct threat to the United States represented by the growing support for the Jihadist movement everywhere in the Islamic world. If the Chechens and other Caucasian mujahedeen reach the shores of the oil-rich Caspian Sea, the only thing that would separate them from Afghanistan will be the neutral state of Turkmenistan. This will form a mujahed Islamic belt to the south of Russia that will be connected in the east to Pakistan, which is brimming with mujahedeen movements in Kashmir. The belt will be linked to the south with Iran and Turkey that are sympathetic to the Muslims of Central Asia. This will break the cordon that is struck around the Muslim Caucasus and allow it to communicate with the Islamic world in general, but particularly with the mujahedeen movement.

Furthermore, the liberation of the Muslim Caucasus will lead to the fragmentation of the Russian Federation and will help escalate the Jihad movements that already ex-

> ist in the republics of Uzbekistan and Tajikistan, whose governments get Russian backing against those Jihadist movements. The fragmentation of the Russian federation on the rock of the fundamentalist movement and at the hands of the Muslims of the Caucasus and Central Asia will topple a basic ally of the United States in its battle against the Islamic Jihadist reawakening.

In addition to destabilizing Russia and establishing strongholds in the Caucasus region and Afghanistan, Zawahiri wants to move the battle to the enemy, meaning the homelands of the US, its allies and Russia. While they have not been able to strike American targets on American soil since 9/11, they have been successful to hit Russia, on a number of occasions, and Madrid. Below, Zawahiri states the rationale why the struggle for the establishment of the Muslim state cannot be launched as a regional struggle:

> It is clear from the above that the Jewish-Crusade alliance, led by the United States, will not allow any Muslim force to reach power in any of the Islamic countries. It will mobilize all its power to hit it and remove it from power. Toward that end, it will open a battlefront against it that includes the entire world. It will impose sanctions on whoever helps it, if it does not declare war against them altogether. Therefore, to adjust to this new reality we must prepare ourselves for a battle that is not confined to a single region, one that includes the apostate domestic enemy and the Jewish-Crusade external enemy.

Considering that Zawahiri wrote the book sometime in late 2001 and at least one and a half years before the US-led invasion against Iraq, his comments proved to be very accurate. And as the anti-Syrian and anti-Iran rhetoric is heating up and the war drums are beating once more, the desire to learn more and listen better to what Zawahiri and Bin Laden are saying about our past policies and deeds is growing by the day.

While Zawahiri's true goals seem to be very clear—entering Cairo triumphantly as the new Saladin after he has crushed the Crusaders of Washington and the Zionists of Tel Aviv—and are mainly politically motivated, Bin Laden's true motives and targets, although very religious in character, are less clear but equally threatening. In August 1996, Bin Laden issued a "Declaration of War against the Americans Occupying the Land of the Two Holy Places" in a very lengthy document full of historical references and religious justifications—vintage Bin Laden communiqué.

> The latest and the greatest of these aggressions, incurred by the Muslims since the death of the Prophet (ALLAH'S BLESSING AND SALUTATIONS ON HIM) is the occupation of the land of the two Holy Places—the foundation of the house of Islam, the place of the revelation, the source of the message and the place of the noble Ka'ba, the Qiblah of all Muslims—by the armies of the American Crusaders and their allies.

Bin Laden begins his declaration of war against America with what he considers the gravest damage and insult to the Islamic faith since the death of the Prophet and he urges the faithful to:

> follow what have been decided by the people of knowledge, as was said by Ibn Taymiyya (Allah's mercy upon him): "People of Islam should join forces and support each other to get rid of the main Kufr [presence of infidels] who is controlling the countries of the Islamic world, even to bear the lesser damage [in order] to get rid of the major one, that is the great Kufr". If there is more than one duty to be carried out, then the most important one should receive priority. Clearly after Belief there is no more important duty than pushing the American enemy out of the holy land. No other priority, except Belief, could be considered before it. The people of knowledge, Ibn Taymiyya, stated: "to fight in defense of religion and Belief is a collective duty; there is no other duty, after Belief, than fighting the enemy who is corrupting the life and the religion". There are no preconditions for this duty and the enemy should be fought with one's best abilities.

Bin Laden goes on next to indict the Saudi royals in a carefully enumerated and detailed statement that includes "the harassment, persecution, and incarceration of reformers; media censorship and manipulation; mismanagement and corruption in the financial and economic sectors; perversion of the Islamic legal system and temporal laws; use of foreign mercenaries; material support to the enemies of Islam; and failure to defend the country. The Muslim [printed] media paid close attention to this detailed dissertation and reminded its readers that bin Laden was calling for armed resistance only because the al-Sauds had rejected all efforts at peaceful reform." [3]

From that point on, Bin Laden begins a systematic and consistent campaign of written, video and audio communications—that continues to this date—stating the grievances of Muslims against the Crusaders and Zionists, and warning the West, especially the United States, of grave consequences if their grievances are not addressed. And to back up his words with deeds, after each major communication, an attack followed. So, with these words and deeds, Bin Laden succeeded to change the nature of discourse in the Islamic world and moved it slowly toward increased militancy and violence against the United States and in many cases against their own rulers.[4]

While Egypt with Hassan El Banna, Sayyid Qutb, Abdel Salam El Farag, and Ayman Zawahiri provided the ideological doctrine, paramilitary strategy and tactics, and a cadre of talented and devoted leaders, Saudi Arabia with its Wahhabism and "petro-dollars" provided the infrastructure (mosques and schools) and substantial funding to create and sustain the Islamic Fundamentalism movement throughout the Muslim world. Both of these factors have proved essential in the emergence and success of the current global terrorist movement. It is ironic that these two countries, Saudi Arabia and Egypt, who gave birth to and nurtured this form of neo-fundamentalism, are the primary targets of Islamic militants.

1. "The Power of Nightmares" Part I: a BBC documentary aired October 20, 2004
2. Ibid
3. Michael Scheuer, *Through our Enemies Eyes*, , pp 11-12
4. Ibid, p 11

Mirror Images

If you don't like the face you see in the mirror, don't break the mirror; change the face.

In Parts One and Two of the book we chronicled the holy wars of Christendom from Constantine the Great in the fourth century to George W. Bush in the twenty first century, and the holy wars of Islam from Prophet Mohamed and Ibn Taymiyya to Sayyid Qutb and Osama Bin Laden. Also we presented the growing presence of politics in religion and the disturbing influence of religion in politics on both sides of the religious divide. Unbridled influence brought power, and unleashed intolerance, adventurism and aggression against the Other. And the more each side accused the other as the Evil one and attacked it, the more it mirrored its alleged opposite. In this section, which we chose to call Mirror Images—for reasons that, hopefully, will become apparent soon—we will unveil the main characters on both sides of these Theo-political wars, place them across each other and expose their seemingly complex, but, in close examination, rather simple and transparent games. We invite the reader to accompany us in the revealing and very sobering final leg of our journey where we present the startling similarities of the ideology, motives, goals and tactics, and deadly effectiveness of both groups in attracting and retaining their naïve and frightened followers.

Throughout the book, we have used various terms, i.e. fundamentalists—Christian and Islamic—neo-fundamentalists, evangelicals, etc. to label the religious and political extremists both in this country and the Muslim world. Fundamentalists seems to be the most appropriate term to use in reference to the religious extremists which, in the original meaning of the word, describes *those who were clinging to the fundamental elements of their faith and resist the pressures and influences of the modern world*—to paraphrase President Jimmy Carter. While this definition describes a benign aspect of religion, below are the prevailing characteristics of the "more intense" form of fundamentalism as President Carter has very accurately portrayed in his book, *Our Endangered Values*:

- ...fundamentalist movements are led by authoritarian males who consider themselves superior to others and...have an overwhelming commitment to subjugate women and to dominate their fellow believers.
- Although fundamentalists usually believe that the past is better than the present, they retain certain self-beneficial aspects of both their historic religious beliefs and of the modern world.
- Fundamentalists draw clear distinctions between themselves, as true believers, and others, convinced that they are right and that anyone who contradicts them is ignorant and possibly evil.
- Fundamentalists are militant in fighting against any challenge to their beliefs. They are often angry and sometimes resort to verbal or even physical abuse against those who interfere with the implementation of their agenda.
- Fundamentalists tend to make their self-definition increasingly narrow and restricted, to isolate themselves, to demagogue emotional issues, and to view change, cooperation, negotiation, and other efforts to resolve differences as signs of weakness.

Alarmingly, it is this "intense" form of fundamentalism that has spread outside the boundaries of religion, seized all branches of the United States government since 2000, and significantly contributed to the creation of a deep and disturbing division among Americans. While the term that is almost universally accepted to describe the ideology of both Christian and Muslim religious extremists—often militant in character—is fundamentalism, there is less agreement on the term that describes political right wing extremists. In the West neo-conservatives or neo-cons is the most common description used for this political form of extremists who are mainly American political theorists whose goal is unrivaled global economic and military superiority. Regardless of the terms one uses to describe this form of political and religious extremism, fundamentalism is the common element that best characterizes them and unifies them against all others, and it applies to both the West and the Muslim world.

Christianism and Islamism

Christianity and Islam are two of the oldest major monotheistic religions in the world. Between them they claim half of the world's population as their followers. And although the long histories of both religions have been marred by tumultuous and, often, bloody conflicts, both are peaceful in their core teachings, and have largely served their followers and mankind well. One can say without hesitation that the world is a better one today than it would have been without Christianity and Islam, or other religions of similar core values and teachings. In practice, however, the leaders and followers of Christianity and Islam have not been immune from human weaknesses and, more frequently than not, have found themselves succumbing to the temptations that power and self-righteousness pose. During the last five decades alone, the world has witnessed repeated attempts by the radical wings of both religions to impose their moral agenda on all of us. When their religious rhetoric aimed at the evils of modernity and spiced with a healthy dose of eternal damnation for the sinners fails to achieve its desired goal, they resort to political activism. And when reform through political means advances either too slowly or fails, the weapons of choice are deceit and violence.

Previously in this book, we introduced the term Christianism as the mirror image of the term Islamism. While in recent years we have come to view Islamists as Muslim Fundamentalists who, although they claim to be followers of Islam, in reality are nothing more than terrorists who use violence to achieve their political ambitions, we do not realize that there are also Christianists who behave exactly the same way as the Islamists. But before the Congregation of the Holy Office convenes an Inquisition on these writings, allow me to compare Islamists and Christianists and let you be the judge as to whether any similarities exist between these two. I would, also, ask the theologians and academics on both sides of the aisle to be forgiving for any unintentional misuse of some terms. It would be prudent to remind everyone that we are not presenting a scholarly diatribe here; we are exploring the misuse of religion and faith for political and economic gain in terms that hopefully the average layman will understand.

The first and foremost fundamental similarity between Islamists and Christianists is that both believe in the infallibility of their holy books—Quran and Bible respectively—the literal interpretation of which dictates every aspect of their spiritual and secular lives. Even though this subject alone deserves volumes—to some extent has been addressed in other sections of the book—we will not pursue it any farther here. It suffices to say that this fundamental belief is the cornerstone of all other tenets held by these two religious factions and the root cause of many problems facing Muslims and Christians alike.

The second similarity is religious intolerance. There are numerous religions in the world today with huge doctrinal differences that manage to coexist and have done so for thousands of years—not implying that this coexistence has always been harmonious. Even the mainstream Christians and Muslims are tolerant of each other and have shown that they can coexist largely peacefully, and sometimes better than they have been able to accept their own sectarian differences. The Islamic wars against Christian Europe from the eighth to the seventeenth century, as shown in previous sections, there were more about territorial gains and imperial expansion and less about religious domination. Similarly the European Crusades were driven by creed, rivalries and, of course, geopolitical control and not aimed solely at liberating the Holy Lands. The religious zealots of Christianity and Islam, though, are totally incapable or unwilling to tolerate the beliefs and religious practices of anyone else than their own. Anyone and everyone outside their sectarian domain is an apostate or heretic and should be eliminated. Contemporary Christianists are a bit more subtle in their practices, while Islamists tend to be cruder—and less hypocritical—than their Christian counterparts.

The third similarity is that both Islamists and Christianists believe that it is their divine and "neglected" duty to impose their brand of moral values on the rest of society by any means including abhorrent violent acts. History is replete of such examples that tragically continue even as I am writing this section. Achieving this, however, requires control of the government which becomes accountable to no one, and the eventual removal of any existing checks and balances. In the US, the Christianists have scored successes during the Reagan and especially the Bush II years in controlling the White House and the Capitol Hill, and are aiming at controlling the courts as well. Their goal has been to pass legislation in support of their repressive moral agenda. In Mohammedom, Islamists have succeeded to have Shariah—Islamic law—as their constitution in Saudi Arabia and Iran, and in Afghanistan during the Taliban. With any luck, they can succeed in Iraq, Egypt, Syria, Turkey and Pakistan as well. The tactics that both groups have been using on their way to various versions of theocracy and domination have been "wedge" issues such as abortion and gay marriage in Christendom and "unifying" issues such as the Palestinian struggle and Iraq War, which have been extremely effective in galvanizing the faithful in Mohammedom.

We hope we have shown that the belief in the divine origin and thus infallibility of the Quran and Bible has led to wholesale religious intolerance and the inevitable goal of establishing a state religion—theocracy—that is totally and exclusively based on Quranic or Biblical doctrine. We intend to show in the following sections, in a mirror image motif, exactly what the masters of both fundamentalist groups have been and are doing to achieve this goal. And, most importantly, how terrifyingly similar these two factions are as they try to convince their followers of their own self-righteousness and the evil nature of the others. Moreover, we plan to stimulate and challenge the rational nature of the reader to recognize where this slippery slope of religious fanaticism might lead, and provide a challenge to all for a rational response to this potential calamity.

What is appalling more than the striking similarities between the Christianists and Islamists, though, is the ultimate hypocrisy of pseudo-morality that characterizes both of them and the absence of true Christian or Islamic values. It seems the high priests and their followers have forgotten that poverty, truth, and the ethics of war are moral values as well, which have been lost, if there were ever present, in the midst of the violence and destruction caused by their abhorrent acts. In the West, there is a fanatical obsession among the public, politicians, religious leaders, and especially the media with preserving the life of fetuses and persons in vegetative state, while no one blinks even an eye at the deaths of millions of helpless persons perishing in Africa, Asia, South America, and even in this country from poverty, AIDS, war, and curable diseases. The Muslim world does not fare any better in this regard. Political and religious leaders and "freedom fighters" care more about advancing their personal or ideological interests, at the expense of the public at large, than providing much needed assistance for the needy and sick. Largely any assistance provided is either superficial or is used as an effective recruiting tool. One wonders how different the Muslim world might have been if the money spent to fund the madrassas in Pakistan and throughout the Muslim world that spewed generations of either assassins or, at best, hypnotized and angry mujahedeen were spent for real and non-religious education, and economic development.

Unholy Alliances

The Republican Party does not have the head count to elect a president without the support of the religious conservatives.
The Rev. Jerry Falwell, September 2004

There is a battle for the public arena and the front line lobbyists are crucial to advancing the agenda of conservative, evangelical Christian America.
National Association of Evangelicals

Let me be very clear about this. We need to vote our values, our beliefs and our convictions. We shouldn't be endorsing candidates. We should be looking for candidates who endorse us.
Richard Land, Southern Baptist Convention

A headline of the March 16, 2005 edition of the Christian Science Monitor read "For Evangelicals, a bid to 'reclaim America'" as a staff writer of the Monitor began her description of a national conference of more than 900 Evangelicals who gathered in Coral Ridge, Florida with the aim to "reclaim America for Christ". According to Rev. D. James Kennedy, Coral Ridge pastor:

> As the vice-regents of God, we are to bring His truth and His will to bear on every sphere of our world and our society. We are to exercise *godly dominion* [emphasis added] and influence over our neighborhoods, our schools, our government...our entertainment media, our news media, our scientific endeavors—in short, over every aspect and institution of human society.

This goal of reclaiming America for Christ, somehow, had a very ominous ring to it. It reminded me of the *Reconquista* of Spain from the Muslims that culminated with the complete expulsion from Spain of all Jews in 1492 and of all Muslims half a century later. Now, there was nothing wrong for the Spaniards wanting to reclaim their land from an invader and occupier and become free again to practice their religion without any persecution. But to expel hundreds of thousands of Spanish citizens on the basis of their religion was wrong and immoral. We are not concerned here, though, with the wrongful decisions of the

Spanish monarchs in the fifteenth century. We are concerned about religious intolerance and the steadily growing force of the Evangelicals who unflinchingly are determined to impose their "godly dominion" on the rest of us whether we like it or not.

Starting with Ronald Reagan in 1980, the Evangelicals have been mobilizing their faithful in support of ultra conservative Republicans in national and local elections with remarkable success. Jerry Falwell's Moral Majority was born in 1979 with the aim to create a voting block of Christian conservatives who would vote and do exactly as Jerry and his cohorts would instruct them. "I have a Divine Mandate to go into the halls of Congress and fight for laws that will save America" declared Jerry Falwell. At the same time, many neo-cons had become political advisers to Ronald Reagan's campaign and as they became more involved, they were able to forge an alliance with the Jerry Falwell's Evangelical foot soldiers that was aimed at the moral regeneration of America.

> The conservative movement, up to that point, was essentially an intellectual movement. It had some very powerful thinkers, but it didn't have many troops. And as Stalin said of the Pope, "where are his divisions?" Well, we didn't have many divisions. When these folks became active, all of a sudden the conservative movement had lots of divisions. We were able to move literally millions of people. And this is something that we had literally no ability to do prior to that time. Paul Weyrich, Religious activist, Republican Party, speaking on BBC's documentary.

The Moral Majority, which was neither moral nor a majority, helped elect Ronald Reagan and did rather well during most of the decade of the eighties as it cleverly wrapped itself with the American flag, and greatly influenced a large segment of God-fearing and patriotic, but naïve ordinary Americans, whose rekindled fear of communism united them once more. But the Moral Majority lost much of its appeal and influence after the collapse of the Soviet Union in the late eighties. The organization was dissolved and Jerry Falwell went back to Liberty University and Thomas Rowe Church. And then came the George Bush senior and Bill Clinton years, and the neo-cons and Christianists found out they were becoming obsolete. Moreover, they realized they could not defeat the liberals and reform America on the basis of their ideology alone. The neo-con strategy, inspired by Leo Strauss' theories, became the political use of religion once again. Together with their old allies—the religious right—they began a campaign to bring morality and religion back into the mainstream of conservative politics.

While the Evangelicals believed in their misguided divine agenda, for the neo-cons religion was a myth. Strauss had taught them that myths were necessary to give ordinary people meaning and purpose.

> For the neo-conservatives, religion is an instrument of promoting morality. Religion becomes what Plato called a "noble lie". It is a myth which is told to the majority of the society by the philosophical elite in order to ensure social order. Michael Lind, Journalist and former neo-conservative in BBC documentary.

Before we get carried away with the Evangelicals, though, we should provide equal opportunity to their mirror image counterparts—the Wahhabites of Saudi Arabia. Our readers should be reminded here that fourteen of the nineteen hijackers involved in the 9/11 attack against the United States were Saudi nationals. Moreover, it was this attack and the background of the hijackers that caught our attention, angered us and eventually propelled us into this enlightening and alarming journey of seeking truth and knowledge. Now, let us return to the Wahhabites. We have covered sufficiently, I believe, the Wahhabism movement and Ibn Taymiyya—whose writings inspired Mohammed ibn Abd al-Wahhab, founder of Wahhabism—in *Stage One: Revival of Islamic Fundamentalism* section earlier in this book and thus we will focus herein mainly on the similarities between the Evangelicals and the Wahhabites.

Wahhabites who are Muslim Sunnis are members of a movement and do not represent a different sect of Islam, as Evangelicals represent a movement and are not a different sect of Christianity. Wahhabi theology advocates a very strict and puritanical stance in matters of faith and religious practice. It is fair to say that Wahhabites are the strictest of all Muslims. They believe in the strict and literal interpretation of the Quran and they see their role as a movement to restore Islam back to the right path. It is worth noting that Wahhabism emerged in late eighteenth century, a period that marks the beginning of the latest major expansion of Western colonialism, which coincided with a wave of uprisings by many Eastern European nations aimed at regaining national independence from the Ottomans. These events seriously challenged Islamic geopolitical dominance, and the notion that Muslims were destined to be the true inheritors of the earth. To many Muslims, this Western dominance and Muslim growing weakness were the result of unfaithfulness, and a sign that Muslims were drifting away from the true path of Islam.

This realization became a convincing and powerful argument that encouraged Muslims to struggle (*Jihad*)—militant approach—to bring the nation (*Ummah*) back to the path of "true" Islam. This new call to arms in the eighteenth century marks, for the first time, a global emergence of Islamic revivalist movement that remains till today the foundation and driving force of all Islamic fundamentalism. The most noteworthy eighteenth century revivalist movement was the Wahhabi movement in Arabia. As Wahhabism spread through Arabia, an alliance of mutual benefits that merged religious zeal with military might was forged between Mohamed ibn Saud, a local tribal chief and ancestor of the current Saudi Royal Family, and Abd al-Wahhab. The former sought unification and control of the Arabian tribes and needed Wahhabism to legitimize his Jihad; the latter desired the spread of Wahhabism through the Muslim world and he needed money and power.

This unholy alliance of politics and religion formed the foundation of the dynasty of the House of Saud, and the enormous wealth that came from late twentieth century oil revenues made it possible for Saudi Arabia to export the puritanical and often militant brand of Wahhabism to all corners of Muslim world and the West. This policy has infuriated moderate Muslim leaders, and recently has caused a great deal of embarrassment to the Saudi Royal Family, because of the growing accusations by the West that Saudis not only tolerate terrorism, but they incubate it and fund it as well. Moreover, in a boomerang effect, the Saudi Royal Family has become one of the main and well-identified targets of Al Qaeda and Islamic fundamentalists who have spawned from the Wahhabism ideology and have been supported by Saudi petrodollars. The evil genie was out of the lamp and Muslims and Christians alike continue till the present time to pay a heavy price for this indiscretion of the Saudi royals.

Back in America, the national elections of 2000 and, especially of, 2004 were another prime example of a Faustian pact between the Evangelicals and George W. Bush. So, in essence what we ended up having in the American government was a crypto-theocracy where our "divinely guided" secular leaders used Christianism to secure the support of the Christianists to solidify their political and military control in pursue of their domestic and international goals. And the Christianists were happy to oblige in exchange for the right to exercise their "divine duty" to impose their brand of "moral values" on the rest of society. Former President Carter describes an event in his book *Our Endangered Values* that illustrates the expectations of the religious right from one who they believed was one of "their own". The time was November of 1979 and while Jimmy Carter was serving as President of the US, he was sort of reprimanded by the then newly elected president of the Southern Baptist Convention who had come to the Oval Office to visit him. President Carter recalls the event. "As he and his wife were leaving, he said, 'We are praying, Mr. President, that you will abandon secular humanism as your religion.' This was a shock to me. I considered myself to be a loyal and traditional Baptist, and had no idea what he meant." Later on and after talking to his pastor, President Carter surmised that "[he] had made some presidential decisions that might be at odds with political positions espoused by leaders of the newly formed Moral Majority and other groups of conservative Christians." And that, of course, was not acceptable by the Christianists who were growing bolder and more impatient. The following year President Carter lost to Ronald Reagan in his bid for re-election. The Moral Majority and the neo-cons had found their new champion.

Although the days that the institutions of church sought world dominance might be over in today's world, the religious zealots continue to exist and their blind obsession to impose their biblical beliefs on everyone is stronger now than it has been since the formation of this Republic. The government, on the other hand, uses religion and "moral values" as a tactic to secure its own power and control over people, and most importantly, to distract the public's attention from real issues—poverty, environmental degradation, unequal distribution of wealth, neo-colonial pursuits, Iraq War—just as the European monarchs used witch hunting and religious differences during the religious wars of Europe in the sixteenth through the seventeenth centuries to distract from the real problems of their time.

There is another alliance—an odd one at best—that exists between a large number of Evangelicals, who we will refer to as Christian Zionists, and Israel and one that deserves particular attention. In his recent book, President Carter said that "One of the most bizarre admixtures of religion and government is the strong influence of some Christian fundamentalists on the U.S. policy in the Middle East." According to a June 8, 2003, article titled "Zion's Christian Soldiers" CBS News reported that American Christian Zionists brag that "they are now a more important source of support for Israel than American Jews or the traditional Jewish lobby." Rev. Jerry Falwell is quoted in the same article as saying "There are 70 million of us. And if there is one thing that brings us together quickly it's whenever we begin to detect our government becoming a little anti-Israel…There is nothing that would bring the wrath of the Christian public in this country down on this government like abandoning or opposing Israel in a critical matter."

Considering that Jews have been persecuted by the Christians repeatedly during the past two thousand years, one has to wonder where the love and support for Israel by the Evangelicals has come from. For the answer to the question, President Carter refers us to the series of novels called *Left Behind.*

> Their religious premise is based on a careful selection of Bible verses…and describes the scenario for the end of world. When the Messiah returns, true believers will be lifted into heaven, where, with God, they will observe the torture of most other humans who are left behind…There are literally millions of my fellow Baptists and others who believe every word of this vision, based on self-exaltation

> of the chosen few along with the condemnation and abandonment, during a period of 'tribulation', of family members, friends, and neighbors who have not been chosen for salvation.
>
> It is the injection of these beliefs into America's governmental policies that is a cause for concern. These believers are convinced that they have a personal responsibility to hasten this coming of the 'rapture' in order to fulfill biblical prophesy. Their agenda calls for a war in the Middle East against Islam (Iraq?) and the taking of the entire Holy Land by the Jews (occupation of the West Bank?), with the total expulsion of all Christians and other gentiles. This is to be followed by infidels (Antichrists) conquering the area, and a final triumph of the Messiah. At this time of rapture, all Jews will either be converted to Christianity or be burned.

Ed McAteer, one of the founders of the Moral Majority and one that many consider as the Godfather of the Christian Right is quoted in the CBS News article as saying "The Bible does not contain the word of God. Listen to me closely. The Bible is the word of God." He believes that the current situation with the Iraq war, the Iran crisis, and the Israeli-Palestinian conflict is the beginning of the final battle. "I believe that we are seeing prophesy unfold so rapidly and dramatically and wonderfully and, without exaggerating, makes me breathless." But not everybody is breathless from excitement. Some may be breathless but for other reasons. "The Jews die or convert. As a Jew, I can't feel comfortable with the affections of somebody who looks forward to that scenario," says Gershom Gorenberg, author of the *End of Days, a book about Christian Evangelicals.* "God save us from these people" says another Jew, Yossi Alfer, former Mossad agent and former Director of the American Jewish Committee. "...they are leading us into a scenario of out and out disaster."

But not all Israelis feel that way about the Evangelical Christians as Alfer does, especially some Israeli leaders who "have utilized this assistance [from the Christian Right] while conveniently ignoring the predicted final plight of all Jews" according to President Carter. What frightens Alfer is that he hears much of Jerry Falwell's and Ed McAteer's world view reflected in the words of the George W. Bush administration. And "it's not good for the Jews, says Alfer. "We have to get God out of this conflict if we're going to have any chance to survive as a healthy, secure Jewish state." President Carter also gives a stern warning about this ungodly alliance between the American Government and the Christian Zionist soldiers. This warning by President Carter had the effect of a major 'wake-up call" on me. I had read many articles and books with theories about the "eschatological" visions of many religious fanatics—American Evangelicals, Iranian Shiites—and their obsession to hasten the coming of Armageddon and dismissed most of them as nonsense and harmless. When I read President Carter's book, though, it had a profound effect on me. Here it was a former president of the United States of America and most importantly a devout, born-again, traditional Baptist and Evangelical Christian himself sounding an alarm about the incestuous relationship between our government and these wackos. It was time to pay attention and heed his warnings.

We could go on for the rest of the book with examples of these totally unholy alliances between rulers of state and religious leaders on both sides—Christians and Muslims—and the catastrophic results they had had on humanity, but instead we will bring this section to a closure by focusing on a pertinent issue that, if left to continue on its current trajectory unimpeded, the potential fallout from its landfall will be unimaginable.

It has been rather obvious in recent history where alliances between secular rulers and religion can lead—Saudi Arabia, Iran, Afghanistan. What has not been very visible though, as it has been moving undetected under the radar, is the steady increase of the power of conservative governments, aided by religious extremists, not only in the West—United States, Canada, Germany, France, Greece, Austria, Italy, Australia—but in Arab Muslim countries as well—Iran, Palestine, Egypt, Turkey—in the past six years. Moreover, the way the Christian West and Muslim East regard each other—putting aside all the pseudo-niceties of the West towards Muslims—has steadily deteriorated. We are moving dangerously closer towards a clash—not of civilizations—but of religions. While Christian Europe and Islam have confronted each other since the seventh century, America has become the newest player in this game of mouse and cat. Another very important difference that exists between the present and the past is that this newcomer comes with a fanaticism and an arsenal of lethal weapons that the world has never known before, and a cowboy trigger-happy attitude that should be bone chilling to the coolest of gun slingers.

The world went through a similarly dreadful situation during the Cold War era. There are two major differences, however, between the Cold War of yesteryear and the current Holy Wars. First, the Cold War was largely political in nature with minor religious undertones—Russians were Christians, after all, even though the communists were atheists. The Soviets, thus, did not fit the description of the Oriental Other. Second, the Soviets were a potent adversary militarily and, thus, the West was content to merely contain them. We have seen the same reaction lately towards the North Koreans by the US. Moreover, the Islamic fundamentalists' power and influence which had been dwindling after the withdrawal of the Soviets from Afghanistan has been rekindled largely thanks to the worsening plight of Palestinians and, of course, because of the invasion of Iraq by the "Mongol Crusaders."

Manipulators of Nationalism and Religious Faith

Mark my word, if and when these preachers get control of the [Republican] party, and they're sure trying to do so, it's going to be a terrible damn problem. Frankly, these people frighten me. Politics and government demand compromise. Put these Christians believe they are acting in the name of God, so they can't and won't compromise. I know, I've tried to deal with them.

Barry Goldwater
US Senator and Republican presidential nominee, 1964

It is not often that some of the best writings about controversial and divisive issues of national interest come from the most unlikely sources. So I was very surprised when I heard Pat Buchanan take on Bush and his neo-con cabal during an appearance in Larry King sometime in the fall of 2004 prior to the presidential election, while he was promoting his new book, *Where the Right Went Wrong*. Over the past twenty years or so, I had developed a rather negative opinion of Pat Buchanan, mostly because of his views on women's and minorities' rights, Reaganomics, religion, and a host of other domestic issues. I always found him to stand diametrically opposite of everything I believed in and supported. This time, though, it was as I was listening to another person—he looked like Pat Buchanan, but what was coming out of his mouth was quite different than anything I had heard before. I felt a little nauseous as I realized that, not only did I not find what he was saying objectionable, I was actually agreeing with him! Buchanan was particularly harsh on Bush for fundamentally shifting American policy from one of containment to one of preemptive war. This is what Buchanan said about Bush's war rhetoric and actions in his book:

> Let it be said: This is utopianism. This is democratic imperialism. This will bleed, bankrupt, and isolate this republic. This overthrows the wisdom of the Founding Fathers about what America should be all about…Americans now assert a right to intervene anywhere to impose democracy.
>
> But George W. Bush did not bring these ideas with him from Crawford, Texas. Before he took his oath, he had probably rarely read or heard such democratic rhetoric before. Who put these ideas in his head? Who put these

words in his mouth? Who got us into this hellish mess in Mesopotamia?

The answer is the neo-cons—the hijackers of American foreign policy, as Buchanan calls them—with the support of the Christian Zionists. On the top of the list stands Paul Wolfowitz, a Leo Strauss disciple, Deputy Secretary of Defense in the first term of George W. Bush and, according to many insiders, obsessed with the removal of Saddam and the main architect of the Iraq War II. Richard Perle, Douglas Feith, Scooter Libby and Dave Wurmser were the other most influential neo-cons with key positions in the White House or Department of Defense. Feith and Wurmser were the ring leaders of a pro-Likud cabal with strong ties to former Israeli Prime Minister Benjamin Netanyahu. All of them had been strong advocates of regime change in Iraq more than a decade prior to the Iraq invasion. Moreover, they supported a realignment of the entire Middle East in favor of Israel as described in "A Clean Break: A New Strategy for securing the Realm", a paper authored by Wurmser under the auspices of the cabal. It is worth noting here that Wurmser was placed in charge of the predecessor of the Special Plans, the Counter-Terrorism Evaluation Group, whose purpose was to gather intelligence on weapons of mass destruction, terrorism and their possible connection to Iraq. This is like tasking the fox to design the fence for the chicken coop!

While Wolfowitz was the leading intellect of the post-September 11 policy, Cheney and Rumsfeld were bureaucratic heavyweights, Cold War veterans and the other two members of the Axis of War, as Senator Edward Kennedy calls them. Both were appointed by previous Republican administrations in Cabinet posts, served in the US Congress and had a rather dark vision of international affairs which, however, they kept for the most part to themselves. Moreover, both had an illustrious and profitable past involvement in the corporate world—Rumsfeld in pharmaceuticals and Cheney in oil—and, most importantly, they believed in American military and economic global superiority. "Before 2000, George W. Bush seemed *a tabula rasa,* a blank slate on foreign policy" says Pat Buchanan. So when the neo-cons were brought into the world of the vastly inexperienced but shrewd new president, they must have been salivating at the prospects of his indoctrination. "The first time I met Bush 43, I knew he was different. Two things became clear. One, he didn't know very much. The other was he had confidence to ask questions that revealed he didn't know very much" said Richard Perle of his first meeting with Bush. And "Thus began the tutoring of George W. Bush" writes Pat Buchanan. The other two persons that Bush brought into his administration were Condoleezza Rice and Colin Powel—the former to become arguably the closest and most trusted advisor to the president, the latter to become the window dressing of America's foreign policy and the perpetual loyal soldier.

In September of 2002 and while the US government was pretending it was going through the diplomatic channels to avoid a military confrontation with Saddam, somewhere in the Pentagon a new unit called the Office of Special Plans was formed with the goal of planning for a post-invasion Iraq. There are several interesting things about this office that are worth relaying to our readers. The person that was brought to head this office was Douglas Feith who up to that point was the Pentagon's undersecretary for policy. "Feith's [prior] political activities and writings were largely devoted to bolstering the hard-line policies of the Likud Party" writes George Packer in *The Assassins' Gate*. Feith, a relatively unknown ideologue whom General Franks has been quoted as calling "the fucking stupidest guy on the face of the earth," with virtually no practical experience in planning, or reconstruction, was recommended for this crucial position on postwar Iraq by none other than his friend and former boss Richard Perle. And the man brought in to direct the operations of the Office of Special Plans was Abram Shulsky, another former Perle aide and housemate of Paul Wolfowitz in Chicago and Cornell. So, one is compelled to ask, why was the Pentagon responsible for reconstruction and nation building instead of the State Department? Why was an inexperienced, Likud party card-carrying member placed in charge of a group tasked with planning and organizing the postwar activities in Iraq?

Things get a lot more interesting. In 1999, Abram Shulsky wrote an essay called "Leo Strauss and the World of Intelligence" in which "Shulsky believed that the writings of his old professor Leo Strauss could be useful antidotes to the narrow-mindedness of the American intelligence community" writes George Packer. Strauss, drawing heavily from classical Greek masters like Plato and Thucydides, theorized that tyrannies cannot be understood in the image of democracies, as tyrants rely on deception. Packer quotes Shulsky saying: "Strauss's view certainly alerts one to the possibility that political life may be closely linked to deception...Indeed, it suggests that deception is the norm in political life, and the hope, to say nothing of the expectation, of establishing a politics that can dispense with it is the exception." George Packer continues with the following passage that I consider being the most insightful analysis in his entire book.

> It isn't such a long step from this insight to the creation of an office that conceals its work behind a deliberately obscure name like 'Special Plans'. There's mirror-imaging of a different kind going on here—not to mistake of seeing your enemy as a reflection of yourself, but the mistake of seeing your enemy as he sees himself until you begin to reflect him. 'When you look into an abyss,' wrote Nietzsche, the bête noire of the Straussians, 'the abyss also looks into you.'

Leo Strauss as a political theoretician considered the classical philosophers—Socrates, Plato, Aristotle, Xenophon—to be wiser than modern thinkers mainly because they had grasped the permanent and necessary inequalities of human condition. One of these inequalities was that only a small group of elite should pursue a philosophic life, as the truths that the philosophical elite may discover were not fit for public consumption. Also, the lesson from Socrates' life and trial is that philosophy is a threat to society and truth is hazardous to philosophers. As a result, classical philosophers and their medieval followers thought in one way—esoterically—and communicated with the masses in code. Recently, Dan Brown's *The Da Vinci Code* has electrified audiences around the world and become a best seller. The book is largely based on this assumption that great thinkers, such as Leonardo Da Vinci, by using metaphors and codes have communicated one message for the elite and another one to the general population. For Strauss, the art of concealment, secrecy and deceit was among the greatest legacies of the classical thinkers. Today, he should be very pleased that his legacy not only is being practiced in the Bush White House by his elite disciples, but it has reached such new highs which arguably Strauss never dreamed of.

At about the same time that Leo Strauss was sowing the seeds of political manipulation at the University of Chicago, another ideologue named Sayyid Qutb was resurrecting Islamic fundamentalism in Egypt. Both men were destined to have profound influence on their followers who in turn would impact global geopolitical events with a magnitude and intensity not seen since the decade leading to WW II. The followers of both used fear as the weapon of choice to control their victims and in a twist of irony each of them would create in the other the image of ultimate external enemy—the essential ingredient of their formula of destruction. The main difference between Strauss and Qutb is in the form of manipulation each of them used—the former used nationalism with the support of religion, and the latter used religious faith with the support of Pan-Arab nationalism.

The Princes of Darkness

Bellum omnium contra omnes.
Thomas Hobbes

> "We really need to get the president-elect briefed up on some things," Cheney said, adding that he wanted a serious "discussion about Iraq and different options." The president-elect should not be given the routine, canned, round-the-world tour normally given incoming presidents. Topic A should be Iraq. Cheney had been secretary of defense during George H. W. Bush's presidency, which included the 1991 Gulf War, and he harbored a deep sense of unfinished business about Iraq.

This is how Bob Woodward describes in his book *Plan of Attack* a message that Cheney sent to William Cohen, outgoing secretary of defense in the Clinton administration, in early January 2001. In another passage, Woodward describes what Powell thought of Cheney.

> Powell thought that Cheney had the fever. The vice president and Wolfowitz kept looking for the connection between Saddam and 9/11. It was a separate little government that was out there—Wolfowitz, Libby, Feith and Feith's "Gestapo office," as Powell privately called it. He saw in Cheney a sad transformation. The cool operator from the first Gulf War would not let go. Cheney now had an unhealthy fixation. Nearly every conversation or reference came back to al Qaeda and trying to nail the connection with Iraq. He would often have an obscure piece of intelligence. Powell thought that Cheney took intelligence and converted uncertainty and ambiguity into fact. It was the worst charge that Powell could make about the vice president. But there it was.

From these two examples, a dark, obsessive and enigmatic personality begins to emerge. And with it, a myriad of questions about the motives and agenda that drive the person who is a heartbeat away from being the president of the most powerful nation on the planet. "The administration's great mystery was

Cheney. With the possible exception of Rumsfeld, no one had a darker, more Hobbesian vision of international affairs." When I read this in George Packard's book *The Assassins' Gate*, I was instantly curious to find out what Hobbesian meant. It was one of these detours I got accustomed taking during this journey I had decided to undertake, what now seems to be, eons ago. It had become one of the most rewarding aspects of the research as I always look for opportunities to expand the field of my knowledge. And I never know what I would find inside these mystifying structures—standing at the end of my detours—as I open the front gate and peek in. This time my detour led me from Dick Cheney to Thomas Hobbes and Leviathan, Robert Kagan and Of Paradise and Power, the Project for the New American Century (PNAC), and back to Dick Cheney. And what I learned was both enlightening and frightening, but not surprising at all. Another piece of the puzzle fit perfectly on the board of the ever becoming clearer mirror image.

Let us begin then with the definition of Hobbism and how this might relate back to Dick Chenney and George W. Bush and the state of perpetual war in which we find ourselves entangled.

Mirriam-Webster Online defines Hobbism as follows:

Main Entry: **Hobbism**

Pronunciation: ˈhä-ˌbi-zəm

Function: *noun*

Date: 1691

: the philosophical system of Thomas Hobbes; especially : the Hobbesian theory that people have a fundamental right to self-preservation and to pursue selfish aims but will relinquish these rights to an absolute monarch in the interest of common safety and happiness.

This definition led me to Thomas Hobbes, British political philosopher of the 17th century and his trade mark book *Leviathan*, titled after the biblical Leviathan. Hobbes theorized that the state of nature (or God's original creation) is one of war. This polemic state of nature is exemplified by the famous motto *Bellum omnium contra omnes*—the war of all against all—and in this state man's condition is defined as misery, or to be true to the quotation: *The life of man, solitary, poor, nasty, brutish, and short.*

Hobbes, moreover, argues for the creation of a sovereign who has absolute power and eventually solves the problem of the state of nature. He conceived absolute monarchy as a lesser evil than chaos and civil war, which are more or less identified with the state of nature. In other words, the natural state of humans is one of perpetual anarchy and war of all against all, and the only counterbalance to this chaos is the existence of a Leviathan power with absolute authority and the necessary powers to control these anarchistic and primitive tendencies of society. Hobbes also argues that people in the interest of common safety will give up their fundamental right to self-preservation and the pursuit of individual aims to an autocrat—or, euphemistically, to a sovereign. The idea here is that the sovereign should keep his hands off his subjects as long as any man does no harm to any other. The problem with this idea is, however, that since there is no power above the sovereign, there is nothing to prevent the sovereign breaking this or any other rule.

Saddam Hussein was an unfinished business to Dick Cheney, Don Rumsfeld and Paul Wolfowitz. Cheney's sense of unfinished business in Iraq, however, was more about oil and less about Hobbesian ideology in the pre 9/11 world. "But September 11 confirmed Cheney in his essential instinct about the nature of the world. His speeches after the terror attacks conveyed almost a sense of relief that here finally was a global enemy on the scale of communism" says Packard in the *Assassin's Gate.* Although the Office of the Vice President (OVP) is shrouded in secrecy, one can learn a great deal about what its focus is by examining who Cheney's top aides are or have been since the Bush administration took control of the White House in 2001. Several of Cheney's lieutenants, as well as the vice president himself, were early supporters of the neo-con manifesto PNAC—Robert Kagan co-authored it—which advocated for a return to a "Reaganite policy of military strength and moral clarity." Moreover, Robert Kagan is married to Victoria Nuland, U.S. ambassador to NATO, who has served as national security adviser in the OVP. Kagan is also the author of *Of Paradise and Power* and of the Policy Review *Power and Weakness.* In both of these landmark writings, Kagan's Hobbesian ideology becomes very clear with the emphasis of the writings on power not morality or democracy.

"My bet from day one—I hope I am wrong—has been that the dominant element of this administration was going to be the neo-realists, Cheney and Rumsfeld, who no more are committed to nation building than this table is committed to go home with me in my back pocket" said senator Joe Biden to George Packard in December 2003. So why did George W. Bush place Rumsfeld—the least interested top level official in Iraq's future—in charge of the postwar in Iraq.? The most probable answer to this question is that President Bush did exactly what Cheney advised him to do, and Cheney knew that Rumsfeld would entrust the planning and administration of the postwar effort in the hands and minds of top aides who had impeccable neo-con credentials and were not the least committed to bringing freedom and democracy to Iraq. To Cheney and company the invasion and occupation of Iraq was not—and still isn't—a matter of ideology. They realized that to maintain power they needed a perpetual enemy. What many consider the failures of postwar Iraq were very probably all calculated failures to ensure our presence in the Middle East—control of the oil, security for the Israelis, and keeping the Chinese at bay—keep the terrorist threat alive—indeed Al Qaeda is present now and operating in Iraq thanks to the invasion—and best of all, have their friends and supporters make a lot of war-money. Cheney throughout this tragedy has not lost sight for a second of the economic gains that war brings to the defense and oil industries—Halliburton's stock has more than tripled since the Iraq invasion.

It is time again to give equal time to the Islamists as there is another dark prince in their midst. His name is Ayman Zawahiri and he is perhaps the most influential, and yet less known to most people, member of Al Qaeda. He is an Egyptian surgeon who has been called the true mastermind behind the vast network of terrorists. As former head of the Egyptian Jihad, he has a long history of terror-related crimes. Zawahiri was greatly influenced by Ibn Taymiyya's and Sayyid Qutb's ideologies. Zawahiri is driven by this warped ideology of Islamism that sees violence as the means to achieving its goal of resurrecting the glory of Islamic empires of yesteryears. Some consider him to be the mastermind of the September 11 assaults on the WTC and the Pentagon.

Many Arab and western analysts agree that Zawahiri's influence in reshaping Bin Laden's thinking and ideology is very profound. Zawahiri was able to convert him from a supporter of the Afghan's Jihad against the Soviets into a strong believer and exporter of the Jihad ideology and making him more violent and anti-West, especially anti-American. Arab analysts have described Zawahiri that to Bin Laden, he is what the brain is to the body. It was Zawahiri who convinced Bin Laden to establish Al Qaeda in 1988, thereby providing "The Base" for training, supplies and operations of militants from Egypt and elsewhere. Moreover, counter terrorism and Islamic militant experts regard Zawahiri to be more intelligent and more dangerous than Bin Laden. To Islamic fundamentalists, he is seen as the main ideological driving force behind Al Qaeda. Bin Laden could be characterized as an Islamic fundamentalist—Wahhabist—and a Mujahed before he met Zawahiri in Afghanistan and became a militant Islamist. In all fairness, it was the US military presence in Arabia during and after the first Gulf War as much as Zawahiri's influence that politicized Bin Laden. Zawahiri has been exploiting Bin Laden's soft spoken manners and strong Islamic fundamentalism credentials to reach and recruit the faithful against the infidel threat.

It would be fairly accurate to compare what Zawahiri is to Bin Laden with what Cheney is to Bush in terms of the personalities of the men, their goals, motives, strategies and tactics. Bush, as Bin Laden, is a champion of the religious fundamentalists and nationalists. He makes biblical references in all his major speeches as Bin Laden does with the Quran. Cheney, on the other hand, rarely speaks directly to the American people. He is the champion of the war and oil industries and the neo-cons and the Bush administration's point man to these groups. Similarly, Zawahiri is the champion and spokesperson of the Islamic polity and Islamic militants as his book *Knights under the Banner of the Prophet* demonstrates. These different but complementing personalities have forged much needed partnerships in their not so Holy wars against the other.

PART THREE

THE END OF THE JOURNEY

Arab rage and American hubris: The fuel to global terrorism

To win the war against terrorism, the United States must overcome the burden of history.

Husain Haqqani,
Visiting scholar at the Carnegie Endowment for International Peace

Why they Hate us

"Why do they hate us?" Perhaps this is the most frequently asked question throughout America since 9/11. It has been the headline in countless newspaper and magazine articles and the subject of numerous TV programs and even larger number of books. Also, it was one of the core questions that motivated us to begin our journey seeking answers to what causes and sustains terrorism. Unfortunately, however, it has also been the question that has provided a golden opportunity to all of those who have sought to promote their agenda by providing answers that justify their dubious actions. "They hate our freedoms" said President George W. Bush in his address to a joint session of Congress and the American people on September 20, 2002. "[They hate] our freedom of religion, our freedom of speech, our freedom to vote and assemble and disagree with each other." This is the reason they hate us, said the President of the world's lone superpower. It was that simple. And by saying so, the president began a campaign of deceit that the neo-cons have long waited for and hoped for. It would define his presidency and become the original theme of his administration's justification for the war against "terrorism".

But the answer to the question, "Why do they hate us?" cannot be communicated in one sound bite, and more importantly, it requires courage, honesty and moral conviction that transcends politics. John L. Esposito in an article titled "History Lessons" said:

> The most serious risk to the future is the continued failure to adequately address the root causes of global terrorism and of anti-Americanism. Although the Bush administration quite correctly talked about a three-pronged strategy (military, economic and public diplomacy), the tendency has been to reduce public diplomacy to a public relations campaign rather than a serious re-examination of American foreign policy and a more multilateral approach.

The fact is that it is not our freedom, or democracy that the Arabs hate and the rest of the world strongly resents. It is our foreign policy and our government's almost juvenile justification for our neo-imperialistic actions that although may be convincing to more than half of the American public, the rest of the world is not buying. Esposito is being polite or diplomatic by characterizing the carefully crafted and methodically implemented propaganda of the Bush administration as a public relations campaign. After their initial successes with their Cold War propaganda under Reagan, the Washington neo-cons went out of style with their limited influence under George Bush I, and eight years of relative obscurity under Bill Clinton brought them to a comatose and near-death state. Then September 11 came, and

Osama Bin Laden, Al Qaeda and Islamic Terrorism became the vital support systems that the neo-cons desperately needed. Their dual goals—American hegemony projected globally through military might, and the sanctity of American-Israeli pact—were back in style. America declared war against terrorism and against any country or entity that harbors terrorism and the whole world, including Muslims, were on our side for a while. But terrorism was not the main neo-con target. It was merely a peripheral issue and a God-sent opportunity that had to be exploited. Neo-imperial interests and oil were the motives, and the US-Israeli interests that had somehow diverged after the end of the cold war, converged against with biblical force against a perpetual adversary for the latter, and a convenient scape-goat for the former.

Should the US, however, have had merely deceived the American public and our allies by expanding her war against terrorism to old neo-con targets—Iraq, Iran, Syria—and been able to crush the enemy as the Soviet Union had done with Hungary and Czechoslovakia, the neo-cons would have won a major battle and the world would have quickly forgotten another American indiscretion. But this was not to be the fate of this war. While the Bush administration had correctly assessed the reaction of Europe—impotent to stand up against the American military and economic superiority, Europeans not only they did not prevent the occupation of Iraq, several of them joined the US in a "coalition of the willing" as Bush often referred to it—it hugely miscalculated the Arab rage and resolve. As the events of 9/11 breathed life into the dying neo-cons, the war against "terrorism"—as fought by the Bush administration— they similarly provided vital life support to the real terrorists instead of weak ening them.

In Part One, "The Evil Image of Terrorism", we traced the historical and causal roots of the resurrection and sustainability of Islamic militancy and we shall not repeat them here. Instead, we shall summarize them and conclude with a few valuable history lessons for President W. Bush and his court of wise men.

In a nut shell, the cardinal cause of the Arab-Muslim rage against Americans can be summarized, in the words of John Esposito, in the following manner:

> In many parts of the Muslim world the war against global terrorism has come to be viewed as a war against Islam and Muslims. The image of America has become that of a neo-imperial power that has sought to redraw the map of the Middle East and the Muslim world, influenced by an unholy alliance of neo-conservatives and the militant Christian right, in an attempt to implement a new American century. US policies have alienated many friends and longtime allies in Europe and the Arab world and fed anti-Americanism within and outside the Muslim world.

"The animosity to Israel and America in the hearts of Islamists is genuine and indivisible." It is an animosity that has provided the Al Qaeda and the epic of Jihad in Afghanistan with a continuous flow of "Arab-Afghans" says Ayman Zawahiri in his book *Knights under the Prophet's Banner.*

The Palestinian Struggle

The Palestinian struggle against the Israeli occupation of their land, although not the root cause of terrorism, is certainly the primary source of fuel that sustains the combustion of terrorism. This ancient conflict between these two adversaries, that resurfaced with the creation of the state of Israel in 1949, the annexation of most of the Palestinian land by Israel and the unwillingness of both sides to resolve it, is the most serious threat to world peace and stability. On one hand, the West created the Middle East mess after World War I and now is unwilling to fix it. Muslims, on the other hand, have exploited the conflict and have made it their war cry to rouse the faithful against the infidels of the West and their own apostates. The Palestinian-Israeli conflict is where the use of deceit, fear, and political and religious manipulation are conjoined with power, wealth, and global control. And ironically and tragically it is a core issue that the West, under Israel's very effective intimidation and threat of accusation—anyone who dares to even address it is anti-Semitic—and America's blind loyalty to Israel, has and continues to ignore it as if it does not exist, or does not matter. Has anyone listened to what the Palestinians have been saying for the past fifty five years?

> Here, then, is another complex irony: how the classic victims of years of anti-Semitic persecution and the Holocaust have in their new nation become the victimizers of another people, who have become, therefore, the victims of the victims. That so many Israeli and Western intellectuals, Jewish and non-Jewish alike, have not faced this dilemma courageously and directly is, I believe, a trahison des clercs of massive proportions, especially in that their silence, indifference, or pleas of ignorance and non-involvement perpetuate the sufferings of a people who have not deserved such a long agony.
>
> Edward W. Said

To most Arabs, Israel, as a Jewish state, is a bone stuck in their throat which they have a very difficult time either swallowing, or coughing out. Even if all Arabs were able to accept the existence of Israel, as few have, to them Israel is an oppressor of Arab rights and one of the worst violators of human rights, in general. And what infuriates the Arabs most is that while the US protests human rights violations in Egypt and constantly criticizes Saudi Arabia for its treatment of women, she remains dreadfully silent about the treatment of Palestinians by the Israelis. In its September 30, 2001 editorial "Roots of Terrorism", the *San Francisco Chronicle* very eloquently echoed this Arab sentiment:

> And then there is Israel. For half a century, the United States has steadfastly championed this tiny nation that emerged from the jaws of the Nazi holocaust. But American support of Israel's occupation of Palestinian territory, as well as its expanding settlements, has intensified Arab and Islamic sympathy for the Palestinian cause. Nearly every night, Arabs and Muslims watch televised broadcasts of Israeli helicopters, missiles and bullets killing Palestinian civilians. These weapons, they protest, are purchased with the annual $3 billion aid provided by the United States.
>
> ...terrorism cannot be tolerated or excused in any way. The United States must identify and eliminate the terrorist network behind the Sept. 11 attacks. Still, understanding

> the historical sources of Arabic and Islamic resentment may help us address the poverty and human misery that fuels fanaticism and acts of desperation.

The Palestinian struggle is important for the world and especially America to understand not only because it is the root cause of Anti-Americanism and the most sustainable fuel to global terrorism, but because it is also a just cause of a nation that has lost its identity and land. "No other movement in history has had so difficult an opponent: a people recognized as the classical victim of history. And no other liberation or independent movement in the post-war period has had so unreliable, and at times murderous, set of natural allies, so volatile an environment, so grudging a super-power interlocutor in the U.S., and so absent a super-power ally" said Edward Said in his book *The Question of Palestine.*

Balfour Renewed

The Middle East that existed in the early years of the twentieth century was very different than the one that even the oldest of us have known. Iraq, Syria, Jordan, Saudi Arabia, and Israel did not exist then as countries. David Fromkin in the introduction to his book *A Peace to End All Peace*, described the 1914-22 period as follows:

> It was an era in which Middle Eastern countries and frontiers were fabricated in Europe. Iraq and what we now call Jordan, for example were British inventions, lines drawn on an empty map by British politicians after World War; while the boundaries of Saudi Arabia, Kuwait, and Iraq were established by a British civil servant in 1922, and the frontiers between Moslems and Christians were drawn by France in Syria-Lebanon and by Russia on the borders of Armenia and Soviet Azerbaijan.
>
> The European powers at that time believed they could change Moslem Asia in the very fundamentals of its political existence, and in their attempt to do so, introduced an artificial state system into the Middle East that has made it into a region of countries that have not become nations even today.

There is no doubt that the Christian West and Islam have never understood each other well and that this is one of the reasons that led to the ill-conceived creation of the Middle East and continues to plague the relations of these two very different worlds to this day. While the major players in the Middle Eastern Settlement were Churchill and Kitchener, and to a lesser extent Woodrow Wilson and Lloyd George, there were others who, although of much less stature and position, left their imprints on the final settlement of the Middle East. Among them were Mark Sykes of Britain and George Picot of France, authors of the Sykes-Picot Agreement signed in 1916 by Britain, France and Russia which divided the Middle East into zones of permanent colonial influence; and British Foreign Secretary Arthur Balfour who issued the controversial Balfour Declaration in 1917 promising Britain's commitment and support for a Jewish home in Palestine. Eighty years later, history is repeating itself and we have again what the Arabs call the New Balfour Declaration of 2004. This time the honor goes not to Great Britain but to Washington.

On April 14, 2004 President George W. Bush endorsed Prime Minister Ariel Sharon's Disengagement Plan and, moreover, he agreed to allow Israel to retain most of the "illegal" settlements in the West Bank, accepted a temporary security fence between Israelis and Palestinians, and denied the Palestinian "right of return" to Israel. In doing so, the President of the United States signaled a major shift in US foreign policy by openly and blatantly aligning the US with Israel on the Israeli-Palestinian conflict, and cemented the widely-held view of Arabs that George Bush's America is no longer the honest broker she once was in the Middle East. But not all news was bad with Bush's endorsement of Sharon's plan. The Israelis and Sharon could not believe their good fortune with George W. whose standing at the polls climbed after his meeting with Sharon.

Calling Sharon's Disengagement Plan "bold and courageous", President Bush said "in light of new realities on the ground," namely the settlements built in violation of at least four UN security Council resolutions, it is "unrealistic" to expect Israel to withdraw all settlements from the West Bank lands it seized in 1967, or to accept the return of millions of Palestinian refugees from the 1958 partition. The initiative to unilaterally withdraw the illegal Israeli settlements in Gaza is a wolf in sheep's clothing because while Israel would withdraw from Gaza, it would incorporate virtually all of the illegal settlements in the occupied West Bank into Israel. And if the President's endorsement was not sufficient source of rage for the Palestinians and all Arabs, the US Congress with a vote 407-9 passed a resolution in support of Sharon's initiative and thus in effect endorsed the annexation of the West Bank settlements by Israel. Professor Stephen Zumes of the University of San Francisco adds:

> More fundamentally, Congress' effective endorsement of an Israeli annexation of land it conquered in the 1967 war is a direct challenge to the United Nations Charter, which forbids any country from expending its territory through military conquest. The vote, therefore, constitutes nothing less than an overwhelming bipartisan renunciation of the post-World War II international system, effectively recognizing the right of conquest.

Now, hold on! What was the reason that we attacked Iraq in the Gulf War? Why shouldn't Saddam Hussein keep Kuwait? He conquered it fair and square and without anybody's military assistance. And what about all these UN Security Council resolutions calling for Israel to withdraw to its pre- 1967 war borders? Is it not what Israel has been doing since 1967 a flagrant violation of these resolutions? But we invaded Iraq for a second time because they had WMDs—which of course they did not have—and because they were in violation of UN Security Council resolutions! And after behaving like this, we wonder "why do they hate us?" Are we to be taken seriously by the world body? I believe we are raising the definition of hypocrisy to new heights.

"In Israel-Palestine...the end result has been the further erosion of America's moral leadership and credibility, increased anti-Americanism among many of its allies and hatred among extremists", says John Esposito. The following excerpt from the 1996 Bin Laden's Declaration of War against the United States confirms Esposito's concerns.

> My Muslim Brothers of The World: Your brothers in Palestine and in the land of the two Holy Places are calling upon your help and asking you to take part in fighting against the enemy—your enemy and their enemy—the Americans and the Israelis. They are asking you to do whatever you can, with [your] own means and ability, to expel the enemy, humiliated and defeated, out of the sanctities of Islam...Our Lord, the people of the cross have come with their horses (soldiers) and [have] occupied the land of the two Holy places. And the Zionist Jews fiddle as they wish with the Al-Aqsa Mosque, the route of the ascendance of the messenger of Allah. (Bin Laden: Declaration of War, 1996)

"If we allow the neo-conservatives to morph our war on Al Qaeda into Israel's war for Palestine, our war will never end" says Patrick Buchanan. "And that is the hidden agenda of the neo-conservatives: permanent war for their permanent empowerment. As Frum and Perle concede, [in *An End to Evil*] this is 'our generation's great cause.'"

American Neo-Imperialism

> *The liberty of a democracy is not safe if the people tolerate the growth of private power to a point where it becomes stronger than their democratic State itself. That, in its essence, is Fascism—ownership of government by an individual, by a group or by any controlling power.*
>
> Franklin Delano Roosevelt

Every imperial power, especially in the past two centuries, has justified in its official discourse which is aimed at appeasing world opinion that its circumstances are special, its mission is to bring order, freedom, and democracy, and that it uses force only as a last resort. Does that sound familiar recently? And sadder yet, there is always a chorus of intellectuals, policy makers and ignorant political analysts "whose world experience is limited to the Beltway, who grind out books on 'terrorism' and liberalism, or about Islamic fundamentalism and American foreign policy, or about the end of history, all of it vying for attention and influence without regard for truthfulness or reflection or real knowledge." *Orientalism* by Edward Said.

In the July/August 1996 issue of *Foreign Affairs* William Kristol and Robert Kagan—two of the "High Priests-in-Training" of the neo-con cabal—wrote an article titled "Toward a Neo-Reaganite Foreign Policy" in which they presented in detail what the United States foreign policy should be in a neo-con-controlled world. These were, of course, the eight lean years of the Clinton White House when the neo-cons could do no more than think—they are supposed to be Washington's pre-eminent think tank—write, and wish Nicolas Machiavelli would be alive to join them in their scheming. "Conservatives will not be able to govern America over the long term if they fail to offer a more elevated vision of America's international role," Kristol and Kagan warn the conservatives. And that role should be "Benevolent global hegemony". Now, that's an oxymoron! Kristol and Kagan, however, were prepared for critics like us, so they went on. "The aspiration to benevolent hegemony might strike some as either hubristic or morally suspect. But a hegemon is nothing more or less than a leader with preponderant influence and *authority over all others in its domain* [emphasis added]. That is America's position in the world today. The leaders of Russia and China understand this." I believe the Arabs and the Islamic fundamentalists understand this, as well and they do not like it a bit. Are we still asking "why do they hate us?"

A year later, in June 1997, the neo-cons founded the, by now famous, Project for the New American Century (PNAC). The Statement of Principles of the PNAC is basically taken out of the Kristol-Kagan article of a year ago. The Europeans were not thrilled about PNAC and some called it "a secret blueprint for US global domination." But the neo-cons were not done yet. They were just warming up. In January 26, 1998 in a letter to then President Bill Clinton they urged him "to enunciate a new strategy that would secure the interests of the US and our friends and allies around the world. That strategy should aim, above all, at the removal of Saddam Hussein's regime from power." And that was in the opening paragraph of the letter. The strategy of the Clinton administration should be in the near term to undertake military action and "in the long term, it means removing Saddam Hussein and its regime from power. That now needs to become the aim of American foreign policy…American policy cannot continue to be crippled by a misguided insistence on unanimity in the UN Security Council." By the way, in case anyone missed the chronology here, the neo-cons were calling for the removal of Saddam Hussein with military means more than three and a half years before 9/11!

Then the tragic events of 9/11 were upon us and as the country grieved and the world sympathized with and stood by America, the neo-cons did not waste any time. Before the dust in ground zero had completely settled, they were writing again, this time to another President—George W. Bush. "US policy must aim not only at finding the people responsible for this incident, but must also target those 'other groups out there that mean us no good'" The neo-cons had not coined the phrase "axis of evil" yet, so they had to settle with "other groups out there that mean us no good." But there were pretty clear about their intentions for Saddam though. In the same letter, they urged President Bush, "It may be that the Iraqi government provided assistance in some form to the recent attack on the United States. But even if evidence does not link Iraq directly to the attack, any strategy aiming at the eradication of terrorism and its sponsors must include a determined effort to remove Saddam Hussein from power in Iraq. Failure to undertake such an effort will constitute an early and perhaps decisive surrender in the war on international terrorism."

George W. Bush was not about to disappoint his neo-con friends, advisors and policy makers in his administration. As he said on February 26, 2003—less than one month before invading a sovereign nation—in a speech at the American Enterprise Institute, "some of the finest minds in our nation are at work on some of the greatest challenges to our nation. You do such good work that my administration has borrowed 20 such minds." On March 20, 2003 the United States of America invaded Iraq and removed Saddam Hussein, just as the neo-cons have been asking since, at least, 1996.

The Invasion of Iraq

Wars throughout history have been waged for conquest and plunder...That is war in a nutshell. The master class has always declared the wars; the subject class has always fought them the battles. The master class had all to gain and nothing to lose, while the subject class had nothing to gain and all to lose—especially their lives.

Eugene V. Debs

We were all wrong.

David Kay

The invasion of Iraq and its subsequent occupation by the US, long before that the decade-long sanctions imposed on Iraq and the devastating effect they had on its people and especially children, have been another major cause of Arab rage against America. "If the Palestinians are Exhibit A, the Iraqis are Exhibit B" says Lisa Beyer in "Why the Hate? Roots of Rage"—her article for Time Magazine *On-Line*. And there are three elements that constitute Exhibit B. First, the past and on-going suffering of the Iraqi peoples caused by the sanctions, invasion and occupation are a major cause of the Arab rage. Second, when we attacked Iraq we not only attacked one nation, we attacked *Dar El Islam*, meaning every Islamic nation and Islam, as a religion, as well. This defines the conflict more than the war raging in Iraq and provides strong justification for those Islamic fundamentalists that advocate that America and the West are waging a crusade against the Muslims aiming to dominate them, even exterminate them. And third, Arabs, from Saddam Hussein and Bin Laden to moderate commentators and intellectuals, have drawn parallels between the Mongol invasion and sacking of Baghdad in 1258 and the 2003 invasion by America, and have coined labels like "American Mongols" and "Bush, the Modern Hulagu". These are some very powerful images for Arabs, especially Iraqis, and resonate greatly throughout the Arab and Muslim world.

The conflict in Iraq has the potential to make Afghanistan's tragedy look trivial, as Iraq has replaced Afghanistan as the center stage of the Islamic Jihad. What a trophy Iraq has been for Zawahiri and bin Laden—going from the most secular of Arab-

Muslim states to potentially the most theocratic. It is not that Saddam Hussein was not a potential threat to American and world peace. He was, but so are the leaders of, at least, a half a dozen of other countries, that given the means and the opportunity would pose the same threat as Saddam Hussein did. This does not give the US the license to attack countries in the name of security, freedom and democracy. Such a behavior by the world's only superpower has weakened the international coalition against global terrorism, strengthened the cause of Islamic extremists, almost ensured another devastating terrorist attack against the US, undermined most of the Arab and Muslim regimes, and greatly weakened the US economy. This is a huge price to pay for a mere "suspicion" of threat. Power and wealth require reason, fairness and restraint. Is this what a "benevolent global hegemon" is all about? Where is the "clear moral purpose" of our foreign policy?

Linking Iraq and Saddam with terrorism, along with the alleged presence of WMD, was the Bush administration's rationale for invading Iraq. In 2005, more than two years after the collapse of Saddam, the same voices in the administration declared that Iraq is the world's center of terrorism. You know what? This time they are correct. Thanks to American intervention, Iraq is now the undisputed hot bed of terrorism where the Islamic fundamentalists receive the best on-job training and inflict the maximum material and human damage on America. Moreover, these terrorists in Iraq will return someday back to their countries with their terrorist's networks and knowledge hugely enriched—just as it happened in Afghanistan during the Soviet invasion. And the Arab Middle Eastern governments will have Bush and America to thank for this great gift bestowed to them by a benevolent empire.

The Iraqi War and how Arabs Reacted

A personal recollection

On April 9, 2003 Baghdad fell to the Coalition forces that marched through the city as liberators. The famous scene of American soldiers pulling down the statue of Saddam Hussein was broadcast all over the world and printed on the front cover of every news magazine published that week. Yet, while the Iraqis were celebrating in the streets of Baghdad, Arabs and Muslims elsewhere were exhibiting different emotions. From Lebanon to Syria to Egypt, the Arabic satellite networks of *Arabiya* and *al Jazeera* (the equivalent of CNN in the Arab world) were broadcasting scenes of young Arabs with tears in their eyes as they were watching another victory of the West, another humiliating defeat for the Arab Muslims.

We happened to be in Egypt at the time and had just completed an assignment for the USAID mission in Cairo. We were staying at the Cairo Inter-Continental hotel just a stone's throw from the US Embassy. Having lived in Egypt since Saddam's invasion of Kuwait in 1990, I had somehow become accustomed to the ever-present uniformed army and police security forces. But these scenes in the center of Cairo were eerie. Traffic within two city blocks from the US and British Embassies was diverted away on a 24/7 basis with cement barricades blocking all accesses to them. Even pedestrians walking to their homes or to businesses or small newspaper and convenience shops were stopped, interrogated and had their bags searched. But it was not the extraordinary security that was strange and unsettling. I had lived and worked in Alexandria, Cairo and Sinai for thirteen years and had experienced in the turbulent period of the early and mid-nineties one of the most violent uprisings of the Muslim Brotherhood, that culminated and came to a halt with the deaths of the tourists in Luxor in 1997. During all this time though I felt very secure, and the Egyptians had been always very warm and friendly towards foreigners and especially Americans. Many of my friends and business associates were Egyptians and I am married to an Egyptian. While I blend easily in a crowd of Egyptians, thanks to my very Mediterranean complexion and very noticeable Bedouin-like nose, this time I was attracting curious, often unfriendly stares. Even at the hotel, where I had been staying months at a time, and where I had got to know very well all the staff from the doormen to the GM, the Egyptian staff was still polite but a little reserved this time. There were many uncomfortable moments for them and for me when, during the continuous barrage of news broadcasts from CNN, *Jazeera*, or *Arabiya*, images of the bombing of Baghdad or the victorious march of American soldiers and hardware towards Baghdad would appear on the TV screens.

I had the most uncomfortable experience, however, during a bus ride to the oasis of Siwa from the coastal city of Alexandria. Siwa had been our favorite destination in Egypt for more than eight years and we had developed, and still have, some very close friendships with a lot of the town's wonderful people. The Siwans are very much like the native Americans—in fact there are amazing similarities in the style and materials they use in the construction of their homes, their clothes, jewelry, and even in their music—and very simple, polite, and extremely warm and friendly folks. All foreigners, especially Americans, had always been welcomed in Siwa. In this, our last trip to Siwa before our repatriation to the US, we experienced something unusual and heart breaking. While my wife and I were chatting, in English, during the nine-hour monotonous bus ride from Alexandria, one of the Siwans riding on the bus asked my wife what nationality was the man with whom she was talking. Now, the question in itself was unusual. Siwans usually keep to themselves; do not ask questions of strangers and especially of an Egyptian woman. The tone of his voice was polite but it had an edge to it. My wife sensed his apprehension and smiling told him—without directly answering his question that—we were on our way to meet with our good friend "*Ostez Abdullah Baghi*". That was the magic answer that changed the almost unfriendly demeanor of this simple and, under different circumstances, always friendly Siwan peasant to the broadest smile we had seen in a very long time, at least since the invasion of Iraq had started two weeks earlier. "Welcome, welcome" he said smiling and bowing. Our friend Abdullah happens to be one of the village elders—his grandfather was the chief of the village—a businessman, one of the best desert safari guides, and, most important, the inspector of all schools districts in the area—the highest ranking government employee in Siwa. He *is Ostez* Abdullah, Mr. Abdullah, a title of high distinction in this simple, peaceful and in many ways primitive corner of the Sahara Desert.

By the time we returned to Alexandria, Americans were marching in Baghdad. The Iraqis were joyous as they trampled on and beat Saddam's statue with their shoes—the ultimate symbol of humiliation and insult for the recipient of such an act in Arab culture. For me, however, was a bitter-sweet experience. On one hand, I was glad that the American soldiers had reached their objective without many casualties and proud of their military victory; on the other, I was witnessing the rage and humiliation of Egyptians in observing a victorious American army crush another fellow Arab nation—even if that nation was ruled by a tyrant like Saddam. I shall never forget, as long as I live, the way people were looking at me, including my close friends and my wife's relatives. At the end of the day, I was an American and it was not just George W. Bush, Donald Rumsfeld and Condoleezza Rice who were responsible for what had happened in Iraq. All Americans shared that responsibility for allowing their government to go ahead with it. I was deeply touched and ashamed of myself and my adopted country. We left from Egypt a couple weeks later—our departure greatly influenced by the events in Iraq and the broader change in American policy that we were witnessing playing out daily in the Arab and international TV channels. It took three and a half years before I could return to the Middle East again for a brief assignment. I want to seal in my memory the better days of the past when people smiled to me in the streets, and I was proud being an American in the belief I was helping ordinary folks with the several infrastructure and institutional development projects, which I had the privilege and opportunity of being a part during perhaps the most rewarding period of my personal and professional life.

Iran, Syria and Lebanon

The road to Damascus lies through Baghdad.
Richard Perle to Benjamin Netanyahu, "Clean Break", 1996

The desert sand had hardly settled from the massive columns of steel that were racing towards Baghdad when the likes of

Rumsfeld, Rice, Cheney, and Wolfowitz were reminding us that we had unfinished business with the other members of the "axis of evil"—Iran, Syria and North Korea. The neo-cons, of course, had never taken Syria and Iran off their sights. In their letter to President Bush on September 20, 2001 they said "any war against terrorism must target Hezbollah…the administration should demand that Iran and Syria immediately cease all military, financial, and political support for Hezbollah and its operations. Should Iran and Syria refuse to comply, the administration should consider appropriate measures of retaliation against these known state sponsors of terrorism." So, the justification has already been made and the war plans, I am certain, have been drawn. They are waiting for the right opportunity. And that opportunity does not necessarily have to come because Iran and Syria did anything to provoke us. The Bush administration is very good at exploiting every situation of potentially damaging news to their advantage. When we get bogged down in Iraq or when the domestic news on the economy is particular bad, they feed "the mass media stooges" with horror stories about Iran's nuclear arsenal, or Syria's support of the Iraqi insurgency and the accommodating public forgets about the real problems. It kind of reminds me of Roman Emperor Nero's tactics of using the slaughtering of gladiators and Christians in the coliseum to detract the attention of the Romans from their domestic problems and military failures abroad. It worked then and it is certainly working now. The Bush administration, of course, is lot more sophisticated than Nero ever was. Not only they are able to divert the public's attention from the real problems the nation faces, they are successfully hyping up the American public as they are gearing up for the next war.

In 1996, Richard Perle co-authored "A Clean Break", a now famous paper urging Benjamin Netanyahu to dump the Oslo Accords, seize the West Bank, and confront Syria. "The road to Damascus lies through Baghdad", Perle told Netanyahu. (*No End to War* by Buchanan) In their book *An End to Evil*, Perle and Frum write, "Iran is itself a terrorist state, the world's worst. North Korea has committed terrorist atrocities too. Both regimes are nightmarishly repressive; both regimes present intolerable threats to American security. We must move boldly against them both and against other sponsors of terrorism as well: Syria, Libya, and Saudi Arabia. And we don't have much time." In his book *The War against the Terror Masters*, Michael Ledeen—another hard core neo-con—suggests that to win the war against the terror masters, we must attack Syria and Iran, invade Saudi Arabia, seize their oil fields and occupy Mecca! The question is not whether we should attack them, Ledeen says, but why has it taken us so long to do it? Let me ask one more time the question. Are we still wondering why they hate us and why Muslims are paranoid about our imperialistic goals? But, of course, we are a "benevolent global hegemon" and not an "evil doer".

In the summer of 2004, one day after the 9/11 Commission announced in its long-awaited report that it found no Iraq-Al Qaeda link, the headlines were "that the same commission found that eight of the 9/11 hijackers had passed between Afghanistan and Iran between October 2000 and February 2001…In other words, the report says: there's been no Al Qaeda link to Iraq (now occupied by US troops), but there has been one to Iran (not occupied by US troops), writes Gary Leupp in his article "Setting up War with Iran". These accusations about potential links between Iran and Al Qaeda came as the administration increased its threats against Iran about the alleged development of nuclear weapons by Iran and amid America's new-found "moralization" of its foreign policy to spread democracy to every corner of the earth. The exact same formula that worked so well with Iraq is applied to Iran with the same disinformation dialectic that was used prior to the invasion of Iraq. There is one noticeable difference here. The Bush administration, after the 2004 election, is bolder, more confident and more hubristic. They know that they have a receptive constituency which will support whatever decision they make. Their justification is aimed more at the history books.

One should note, however, that in the case of Iran the neocons are clever enough not to push too much for regime change in Tehran on the grounds of bringing democracy to the Iranian people. Whether we like it or not, Iran has an elected government after all. So, they will keep the freedom and democracy rhetoric for Syria and North Korea. By the way, why aren't we attacking North Korea? Its government has, in a number of occasions, admitted they have developed nuclear weapons. The United States refuses to even enter into unilateral talks with

North Korea to address this "threat" and I would guess we are not developing any serious war plans for attacking North Korea. First, Koreans aren't Muslims and second, they will be a much tougher adversary than Iraq or Syria, as our experience in the first Korean War taught us more than fifty years earlier.

After the Iraqi elections in January 2005, the administration's rhetoric against Syria and Iran heated up even more and increased in frequency. In addition to the official statements from the administration, the neo-con think tank has not remained silent. In "Syrious Threat" published in National Review Online on March 11, 2005, Michael A. Ledeen—a Freedom Scholar at AEI—said that "Calling for the quick departure of Syrian troops and intelligence officials from Lebanon is all to the good, but it is only a small step in the necessary campaign to remove the terror masters in Damascus and Tehran...The president has committed himself and his administration to the liberation of Syria, Lebanon, and Iran [someone must have forgotten to tell Ledeen that Iran has an "elected" government]. This cannot remain a merely rhetorical commitment. If his fine words are not followed by effective action, we may yet again be branded 'paper tigers.' [The US, a paper tiger? That's another interesting oxymoron!] The revolutionary changes in the Middle East are the ripple effects of the serious action we took in Afghanistan and Iraq, and people are now risking their lives for freedom in the belief that the United States will stand beside them. We must show them we are serious. It isn't very hard, and there are plenty of people in the government and in the armed forces who know how to do it. They are awaiting their orders." What are you waiting for Mr. President? The neo-cons are getting restless. It is only a year and a half before the next mid-term elections and they need sufficient time to promote their next round of disinformation.

While the Bush administration was issuing stern warnings to Syria and demanding they withdraw their troops from Lebanon, precipitated largely from the February 14, 2005 assassination of Rafik Hariri, the former Lebanese prime minister, a massive pro-Syrian and pro-Hezbollah demonstration took place on March 8 in Beirut. Hundreds of thousands of demonstrators organized by Hezbollah took the streets shouting anti-American and anti-Israeli slogans and demanding that American and

French intervention in their internal affairs comes to an end. "The opposition wants to open the door to the Americans and to foreign intervention. We will stop them" declared one of the student leaders. To Hezbollah and its followers, the foreign threat to Lebanon comes not from Syria but from Israel and its ally, the United States. "Many Lebanese Shiites believe that Israel still has designs on their land and that the American-backed democracy movement is simply another form of American imperialism" reports the New York Times. There is no better catalyst in energizing the Arab Muslim world in support of any of our "declared enemies" than having the US attack those enemies. Such an action is guaranteed to rally the Muslims against whatever and whomever we support. Why? Simply because they do not trust the American benevolent hegemony. They have studied the history of American imperialism and its unjust intervention in the Middle East a lot closer than we Americans have.

The Crusades and Western Colonialism

After the Palestinian struggle and the occupation of Iraq—in that order—the next issue that unites all Arabs and Muslims against America and the West is the memory of the Crusaders against the Muslims in the Middle Ages. The Crusades while only a faint event—and a misrepresented at that—lost in the Western consciousness, it still looms large in the cultural memory of the Muslim world, says Andrew Curry in an article published in U.S News on April 8, 2002. There has not been any communication issued from Osama Bin Laden or Ayman Zawahiri that does not make a reference to the war waged against the Islamic nation by the American Crusaders and the Zionists. "Their words tap into a reservoir of ill will. 'The impact of the Crusades created an historical memory which is with us today—the memory of a long European onslaught,' says Akbar Ahmed, chair of Islamic studies at American University in Washington, D.C. Its legacy was profound. For Muslims, then probably the strongest and most vibrant civilization on the globe, the Crusader victories and the destruction that followed were a confidence-shaking blow", continues Andrew Curry.

The Muslims were defeated and the survivors slaughtered within the walls of Jerusalem in the First Crusade. After a hundred years, Saladin retook Jerusalem and the European Christian knights failed to liberate the Holy City in three subsequent crusades. The best remembered is the Third Crusade most probably because of the participation of the legendary Richard the Lion-Hearted, king of England. After battling Saladin for sixteen months and having failed to defeat the Muslim armies, King Richard signed a truce with Saladin and headed back to England.

But although Richard the Lion-Hearted failed to capture Jerusalem the unfulfilled goal of the crusades never evaporated and "Richard did come back in the popular imagination—if in a different guise" writes Andrew Curry. "Marching into a Jerusalem captured from the Turks in 1917, a British general, Sir Edmund Allenby, proudly declared 'today the wars of the Crusades are completed', and the British press celebrated his victory with cartoons of Richard the Lion-Hearted looking down at Jerusalem above the caption 'At last my dream come true'. The colonial powers glorified the Crusades as their ideological forebears."

The Crusades also ushered an era of European colonialism that ended ten centuries of great Arab and Muslim military and cultural achievements with the dismemberment of the Ottoman Empire and the creation of the modern Middle East. "Colonialism and the advance of Western modernity have nurtured the modern version of Islamic fundamentalism", says Lisa Beyer. "If Islam is perfect and its kingdom is in retreat, it must be that its practitioners have strayed from the fundamental of the faith." This notion has been the cornerstone of the ideologies of all Islamic neo-fundies from Hassan El Banna to Sayyid Qutb. So, fear of the "evils" of modernity, rage over the Crusades and Western colonialism, the Palestinian struggle, the Iraq war, and the Arab-Muslim sense of impotence against the hostile super powers of crusaders and Zionists has been the root cause and the fuel that has sustained their rage.

Brief History Lesson for George W. Bush

And this is no small conflagration we contemplate. This is no simple attempt to defang a villain. No. This coming battle, if it materializes, represents a turning point in U.S. foreign policy and possibly a turning point in the recent history of the world.

US Senator Robert Byrd on the eve of the Iraq War

"We are truly 'sleepwalking through history'" said Senator Byrd on February 12, 2003 on the floor of the US Senate. And even if the entire nation has not been sleepwalking, the President of the United States has certainly been sleepwalking through history since he took office in January 2001. If the citizens of America are not students of history, it is OK. After all, the job of being a citizen does not require knowledge of world history—although it might be extremely helpful at times as the present. But it should be a prerequisite for the President of the United States to have at a minimum some rudimentary knowledge of history. To that end, we will offer President George W. Bush a short history lesson, *gratis*, of course.

About Democracy

No amount of charters, direct primaries, or short ballots will make a democracy out of illiterate people.

Walter Lippmann

The first question that came to mind when I started thinking about the first lesson for President Bush—Democracy—was, why do we want to democratize Iraq, and the rest of the world for that matter? Democracy isn't exactly what it's cracked up to be and hasn't worked all that well here, especially in the last four years. It has been a very long time since my last civics course in the public schools in post-war Greece, and I thought I better do my homework before I show off to the President of the United States—I heard that he is a graduate of Yale! So, I googled the word "democracy" and was reminded that democracy does not simply mean "rule by the people." It is a good thing that people should choose their government, but democracy implies a few more things than that. For example, the election of public officials should be conducted in a free and just manner. But then I thought about the 2000 election in the United States. Also democracy requires a constitution, which limits the powers and controls the formal operation of government, equality before the law and due process under the rule of law; and then, I thought about the Patriot Act and Guantanamo Bay. One of the prerequisites of democracy, I learned, is freedom of the press and access to alternative information sources; and then FOX News, CBS, ABC, CNN, and NBC popped into my head. Finally, I learned that democracy can be very risky form of government unless there are educated citizens informed of their rights and civic responsibilities. At this point I was ready to ditch democracy, but just in time I thought of the wise words of Winston Churchill who said: "Indeed, it has been said that democracy is the worst form of government except all those other forms that have been tried from time to time."

These words of Winston Churchill convinced me that we better stick with democracy here in the United States. But what about Iraq and the rest of the Middle East? By asking that question, by the way, I do not mean to suggest, even remotely, that Iraqis, or anybody else, do not deserve the right to choose their form of government and their leaders. But, is it really our God-given duty to impose our form of government to other nations, and do so by invading and occupying them? And here is where the real lesson for George W. Bush begins with no better introduction than the following quote:

> The question before the neo-conservatives behind Bush is how to implement democracy in a country that has no democratic culture; implant liberal secular values (on which democracy depends) where values are strictly religious, indeed Islamic; and plant a US-style market economy where the geography allows largely for a single commodity (oil) economy; and indeed how to sell Western culture (Read Judeo-Christian culture) in the middle of a region where *Islamic theocracy generally holds sway*. [Emphasis added] Cornelius Thomas,
> www.dispatch.co.za/2003/04/17/editorial

For someone in the West who has not been exposed to Arabic and Islamic cultures it is very difficult, if at all possible, to fully comprehend the extent that religion and culture impact every aspect of the lives of their people. One does not question authority and most importantly, does not question religion. Period. These were two things that I had a very hard time comprehending, even believing in the beginning of my tour of Middle East, having being raised in a culture that teaches you "to believe and question" everything from the government institutions to the religious institutions. To illustrate this point, I would like to share with you a discussion I had in Alexandria, Egypt in the mid-nineties over dinner with a group of intellectuals and academics. We were discussing cultural differences between Westerners and Arabs (in this case Egyptians). What caught my attention and has remained in my memory since then, is how one of the guests—a professor of management at the Sadat Academy of Management—described the influence that his father had and still has on him, and his own dependency on what his father says. "Let me give you an example", the man said. "I am in my mid-fifties and a professor at one of the prestigious universities in Egypt; I lived in the US for more than ten years where I got my Master's and PhD degrees. When I lived in the US, I always asked for my older brother's advice before I made any serious decisions. Even now that I am married and have my own children, any time I have to make an important decision, I still go and talk to my father. I know that this might sound kind of strange to you, but it is extremely difficult for me to make a decision that I know may be contrary to my father's wishes or advice. I feel I need his approval."

The images of the father, an older brother, a teacher, and especially of a religious scholar are revered in Muslim societies. Unfortunately, with the probable exception of their immediate relatives, not all figures of reverence and authority have their best interests in mind. On the contrary, Islamic history is full of examples of treachery and manipulation—no more, however, than Western Christendom—and given the relatively high level of illiteracy, intellectual isolation, limited sources of alternative knowledge—other than Islamic ones—the average citizen is an easy prey to any form of manipulative religious extremism. We have seen examples of this in Afghanistan and Iran. I came across an article *in Al Jazeera* shortly after the Iraqi elections in January 2005 that highlighted an interview with Iraq's influential Association of Muslim Scholars. "The voter goes to the polling stations not knowing who he is voting for in the first place. There are more than 7700 candidates and I challenge any Iraqi voter to name more than half a dozen" said Muhammad al-Kubaysi. "Even 80% of Iraqis living abroad in complete safety refused to register [to vote]. This shows that the low turnout in many areas is not a security problem. Rather, it demonstrates a growing Iraqi awareness that these elections are indeed an American and not an Iraqi initiative."

Even if we accept that the voter turnout was acceptable, if the voters do not know who the candidates are—and obviously not what their qualifications and position on various issues—how can they make the "right" choice for themselves and Iraq? If the objective of the United States government was to check off another item in their list –Democratization of the Middle East--and broadcast to Americans, first, and the world, second, that the winds of freedom and democracy are blowing through the Middle East, then they have succeeded. Otherwise, to think that by merely holding "free" elections we have brought freedom to these people is potentially one of the most irresponsible and criminal acts we are committing against these people. We might have thrown them into the jaws of theocracy.

The Age of Enlightenment is described in encyclopedias as an 18th century movement that led the world toward progress, out of a long period of irrationality, superstition, and tyranny which began during the historical period we call the Dark Ages. It was an age where prominent philosophers, such as Voltaire and Jean-Jacques Rousseau questioned and attacked existing institutions of both Church and State. Moreover, it was a movement that provided the framework for the American and French Revolutions and for the independence wars in Ottoman Europe. The Arab Muslim world has not had yet its own Age of Enlightenment. We should allow it to do so, first by stopping intervening in its affairs and second by encouraging its people to have their Age of Reason and Enlightenment. We can do that by assisting them in their economic and educational development, and inviting them (even the Islamic extremists) to participate in peace-seeking dialogues with the West.

So, Mr. President, it is counterproductive and highly hypocritical to label most of them as barbarians and members of the "axis of evil", refuse to engage in diplomacy with their elected governments—as in Iran or Palestine—and change their "regimes" by brute force because they are not "friendly" to our "benevolent global hegemony", on one hand, and then pretend that we are the guardians of global freedom and democracy, on the other.

About Imperial Hubris

... the invasion of Iraq and the war to impose democracy upon that Arab and Islamic nation that has never known democracy may yet prove a textbook example of the imperial overstretch that brought down so many empires of the past.
Patrick J. Buchanan in *Where the Right went Wrong*

Troathes (The Women of Troy): The Athenian Experience

> A fool is he who sacks the cities of men, with shrines and tombs—sacred places of the dead—he demolishes them, but then he too falls

With these words Poseidon assures Athena that he will grant her request to "make the Aegean strait to roar with mighty billows and whirlpools, and fill Euboea's hollow bay with corpses, the Achaeans (Greeks) may learn henceforth to reverence my temples and regard all other deities" and they both exit the stage in the opening part of Euripides's tragedy *Troathes* (Women of Troy) presented in 415 BC in Athens. The audience has been forewarned of the inevitable punishment (catharsis) of the Greeks and, thus, somewhat morally satisfied may be able to watch their atrocities in the following acts.

The *Troathes* is a unique tragedy about pain--pain that war brings to men. It is one of the most depressing tragedies of Euripides. It is a play full of murder, slavery, and destruction where human dignity is trampled to the maximum. Euripides masterfully chose Hecabe, wife of Priam, queen of Ilium (Troy), but most importantly mother of many sons and daughters, to draw in the audience in feeling her sorrow for what was lost and her pain for what awaits them all. It is not merely about the mourning of Troy. It is about the indictment of Greeks as war criminals. It is a warning of what is in store for the Greeks for all their atrocities. It is a prophetic message about the crushing defeat of the Athenian armies in Sicily two years later. It is about the decay of the human values as a result of war. It is about revolting war crimes that are repeated to this date. It is about imperial Hubris at its worst. And it is a relevant and very important lesson for Americans who just like the Athenians ignored the warnings of the wise and embarked in an immoral and dangerous war in Iraq. But let us hear for ourselves the words of a mother and her daughters as one by one fall victims to the whim of the victors, and try to feel the pain and despair that they surely must have felt.

Hecabe has just learned that one of her two unmarried daughters, Cassandra, will be taken by King Agamemnon to "share with him his stealthy love", and, the other, Polyxene, has been decreed to "minister (be sacrificed) at Achilles' tomb". Andromache, wife of Hector, crown prince of Ilium and fallen hero, "she too was a chosen prize; Achilles' son did take her." Fearing the worst for herself, Hecabe asks Talthybius, the Greek herald and implementer of these atrocities, "as for me whose hair is white with age, who needs to hold a staff to be to me a third foot, whose servant am I to be?"

Talthybius:

Odysseus, king of Ithaca, hath taken thee to be his slave.

Hecabe:

O God! Now smite the close-shorn head! Tear your cheeks with your nails. God help me! I have fallen as a slave to a treacherous foe I hate, a monster of lawlessness, one that by his double tongue hath turned against us all that once was friendly in his camp, changing this for that and for this again. Oh weep for me, ye Trojan dames! Undone! Undone and lost! Ah woe a victim to a most unhappy lot!

Cassandra, half crazed from the news of becoming Agamemnon's concubine and carrying torches, enters the stage.

Cassandra:

Bring the light, uplift and show its flame! I am doing the god's service, see! I making his shrine to glow with tapers bright. O Hymen, king of marriage! Blest is the bridegroom; blest am I also, the maiden soon to wed a princely lord in Argos. Hail Hymen, king of marriage! Since thou, my mother, art ever busied with tears and lamentations in thy mourning for my father's death and for my country dear, I at my own nuptials am making this torch to blaze and show its light, in thy honor, O Hymen, king of marriage! Grant thy light too, Hecate, at the maiden's wedding, as the custom is. Nimbly lift the foot aloft, lead on the dance with cries of joy, as to greet my father's happy fate. To dance I hold a sacred duty; come, Phoebus, lead the way, for 'tis in thy temple mid thy bay-trees that I minister. Hail Hymen, god of marriage! Hymen, hail! Come, mother mine, and join the dance, link thy steps with me, and circle in the gladsome measure, now here, now there. Salute the bride on her wedding-day with hymns and cries of joy. Come, ye maidens of Phrygia in raiment fair, sing my marriage with the husband fate ordained that I should wed.

Hecabe:

Though god of fire, 'tis thine to light the bridal torch for men, but piteous is the flame thou kindlest here, beyond my blackest bodings. Ah, my child! How little did I ever dream that such would be thy marriage, a captive, and of Argos tool. Give up the torch to me: thou dost not bear its blaze aright in my wild frantic course, nor have thy afflictions left thee in my sober senses, but still art thou as frantic as before. Take in those torches, Trojan friends, and for her wedding madrigals weep your tears instead.

Cassandra:

O mother, crown my head with victor's wreaths; rejoice in my royal match; lead me to my lord; nay, if thou find me loth at all, thrust me there by force; for if Loxias be indeed a prophet, Agamemnon, that famous king of the Achaeans, will find in me a bride more fraught with woe to him than Helen. For I will slay him and lay waste his home to avenge my father's and my brethren's death.

Talthybius and Cassandra exit and Hecabe mourns Cassandra's and Polyxene's fate:

Hecabe:
O my daughter, O Cassandra! Whom gods have summoned to their frenzied train, how cruel the lot that ends thy virgin days! And though, Polyxene! My child of sorrow, where, oh! Where art thou? None of all the many sons and daughters have I born comes to aid a wretched mother. Why then raise me up? What hope is left us? Guide me, who erst trod so daintily the streets of troy, but now am but a slave, to a bed upon the ground, nigh some rocky ridge, that thence I may cast down and perish, after I have wasted my body with weeping. Of all the prosperous crowd, count none a happy man before he die.

Andromache with her young son enters the stage and learns from her mother the fate of her sister Polyxene, who has been sacrificed in the tomb of Achilles. "Her death was even as it was, and yet that death of hers was after all a happier fate than this my life" Andromache tells her mother, as she laments her fate to be taken captive by the son of Achilles who killed Hector, her husband. But the worst is yet to come for Andromache as Talthybius enters the stage once more.

Talthybius:
Oh hate me not, thou that erst wert Hector's wife, the bravest of the Phrygians! For my tongue would fain not tell that which the Danai and sons of Pelops both command.

Andromache:
What is it? Thy prelude bodeth evil news.

Talthybius:
Tis decreed thy son is-how can I tell you the news?

And with great hesitation, Talthybius tells Andromache that, at the advice of Odysseus, the Greek command has decreed that young Astyanax must be thrown from the walls of Troy. "He said they should not rear so brave a father's son." Andromache runs to her son, holds him tight to her bosom and begins to mourn him alive. It tears your heart. A forceful indictment of genocides and a brilliant description of the endless pain of a mother losing her son are these verses written by Euripides nearly two thousand five hundred years ago.

> My child! My own sweet babe and priceless treasure! Thy death the foe demands, and thou must leave thy wretched mother. That which saves the lives of others, proves thy destruction, even the sire's nobility; to thee thy father's valiancy has proved no boon. O the woeful wedding rites, that brought me erst to Hector's home, hoping to be the mother of a son that should rule o'er Asia's fruitful fields instead of serving as a victim to the sons of Danaus! Dost weep, my babe? Dost know thy hapless fate? Why clutch me with thy hands and to my garment cling, nestling like a tender chick beneath my wing? Hector will not rise again and come gripping his famous spear to bring thee salvation; no kinsman of thy sire appears, nor might of Phrygian hosts; one awful headlong leap from the dizzy height and thou wilt dash out thy life with none to pity thee! Oh to clasp thy tender limbs, a mother's fondest joy! Oh to breathe thy fragrant breath! In vain it seems these breasts did suckle thee, wrapped in thy swaddling-clothes; all for naught I used to toil and wore myself away! Kiss thy mother now for the last time, nestle to her that bare thee, twine thy arms about my neck and join thy lips to mine! O ye Hellenes, cunning to device new forms of cruelty, why slay this child who never wronged any?

As Talthybius exits with Andromache and Astyanax, Hecabe mourns her grandson and a lost city. "O child, son of my hapless boy, an unjust fate robs me and thy mother of thy life. How is it with me? What can I do for thee, my luckless babe? For thee I smite upon my head and beat my breast, my only gift;

for that alone is in my power. Woe for my city! Woe for thee! Is not our cup full? What is wanting now to our utter and immediate ruin?

But Euripides is not done yet. In the climax of the play, Talthybius enters with soldiers carrying Antyanax's little lifeless body on Hector's shield. Hecabe now mourns her dead grandson. Talthybius orders the city to be torched. Hecabe tries to throw herself to the flames of the burning city and in her desperation becomes angry with the gods. "Lo! They are burning thee, and leading us e'en now from our land to slavery. Great gods! Yet why call on the gods? They did not hearken e'en aforetime to our call. Come, let us rush into the flames, for to die with my country in its blazing ruin were a noble death for me." The citadel collapses. The soldiers drag the captive women towards the ships. The wailing of women and the flames of the burning city penetrate a sky full of smoke and dark clouds. This is the tragedy of Troathes and of humanity at war.

> A fool is he who sacks the cities of men, with shrines and tombs—sacred places of the dead—he demolishes them, but then he too falls.

As the Athenian Assembly was debating the invasion of Sicily during the Peloponnesian War and as Athens was swept by a deadly plague, Euripides confronts his countrymen by unveiling the Athenian imperialistic motives and their impending collapse using the burning Troy as his backdrop. By condemning not only the Trojan War as aggressive and morally without foundation but also the atrocities committed by the Greeks, Euripides accuses indirectly but substantially the politics of the war and the behavior of his countrymen. Two thousand four hundred eighteen years later, another brave statesman was warning the lawmakers and his countrymen of another impending political and military disaster—the invasion of Iraq. In his landmark speech on the Senate floor on Wednesday, February 12, 2003, US Senator Robert Byrd had this to say:

> To contemplate war is to think about the most horrible of human experiences. On this February day, as this nation

stands at the brink of battle, every American on some level must be contemplating the horrors of war.

Yet, this Chamber is, for the most part, silent – ominously, dreadfully silent. There is no debate, no discussion, no attempt to lay out for the nation the pros and cons of this particular war. There is nothing.

We stand passively mute in the United States Senate, paralyzed by our own uncertainty, seemingly stunned by the sheer turmoil of events. Only on the editorial pages of our newspapers is there much substantive discussion of the prudence or imprudence of engaging in this particular war.

And this is no small conflagration we contemplate. This is no simple attempt to defang a villain. No. This coming battle, if it materializes, represents a turning point in U.S. foreign policy and possibly a turning point in the recent history of the world.

This nation is about to embark upon the first test of a revolutionary doctrine applied in an extraordinary way at an unfortunate time. The doctrine of preemption – the idea that the United States or any other nation can legitimately attack a nation that is not imminently threatening but may be threatening in the future – is a radical new twist on the traditional idea of self-defense. It appears to be in contravention of international law and the UN Charter. And it is being tested at a time of world-wide terrorism, making many countries around the globe wonder if they will soon be on our – or some other nation's – hit list. High level Administration figures recently refused to take nuclear weapons off of the table when discussing a possible attack against Iraq. What could be more destabilizing and unwise than this type of uncertainty, particularly in a world where globalism has tied the vital economic and security interests of many nations so closely together? There are huge cracks emerging in our time-honored alliances, and U.S. intentions are suddenly subject to damaging worldwide speculation. Anti-Americanism based on mistrust, misinformation, suspicion, and alarming rhetoric from U.S. leaders is fracturing the once solid alliance against global terrorism which existed after September 11.

We are truly "sleepwalking through history." In my heart of hearts I pray that this great nation and its good and trusting citizens are not in for a rudest of awakenings.

> To engage in war is always to pick a wild card. And war must always be a last resort, not a first choice. I truly must question the judgment of any President who can say that a massive unprovoked military attack on a nation which is over 50% children is "in the highest moral traditions of our country". This war is not necessary at this time. Pressure appears to be having a good result in Iraq. Our mistake was to put ourselves in a corner so quickly. Our challenge is to now find a graceful way out of a box of our own making. Perhaps there is still a way if we allow more time.

America, as ancient Athens, did not listen to the call of the wise. America attacked Iraq as Athens attacked Sicily. It is interesting to note here that the historian Thucydides in writing about the invasion of Sicily, he reports that most of the members of the Athenian Assembly who were deliberating the war had no knowledge where Sicily was or how large it was. It can be argued that most of the American public had limited, if any, knowledge of where Iraq was and the problems we may face by going there. In 413 BC, the entire Athenian army was defeated and captured and a large part of the great and powerful fleet of the Athenians was destroyed in the harbor of Syracuse. Athenian power since the Persian Wars had rested solely on its naval superiority. The disastrous Sicilian expedition left Athens almost completely powerless. Spartans—the perennial rivals to the Athenian dominance—took advantage of this weakness and attacked Athens. By 405, the rest of the Athenian navy was destroyed and a year later the Athenians surrendered to the Spartans, who tore down the walls of the city, barred them from ever having a navy, and installed their own oligarchic government in Athens. The Age of Athens, the Age of Pericles—the Golden Age—the Athenian Empire had come to an end. Will the American Empire follow the fate of ancient Athens? We hope not, but the careless and imperialistic policies of George W. Bush and his neo-cons point to an inevitable weakening of the American Empire.

While some of us might not be around to witness this decline of PAX Americana, for the benefit of the younger generation, there is no better way to draw the curtain on this section than to give some advice in the words of James Carrol, not to

President Bush this time, but to the American people, for they are the ones that need to take action, and soon.

> Given how they have been so dramatically unfulfilled, Washington's initial hubristic impulses toward a new imperial dominance should not be forgotten. That the first purpose of the war—Osama "dead or alive"— changed when Al Qaeda proved elusive should not be forgotten. That the early justification for the war against Iraq-Saddam's weapons of mass destruction changed when they proved nonexistent should not be forgotten...That Afghanistan and Iraq are in shambles, with thousands dead and hundreds of thousands at risk from disease, disorder and despair, should not be forgotten. That a now-disdainful world gave itself in unbridled love to America on 9/11 should not be forgotten.
>
> James Carrol, "The Bush Crusade", September 20, 2004, The Nation.

World is not a Safer Place

On April 9, 2003 Baghdad fell to the Coalition forces that marched through the city as liberators. For the administration of George W. Bush nothing could have been more victorious. Three weeks later, on May 1, 2003 the president donned in a pilot's flight suit landed in an aircraft carrier in a fighter jet and declared victory—Mission Accomplished—and the end of major military combat in Iraq. The joyous neo-cons applauded and the Arabs clenched their teeth and fists. The tears were gone from their eyes, but one could see in them the piercing fire of the desert fighters.

At the dawn of the twentieth century, the US had fought two wars in less than three years with the purpose, as we were told, of combating terrorism. With these two wars fought and won, one would have expected the world to become a more peaceful place where stability and security would have been brought back to our lives and the lives of millions Iraqis and Afghanis. Unfortunately the wars that brave American soldiers fought and died for in Afghanistan and Iraq with the purpose of eradicating the roots of terrorism, accomplished none of their objectives. Other than the fact that US forces still occupy both countries, terrorism is still the biggest threat to world peace and security. Even the much-publicized capture and execution of Saddam Hussein or the death of Zarqawi did not reduce the threat of terrorism.

With the fall of Saddam's statue on 9 April 2003, the Iraqis celebrated the end of the tyrant's regime and were filled with hope for a better future. However, as the days passed it became obvious the US didn't have a clear post-war plan for Iraq. America became in the eyes of the Iraqis and the rest of the world, an occupying power. This gave birth to the resistance movement against the American and coalition presence in Iraq.

Moreover, the American occupation of Iraq has left the Iraqis jobless, insecure and in much worse living conditions than before the war. Under Saddam's regime, most people had jobs with the government. By the end of 2003, the rate of unemployment was estimated at around 80% and Iraqis live in fear of a civil war that could tear their country apart. A Gallup poll found that fewer than 10% of the Iraqis believe that the US invasion was done to help Iraqis, and even fewer believe the objective of the US was to establish a true democracy in their land. And there is another reason for Iraqis to be resentful of the American invasion and occupation. In a report from doctors from Johns Hopkins University published in the prestigious British medical journal, *The Lancet*, a shocking statistic emerged in late October 2004. The journal reports that more than 100,000 Iraqis, most of them women and children, have died since the US-led invasion of the country than would have died otherwise. "We were shocked at the magnitude but we're quite sure that the estimate of 100,000 is a conservative estimate," said Dr. Gilbert Burnham of the Johns Hopkins study team. Since that report, the fatalities of Iraqi civilians are estimated above half a million.

The resistance against the Americans and the coalition forces continues to intensify by the day and gain strength and sophistication to the extent that it has become uncontrollable. And although the American administration claims that Jihadists lead the insurgency, American military officials say that well-armed Sunnis angry about losing power are behind the resistance movement.

It would be an error, however, to try to paint the insurgency in broad-brush strokes, as the movement is complex and multifaceted. While the movement may be sustained by the fierce Iraqi nationalists who oppose the occupation of their soil by foreign forces, it is constantly fueled by Jihadists and Shiite militants whose aim is undoubtedly to create an Iranian style, or, worse, a Taliban style theocratic Islamic republic. *Ansar al Islam*, a home grown militant Islamic group, inspired by Al Qaeda, did not take much time to reorganize, regroup and start its resistance operations against the American and coalition forces shortly after the collapse of Saddam's regime. Members of *Ansar al Islam*, several of whom are veterans of the Afghani resistance against the Soviets, share Bin Laden's ideology of founding an Islamic nation. The regime of Saddam Hussein used *Ansar al Islam* to destabilize northern Iraq and to assassinate Sadam's Kurdish opponents. No further connection has been found between Saddam and Al Qaeda. Reports issued in the summer of 2004 by the 9/11 Commission and the congressional committee on intelligence have concluded, to the disappointment of the Bush administration, that there was never a connection between Saddam and Bin Laden.

The war in Iraq has stimulated more debate globally than anything else since the Viet Nam war. While most of the debate has focused on whether the US should have invaded Iraq, whether the US had a good plan for the war and for the peace, whether it should have more or less troops on the ground, whether the Iraqis deserved a better life without Saddam, and so forth, the central issue of the debate should be "is the US and the world a safer place today than before the war?" After all this was the core reason given to the American people and the world community by the Bush administration.

The emergence of ISIS (ISIL) in the summer of 2014 and the streak of its victories in Iraq and Syria should have answered that question with an emphatic, "NO the world is not a safer place!" Nor it is more democratic, unless we confuse democracy with chaos. By invading Iraq and removing Saddam Hussein the US destabilized the entire region. Iran and Saudi Arabia are scrambling to fill the vacuum created in the region. And the physical presence of US forces has caused Al Qaeda and its medieval mutation ISIS to establish their so called Caliphate in Iraq and Syria. Russia is drawn in as well. And after the November 2015 terrorist attacks on Paris by ISIS, France has now declared war on ISIS.

In his book, *Where the Right went Wrong*, Pat Buchanan referring to President Bush's address to the graduates at West Point on June 2, 2002 as the "West Point Manifesto" points to a very chilling statement made by President Bush and one that most likely has escaped the attention of most Americans. Bush said" Competition between nations is inevitable, but armed conflict in our world is not…America has, and intends to keep, military strengths beyond challenge—thereby making the destabilizing arms races of other eras pointless, and limiting rivalries to trade and other pursuits of peace." Buchanan correctly highlights what this statement means. "This is breathtaking", he says. "President Bush was saying to Beijing, Moscow, New Delhi: You may compete with us in trade, but we will not allow you to increase your strength to where it challenges America's power."

As a footnote to this section, comes the assessment of all 16 U.S. intelligence agencies which serves as the leading security reference for policymakers and Congress. On February 13, 2009, *The New York Times* reported the following:

> The new director of national intelligence told Congress on Thursday [February 12] that global economic turmoil and the instability it could ignite had outpaced terrorism as the most urgent threat facing the United States. The assessment underscored concern inside America's intelligence agencies not only about the fallout from the economic crisis around the globe, but also about the long-term harm to America's reputation. The crisis that began in American markets has already "increased questioning of U.S. stewardship of the global economy," the intelligence chief, Dennis C. Blair, said in prepared testimony.
>
> Mr. Blair's comments were particularly striking because they were delivered as part of a threat assessment to Congress that has customarily focused on issues like terrorism and nuclear proliferation. Mr. Blair singled out the economic downturn as the "primary near-term security concern" for the country, and he warned that if it continued to spread and deepen, it would contribute to unrest and imperil some governments. "The longer it takes for the recovery to begin, the greater the likelihood of serious damage to U.S. strategic interests," he said.

This assessment should not come as a surprise to anyone who has been awake and following domestic and international news in the last eight years. The preoccupation of the Bush administration with the Iraq war at the expense of any and all other issues has brought us to this dire global economic situation we are in that ironically has become the most serious national security threat since the peak of Cold War.

An End to Evil

In late 2003, David Frum and Richard Perle, two of American Enterprise Institute's (AEI) fellows and neo-con high priests wrote a book titled *An End to Evil.* The book attracted headlines and spurred up controversy among neo-con opponents. Regardless of one's political affiliation, one thing is certain: this book should be read carefully by everyone. Pat Buchanan in a March 1, 2004 article in the American Conservative writes that "on putting down Perle's new book the thought recurs: the neo-conservative movement may be over. For they are not only losing their hold on power, they are losing their grip on reality." It may be arguable that they are losing their grip on reality, but it is highly doubtful that they are losing their grip on power. On the contrary, as one watches and listens to the Bush campaign rhetoric cannot ignore the fact that it sounds frighteningly similar to the same talking points that *An End to Evil* presents.

Joshua Micah in his January 7, 2004 review of the book writes: "*An End to Evil* is propaganda at its most crude, most deceptive, and most damaging. As such, this book can be read both as a masterpiece of contemporary propaganda and a policy statement with far reaching effects." Micah continues with his analysis of the book's propaganda techniques. "One of the most fundamental functions of propaganda is to provide the mass with a set of beliefs that they can rely on to analyze the world. In the case of Perle and Frum, the goal is to homogenize American public opinion behind Bush. In a sense, the function of propaganda is to give the largest number of people the exact same talking points...It is essential that we do not dismiss this as an unimportant work – instead, it is precisely the high level of propaganda that makes this book a terrifying reminder that America is close to being dragged into depths of neo-conservative insanity."

The following statement from *An End to Evil* is highlighted in the Foreign and Defense Policy area of the web site of the AEI, as it clearly represents the foreign policy of its think tank and of the United States, for that matter:

> For us, terrorism remains the great evil of our time, and the war against this evil our generation's great cause. We do not believe that Americans are fighting this evil to minimize it or to manage it. We believe they are fighting to win—to end this evil before it kills again and on a genocide scale. There is no middle way for Americans: It is victory or holocaust. This book is a manual for victory.

If there is any doubt about the goals of neo-cons regarding America's hegemonic role in the world, in the article "Fighting a Global Insurgency" that appeared on AEI's web site on December 4, 2003, the imperial aim of the US becomes clear.

> Defense transformation must bring about a change in the military mindset from what Eliot Cohen calls a "mass army" to that of an "imperial army": The mentality of an imperial army is, of necessity, utterly different from that of a mass army…The former accepts ambiguous objectives, interminable commitments and chronic skirmishes as a fact of life; the latter wants a definable mission, a plan for victory and decisive battles. In the imperial army the trooper finds fulfillment in the soldier's life; in the mass army in the belief that he exists to fight and win America's wars.

Are the neo-cons with their noble lies preparing America for the perpetual wars that will bring perpetual peace? If the answer is yes, then the next question Americans should be asking is "which evil must we end?"

In another ironic chapter of neo-con *History Re-written*, Richard Perle, the neo-con high priest, or Prince of Darkness as he was known in the Reagan years, came out of several years of hiding and gave a very interesting…well, read for yourselves…

Prince of Darkness Denies Own Existence

Washington Sketch: Richard Perle in Wonderland

Dana Milbank sketches the intellectual godfather of the Bush doctrine and the Iraq war as he disavows neo-conservatism.#

By Dana Milbank

"Prince of Darkness denies Own Existence" by Nana Milbank of the *Washington Post*, Friday, February 20, 2009; Page AO3

…Jacob Heilbrunn of *National Interest* asked Perle to square his newfound realism with the rather idealist title of his book, *An End to Evil.* "We had a publisher who chose the title," Perle claimed, adding: "There's hardly an ideology in that book." (An excerpt: "There is no middle way for Americans: It is victory or holocaust. This book is a manual for victory.")

Friday, February 20, 2009; Page A03

Listening to neo-conservative mastermind Richard Perle at the Nixon Center yesterday, there was a sense of falling down the rabbit hole. In real life, Perle was the ideological architect of the Iraq war and of the Bush doctrine of preemptive attack. But at yesterday's forum of foreign policy intellectuals, he created a fantastic world in which:

1. Perle is not a neo-conservative.
2. Neo-conservatives do not exist.
3. Even if neo-conservatives did exist, they certainly couldn't be blamed for the disasters of the past eight years.

"There is no such thing as a neo-conservative foreign policy," Perle informed the gathering, hosted by National Interest magazine. "It is a left critique of what is believed by the commentator to be a right-wing policy."

So what about the 1996 report he co-authored that is widely seen as the cornerstone of neo-conservative foreign policy? "My name was on it because I signed up for the study group," Perle explained. "I didn't approve it. I didn't read it."

Mm-hmm. And the two letters to the president, signed by Perle, giving a "moral" basis to Middle East policy and demanding military means to remove Saddam Hussein? "I don't have the letters in front of me," Perle replied. Right. And the Bush administration National Security Strategy, enshrining the neo-conservative themes of preemptive war and using American power to spread freedom? "I don't know whether President Bush ever read any of those statements," Perle maintained. "My guess is he didn't."

The Prince of Darkness—so dubbed during his days opposing arms control in the Reagan Pentagon—was not about to let details get in the way of his argument that "50 million conspiracy theorists have it wrong," as the subtitle of his article for National Interest put it. "I see a number of people here who believe and have expressed themselves abundantly that there is a neo-conservative foreign policy and it was the policy that dominated the Bush administration, and they ascribe to it responsibility for the deplorable state of the world," Perle told the foreign policy luminaries at yesterday's lunch. "None of that is true, of course."

Of course.

He had been a leading cheerleader for the Iraq war, predicting that the effort would take few troops and last only a few days, and that Iraq would pay for its own reconstruction.

Perle was chairman of Bush's Defense Policy Board—and the president clearly took the advice of Perle and his fellow neo-cons. And Perle, in turn, said back then that Bush "knows exactly what he's doing."

Yesterday, however, Perle said Bush's foreign policy had "no philosophical underpinnings and certainly nothing like the demonic influence of neo-conservatives that is alleged." He also took issue with the common view that neo-cons favored using American might to spread democratic values. "There's no documentation!" he argued. "I can't find a single example of a neo-conservative supposed to have influence over the Bush administration arguing that we should impose democracy by force."

Those in the room were skeptical of Perle's efforts to recast himself as a pragmatist. Richard Burt, who clashed with Perle in the Reagan administration, took issue with "this argument that neo-conservatism maybe actually doesn't exist." He reminded Perle of the longtime rift between foreign policy realists and neo-conservative interventionists. "You've got to kind of acknowledge there is a neo-conservative school of thought," Burt challenged.

"I don't accept the approach, not at all," the Prince of Darkness replied.

At times, the Prince of Darkness turned on his questioners. Fielding a question from the *Financial Times*, he said that the newspaper "propagated this myth of neo-conservative influence." He informed Stefan Halper of Cambridge University that "you have contributed significantly to this mythology."

"There are some 5,000 footnotes," Halper replied. "Documents that you've signed."

But documents did not deter denials. "I've never advocated attacking Iran," he said, to a few chuckles. "Regime change does not imply military force, at least not when I use the term," he said, to raised eyebrows. Accusations that neo-conservatives manipulated intelligence on Iraq? "There's no truth to it." At one point, he argued that the word "neo-conservative" has been used as an anti-Semitic slur, just moments after complaining that prominent figures such as Dick Cheney and Donald Rumsfeld—Christians both—had been grouped in with the neo-conservatives.

"I don't know that I persuaded anyone," Perle speculated when the session ended. No worries, said the moderator. "You certainly kept us all entertained."

EPILOGUE

We can deny our heritage and our history, but we cannot escape responsibility for the result. There is no way for a citizen of a republic to abdicate his responsibilities. As a nation we have come into our full inheritance at a tender age. We proclaim ourselves, as indeed we are, the defenders of freedom, wherever it continues to exist in the world, but we cannot defend freedom abroad by deserting it at home.
Edward Murrow, March 9, 1954

...it is not the level of security that is the core issue for me. My problem is not with the metal detectors and screenings. My problem is that there's been nothing waiting on the other side. There has been way too little vision for an American of 9/12 and way too much 9/11—over and over and over.
I would go through a gauntlet of five airport metal detectors every time I flew out of Washington, D.C., if I thought that there was some great project, worthy of America, on the other side—not just the "war on terrorism." Even in the Cold War, when we were doing nuclear drills in my school basement, we were also figuring out how to lunch men into space—probing the next frontier and inspiring a young generation. We need America, and the world needs America, to be something more than just the "United States of Fighting Terrorism." Yes, we must never forget who our enemies are, but we must always remember who we are. "They" are the people who perpetrate 9/11s. "We" are the people who celebrate the Fourth of July. That's our national holiday—not 9/11.
Thomas Friedman, Hot, Flat, and Crowded

We started this improbable journey in the fall of 2001 shortly after the 9/11 attacks when we were still living in Sinai. More than seven years later and after the George W. Bush presidency came to a much welcomed conclusion, I decided it was time to bring our journey to a closure as well. This time our home was half way around the world and thousands of miles from the Middle East in another desert landscape—Arizona. Our journey started because of a threat that had originated not far from our home in Sharm El Sheikh and ended in our home in John McCain's and Jon Kyl's state. During this journey we were introduced and became well acquainted with the first image of evil—Islamic fundamentalism—and along the way, as we traversed the globe, we met its mirror image—neo-conservatism and Christian fundamentalism. It was a journey that hugely challenged our intellect and core personal and faith values. At the end, our search raised more questions than it answered.

There were two issues that dominated the content of this book—the war on terrorism and the Iraq war. The former was the reason we decided to embark in this journey. The latter was a war of choice and the tragic legacy of George W. Bush and as such it became unavoidable for us not to include. We will begin our "closing arguments" with the Iraq war first, as it is an event that sooner or later will come to an end, and finish with the war on terrorism, which is an open-ended event of which the *When* and *How* it will end depend on several complex and interwoven issues. Moreover, the broader issues of democracy and civil liberties, and vision of America, which Murrow's and Friedman's excerpts above address, emerged as the true stories behind the initial story of the threat of terrorism.

The issues that were dominating the pre- 9/11 agenda of the developed world were global warming, world hunger, globalization, assistance to developing nations with money, food, medicine, cure for AIDS, etc. And then after 9/11 and with Bush declaring war on terrorism, the world regressed to a state not seen since World War II and the Cold War that ensued. Primal fear took over everything. People feared for their lives, homes, and overall safety. The American Dream was threatened. Folks across America demanded security from their military and law enforcement agencies. Instead, their government not only neglected the "business of the people", it betrayed them as well;

it made the Iraq war the single most important issue and ignored, or worse manipulated, everything else. National security is a lot more than protection from Islamic fundamentalists. National security means having a job; national security means not losing our homes; national security means being able to send our kids to college; national security means protecting the air we breathe, the water we drink, our forests, lakes and rivers; national security means being able to see a doctor and buy medicine when we get sick; national security means being able to care for the elderly and disabled; national security means providing food and shelter to ALL Americans.

Iraq War was a war of choice and—no matter how you dress it up and how much make up and perfume you put on it—it was still an ugly, dirty, violent, illegal and immoral war. And that is a pretty serious indictment. The war against Iraq, however, is not only an indictment against the Bush administration. It is an indictment as well against the major information media, especially the TV networks, for relinquishing their duty to question, investigate, and criticize the actions of the government when criticism was necessary. It seems they all drank the cool aid and became cheer leaders of the Bush foreign policies. What is indeed astonishing, even after nine years from the invasion of Iraq, is the fact that an official "Inquiry on the War" is still missing. A country invades another country for no reason at a great cost of blood and treasure and nobody asks why? The media and the Administration have debated a lot more whether we should have a surge and much less, if at all, why we allowed ourselves to go to war. We should have an inquiry on the war and people should be held accountable. This is not a trivial matter to be sidestepped.

Unfortunately, electronic media have become tools of corporate America and a platform of government propaganda. The printed media may be somewhat better, but unfortunately a small percentage of Americans still read newspapers and magazines. And we, the American public, should be found as nothing less than co-indictors as we share a great deal of this lapse of civic responsibility. The question that gnaws me is this; are we really so disengaged from the political process that we are easily fooled and manipulated, or is it that we are indeed ideologically aligned with the imperialistic motives of the Bush administration and of the neo-cons? I guess we will never know for certain, but either case is an alarming and frightening prospect to be happening in any society that espouses to be democratic and protector of liberty. It is time to acknowledge the timeless axiom that when knowledge of and participation by the People in the affairs of the government is absent, democracy for the People cannot exist as well.

The biggest hypocrisy of Bush and his Christian Coalition is that they took us to Iraq to liberate Iraqis—who are mostly Muslims—and bring them freedom of choice and democracy, while Muslims and people of other faiths in this country have to comply with the "biblical worldview" of the Evangelicals who are determined to restore America to a Christian nation by applying biblical moral truth and the Gospel to every area of society. This hypocrisy and the ways the war was justified and has been conducted are appalling. The American people are one of the most patriotic, caring and religious peoples in the world, if not the most. A very strong pioneer spirit of working hard, helping each other, defending themselves against external enemies and paying tribute to God still reigns supreme in contemporary America. The vast majority of Americans, though, are not very cognizant of the destructive path that war leaves behind and a bit naive in believing in their leaders. The rest of the world has been invaded, occupied, looted, and ravaged for countless times in the thousands years-old history. The result is that the people in Europe, Africa and Asia are more resilient but also, wearier, more pragmatic, more fearful of the cruelty and destruction of war, and a lot more skeptical of their leaders who time and time again have taken them to bloody and senseless wars.

I had started reading Bob Woodward's latest book *The War Within* as I was wrapping up this book. I was struck by the comments Woodward made in the Epilogue of his book. It is not that I was surprised by them as throughout this book I have made similar comments. But to read the verdict of Bush's conduct of the war by one of our generation's best investigative reporters, it is something else. By the way, I highly recommend all four books that Bob Woodward wrote about the Bush presidency and couldn't find anything more suitable to summarize the tragedy of this war than a few excerpts from the Epilogue of his latest book. Here they are:

> For at least seven months during 2006, President Bush had known that the existing strategy in Iraq was not working. No matter how he tried to dress it up with positive language and sugar coat it to the American public, he was losing the war. But somehow he had set no deadlines, demanded no hurry, avoided any direct confrontation with Secretary Rumsfeld, General Pace or General Casey about the need for change...The president delegated the responsibility for finding a new strategy to Steve Hadley, his national security adviser, according to my reporting and to the president's own words..."you've got to understand Steve. I'm telling you, he drove a lot of this, you want to get it right in the book."
>
> Bush had done exactly that. The commander in chief had handed off a war he was losing to his national security adviser.
>
> Again, his faith and his instincts meant more than the concerns of his war cabinet and the international community.
>
> My second book on Bush, *Plan of Attack*, recounted the president's decision making during the 16 months from November 2001 to the invasion in March 2003. During this period, Rumsfeld and the Central Command commander at the time, General Tommy Franks, gave the president a dozen detailed briefings on the invasion plan. Every meeting was about how to go to war. There was no meeting to discuss whether to go to war. The president had never questioned its rightness, and its rightness made it the only course.
>
> I have never doubted the sincerity of the president's convictions. But convictions alone are not enough. The decision to go to war is momentous. The decision to launch a preemptive war is doubly so and carries with it a great weight of responsibility.
>
> In my 1991 book, *The Commanders*, on the invasion of Panama and the first Gulf War to oust Saddam from Kuwait, I wrote, "The decision to go to war is one that defines a nation, both to the world and, perhaps more importantly, to itself. There is no more serious business for a

> national government, no more accurate measure of national leadership."
>
> A president must be able to get a clear-eyed, unbiased assessment of the war. The president must lead. For years, time and again, President Bush has displayed impatience, bravado and unsettling personal certainty about his decisions. The result has too often been impulsiveness and carelessness and, perhaps most troubling, a delayed reaction to realities and advice that run counter to his gut.
>
> This was most evident in the three years after the invasion, the period covered by my third Bush book, *State of Denial*, published in September 2006. Bush and his administration had not openly acknowledged the severity of escalating violence and deterioration in Iraq. "With all Bush's upbeat talk and optimism," I wrote the book's last line, "he had not told the American public the truth about what Iraq had become."
>
> My reporting for this book showed that to be even more the case than I could have imagined.
>
> One final question: Who pays the price of war? I don't mean the billions of dollars spend each year on it. I mean the human cost. That falls to the 140,000 service members and to their loved ones. They are the ones losing limbs, losing lives, and losing years to deployments half-way around the world. A friend of mine labeled this the "ripple of human misery" that disperses slowly, quietly throughout every corner of the country, often unnoticed by the majority of Americans.
>
> Those who serve and their families are the surrogates of all Americans. They bear the risk and the strain of a year or more in a violent foreign land. So many have spent their youth and spilled their blood in a fight far from home. What do we owe them? Everything. And what have we given them? Much less than they deserve.

America invaded Iraq under the pretext of fighting the "broader" war against terrorism but Iraq as a member of the "axis of evil" had been at the crosshairs of senior Bush administration officials, like Cheney and Rumsfeld, long, long before 9/11. The realization of this "small" detail, leaves one wondering if the global engagement of Islamic fundamentalists would have been so potent and durable, if at all, without this provocation by the

US. An examination of the "theater of engagement" for all Islamic fundamentalist groups prior to the Soviet occupation of Afghanistan and the presence of American forces on Muslim soil in 1990, shows that there were no attacks of any type outside the Muslim world—particularly Egypt. The Jihadist activities were confined mainly against high government officials and heads of state who were determined to be apostates by the fundamentalists.

Their radical ideology and militant tactics had not resonated that much in moderate Arab states, prior to the invasion of Afghanistan by the Soviets and the invasion of Lebanon by Israel. The aggressive Israeli policies towards Palestine, the increasing settlements in West bank and Gaza, the second Intifada, and, the "icing on the cake", the invasion of Iraq tipped the scales in favor of the Islamists and legitimized their "struggle" against the aggressor crusaders in the minds of even the most moderate Muslims. The failure of the US and the West in general to resolve the Palestinian issue, and the hubris of American foreign policy and the hot rhetoric of the Bush and his neo-con zealots have hugely created and fueled their Holy War.

One of the arguments that was used by the architects of the Iraq war was that we wanted to make the world safer and more democratic. The emergence of ISIS (ISIL) in the summer of 2014 and the streak of its victories in Iraq and Syria should have answered that question with an emphatic, "NO the world is not a safer place!" Nor it is more democratic, unless we confuse democracy with chaos. By invading Iraq and removing Saddam Hussein the US destabilized the entire region. Iran and Saudi Arabia are scrambling to fill the vacuum created in the region. And the physical presence of US forces has caused Al Qaeda and its medieval mutation ISIS to establish their so called Caliphate in Iraq and Syria. Russia is drawn in as well both because to defend their long-time ally Bashar Assad but most importantly to ensure her presence in the region. And after the November 2015 terrorist attacks on Paris by ISIS, France has now declared war on ISIS. It will not be long before the rest of Europe will join in.

One cannot help but think of the medieval Assassins when discussing Al Qaeda and its subsidiaries. In reviewing the origin of the Assassins, their tactics and their impact on their world, and then try to draw parallels between them and the modern terrorists, one should not overlook an, not so obvious, observation. The Assassins although they never won any military victories and didn't gain or occupied any land, with the exception of the Alamut fortress, they terrorized the Islamic and part of the European world of crusaders for the large part of two hundred years with great success. And they accomplished all this even though they didn't have a political agenda or the broad public support that the recent Islamic fundamentalism movement is enjoying. The modern Assassins too without the issues of Palestine and Iraq would have been just that—modern Assassins—without a loyal ecumenical following.

We can debate endlessly whether America provoked the actions of Al Qaeda. Regardless of the core cause of global Islamic terrorism, however, America has handed them a priceless gift since 9/11. Without this gift from America, Al Qaeda would eventually have fallen into the dustbin of history and the achievements of the modern Assassins might have not been much more than political assassinations, much of the same as the targeted assassinations in the Islamic medieval world of the original Assassins. This is not to say that political assassinations are fine, don't cause much damage and should be ignored. There is a big difference, however, between targeted assassinations, mainly against unpopular Muslim military and political leaders branded as apostates and a full scale holy war between Islam and the West. The former is an important national issue for many Arab states that should be addressed by each Arab country for the sake of its own stability; the latter is a much more critical issue of global peace and stability.

After the disastrous Iraq war, America had high expectations from the Obama administration. That has not turned out to be the case and it makes one wonder how can a president with so much talent and good intentions place at the helm of his foreign policy team such inept persons? Bob Woodwork mentioned in his last book about George W. Bush that "The commander in chief had handed off a war he was losing to his national security adviser." President Obama has handed off the Middle East conflicts that he is not winning to his national security adviser Susan Rice. The list of blunders is long. First was Egypt and the failure to recognize the threat posed to Egypt and the region by Mohamed Morsi and his Muslim Brotherhood extremists. Were it not for the timely intervention of Abdel Fatah El Sisi, Egypt would have joined the long list of failed states in the Middle East. But we lost the respect and support of Egyptians and her leaders and pushed her to the arms of a very accommodating Vladimir Putin and Russia. Second, was the stubborn insistence to oust Bashar Assad of Syria at any costs. There is no argument that Assad has been a butcher to his own people, not unlike Saddam Hussein had been to Iraqis. Granted Obama didn't invade Syria, but his support of the rebels (infiltrated by Al Qaeda and ISIS) contributed to the strengthening of ISIS in Syria and Iraq. Finally, the hypocrisy of the US (not only during the Obama administration) to preach democracy and human rights in the Middle East while allowing Saudi Arabia, mainly, and Qatar to have authoritative regimes is not going unnoticed around the world. I would be remiss if I did not mention that Turkey, the darling of the US since the cold War, seems to be playing a sinister game with her overt support of Muslim Brotherhood and covert support of ISIS while the US is napping.

Frequently during the research and writing for this book, one thought kept challenging me—Islam has not had its Age of Enlightenment yet. It seems that what Islam is experiencing now resembles the Religious Wars of Europe of the sixteenth and seventeenth centuries. The Age of Enlightenment is described in encyclopedias as an 18th century movement that led the world toward progress, out of a long period of irrationality, superstition, and tyranny which began during the historical period we call the Dark Ages. It was an age where prominent philosophers, such as Voltaire and Jean-Jacques Rousseau questioned and attacked existing institutions of both Church and State. Moreover, it was a movement that provided the framework for the American and French Revolutions and for the independence wars in Ottoman Europe. The Arab Muslim world has not had yet its own Age of Enlightenment. We should allow it to do so, first by stopping intervening in its affairs and second by encouraging its people to have their Age of Reason and Enlightenment. We can do that by assisting them in their economic and educational development, and inviting them (even the Islamic extremists) to participate in peace-seeking dialogues with the West. And most important we should at all costs avoid regressing to the Dark Ages of tyranny and religious persecution.

So, where are we headed? What is in store for the future generations? Is the US turning into an imperial power? Are we headed towards a major collision between the West and the Arab/Muslim world? Are Benjamin Netanyahu and his zealots, and the fundamental Christians and neo-conservatives planning to re-map the Middle East one more time, and create a dominant pro-American, pro-Israeli presence around and in the midst of the Arabs? Will the Muslim fundamentalists succeed in terrorizing the West and will ISIS ultimately establish their fallen Caliphate within the Arab/Muslim world? What will the "Arab Spring" ultimately bring to Arab nations? Will the increased polarization of peoples here and elsewhere come to an end? Will we return to the dialogue of climate change, world hunger, women's and children's rights which was abruptly paused with 9/11 and the global economic crisis of 2008? Are we witnessing the rise and fall of the PAX AMERICANA in a single generation? We certainly do not have answers to these and many more questions. We hope and pray that our leaders do.

As I am writing the closing pages of this book, I am having mixed emotions. I feel sad parting with something that has become part of me—a similar feeling I experienced when I completed my work in the Middle East—but at the same time I feel relieved and hope that my "nightmares" about these two evil images, that haunt me every time I return to my writings, may be less frequent and less taunting. In a strange and wishful way, I believe that by bringing my work to an end America and the world will start writing a new book, one of peace and acceptance. It is time to capture, chain and imprison both images of evil in *Hades*—the dark underworld.

George A. Kinias
November 2015

George Kinias, a native of Greece, was educated in the United States where he has spent most of his adult life. An environmental engineer by profession, he was fortunate to have the opportunity to live and work in the Middle East for fourteen years. He arrived in Egypt three days after the Invasion of Kuwait by Saddam Hussein, lived through the turbulent years of the uprising of Muslim Brotherhood in the nineties, and returned to the U.S. after the Iraq invasion in 2003. Always interested in history and geopolitics, it was during this violent period that he became even more interested and engaged in Middle Eastern affairs. The events of 9/11 were the culmination of this passion and the beginning of a virtual spiritual and cultural journey into the heartlands of Islam.

He is married to Alexandra Kinias, a native Egyptian, and they live in Scottsdale, Arizona and Greece.

www.ingramcontent.com/pod-product-compliance
Lightning Source LLC
Chambersburg PA
CBHW030249290526
45785CB00001B/20